Search These Commandments

Melchizedek Priesthood
Personal Study Guide

Published by
The Church of Jesus Christ
of Latter-day Saints
Salt Lake City, Utah

Contents

Comments and Suggestions

Your comments and suggestions about this manual are appreciated. Please submit them to—

Office of the First Quorum of the Seventy
Attention: Adult Curriculum
47 East South Temple Street
Salt Lake City, Utah 84150
USA

Identify yourself by name, address, ward, and stake. Then identify the name of the manual, how you used it, your feelings regarding its strengths and weaknesses, and any recommended improvements.

Message from the First Presidency

Beloved Brethren:

Speaking of the Doctrine and Covenants, the Lord told a special conference of elders in the early days of the Church that they should "search these commandments, for they are true and faithful" (D&C 1:37).

It is appropriate that this divine counsel should be followed by you who are holders of the priesthood in our day. This year you will have the opportunity of *searching* the Doctrine and Covenants in an effort to increase your faith, spirituality, and understanding of the gospel of Jesus Christ.

The word *search* indicates that your study of the scriptures should be more than a shallow reading of words. Your search should be an in-depth probe, a spiritual feast in which you come to know not only the gospel but also Him whose name it bears and the Father who sent Him to redeem us.

Along with your study of the scriptures, we hope that you will take the time to read and ponder the contents of this personal study guide. In it you will find teachings from the scriptures and the General Authorities that can help you to become better husbands, fathers, and bearers of the holy priesthood.

May you live to be worthy of the priesthood you bear and heed the Lord's command to "search these commandments."

Faithfully your brethren,
The First Presidency

Suggested Doctrine and Covenants Reading Schedule

The Churchwide scripture study for 1985 is the Doctrine and Covenants. The Gospel Doctrine class will study the Doctrine and Covenants and the supplemental text, *My Kingdom Shall Roll Forth* (MKSRF), during the same period of time. Following is the suggested reading schedule:

January	Joseph Smith—History; Introduction to the Doctrine and Covenants; D&C 1–10	August	D&C 107–123
		September	D&C 124–135; MKSRF, pp. 1–15
February	D&C 11–27	October	D&C 136; Official Declaration—1; MKSRF, pp. 16–72
March	D&C 28–42		
April	D&C 43–57		
		November	D&C 138; MKSRF, pp. 73–114
May	D&C 57–75		
June	D&C 76–92, 137		
		December	Official Declaration—2; MKSRF, pp. 115–156
July	D&C 93–106		

It is recommended that families with small children obtain copies of the *Doctrine and Covenants Stories* (PBIC037A). This pictorial history covers the same material as the adult reading schedule and enables parents to discuss it with their children.

Personal Study Schedule 1985

As your instructor announces the lessons which your quorum leaders have assigned for coming weeks, note them below so that your personal study will prepare you for quorum meeting.

January

Sunday	Lesson Number and Title
6	
13	
20	
27	

February

Sunday	Lesson Number and Title
3	
10	
17	
24	

March

Sunday	Lesson Number and Title
3	
10	
17	
24	
31	

April

Sunday	Lesson Number and Title
7	
14	
21	
28	

May

Sunday	Lesson Number and Title
5	
12	
19	
26	

June

Sunday	Lesson Number and Title
2	
9	
16	
23	
30	

July

Sunday	Lesson Number and Title
7	
14	
21	
28	

August

Sunday	Lesson Number and Title
4	
11	
18	
25	

September

Sunday	Lesson Number and Title
1	
8	
15	
22	
29	

October

Sunday	Lesson Number and Title
6	
13	
20	
27	

November

Sunday	Lesson Number and Title
3	
10	
17	
24	

December

Sunday	Lesson Number and Title
1	
8	
15	
22	
29	

How To Use This Study Guide

Each lesson in this study guide is divided into two parts—the personal study material for your use and the quorum training suggestions for the use of your quorum leaders and instructors.

You may profitably study the personal study material during the week as you look up the scriptures cited and as you try to answer the questions asked. The scriptures should be looked upon as your manual and the study guide as a means of assisting your understanding of the scriptures. Your instructor should announce the lesson topics which have been assigned by the quorum leaders to be discussed in coming weeks (see p. vii) so that you may use your personal study time to prepare for quorum meeting. With the exception of lesson 1, these lessons need *not* be given in sequential order.

The quorum training suggestions give quorum leaders some ideas for helping you apply at home the doctrines you study. In some instances, the training suggestions provided in a single lesson could profitably occupy two or more successive quorum meetings. Normally, most of the quorum time should be spent on the quorum training suggestions rather than on the personal study material.

To the Quorum Leader

Teach According to the Covenants

As a quorum leader, you are to "sit in council" with your quorum members and "teach them according to the covenants" (see D&C 107:89). You are responsible for planning quorum instruction. You may teach your quorum members yourself or you may delegate that responsibility to others. In either case, see that the teaching in each quorum meeting is directed toward the particular needs of your quorum members and is in harmony with the teachings of the Church.

Prayerful discernment and what you learn in personal priesthood interviews will help you select lesson topics. Decide in advance, with the help of your counselors, what topics will be discussed and who the instructor should be. Inspiration may guide you to choose topics not included in this study guide. Previous study guides may provide the material you need for those topics.

You may sometimes devote quorum meetings to special workshop sessions. In addition, if you feel so inspired, you may devote more than one quorum meeting to a single topic. For example, after presenting a lesson on family prayer, you may want to use a second quorum meeting to teach how family prayer might be taught in the home.

Share your testimony and conviction of the principles taught, even if you do not personally teach the lesson.

Encourage Use of the Scriptures

Quorum study is an extension of personal study. Encourage each quorum member to carry out a program of personal scripture study. Usually, you should tell quorum members about upcoming lessons so they can study the personal study portion of each lesson before quorum meeting. The personal study material is designed to encourage your quorum members to study the scriptures.

In addition, by both teaching and example, encourage quorum members to bring their standard works to quorum meetings and to use them there. You might also suggest ways for them to use the scriptures in their homes.

Encourage Quorum Members to Hearken to the Words of the Living Prophets

You should also teach your members to listen to the words of the General Authorities living now and obey their inspired counsel. Two general conference inserts in this study guide suggest ways to take advantage of the messages delivered in the general conferences each April and October. These should be used as close to conference as conveniently possible.

"Those, and I testify to this out of my own experience, who will through mighty prayer and earnest study inform themselves as to what these living prophets say, and act upon it, will be visited by the spirit of the Lord and know by the spirit of revelation that they speak the mind and will of the Father" (Marion G. Romney, in Conference Report, Apr. 1945, p. 90).

Planning Additional Melchizedek Priesthood Quorum Lessons

Use the following ideas to expand on a particular lesson, to address a special need of the quorum, or to prepare supplementary lessons if the study guide does not provide enough for the curriculum year:

- Select topics from the Church magazines, especially from general conference issues, to discuss in quorum meeting. Use the magazines and the *Church News* as supplemental sources for other lessons.

- Carefully set the stage for and conduct a testimony meeting during the quorum hour two or three times during the year. It will help to increase the brotherhood and unity in the quorum. Ask the brethren to describe how they received their testimony. Teach them to write their testimonies and to share their written and verbal testimonies with their families.

- Discuss how to increase personal spiritual strength, and ask the quorum members to share individual experiences with this.

- Have selected quorum members present ideas for personal scripture study programs. Have a demonstration of ideas for marking and referencing personal copies of the scriptures.

- Discuss the importance of family leadership, and ask two or three successful fathers to share their ideas on various aspects of fatherhood. You may want to have them hold a panel discussion.

- Discuss the responsibility of each husband and father to teach the gospel to his family, and examine ways to do that. Include such ways as informal mealtime and bedtime discussions, one-to-one time when traveling, and personal example.

- Have a brainstorm session with quorum members to generate ideas for improving family home evening. Include ideas for involvement of family members, lesson topics and approaches, games, and so forth.

- Hold a workshop session to discuss family councils—their purposes, agendas, techniques, schedules, and so forth. Have home teachers follow up appropriately with families.

- Hold a session on how to be a better husband. Include in the discussion how to show more courtesy, concern, and helpfulness at home. Focus also on how to encourage the education and personal development of the quorum members' wives.

- Discuss with the quorum members their responsibility to prepare themselves for Church leadership responsibilities. Discuss spiritual preparation, leadership principles, Church procedures, and family and work priorities.

- Discuss one priesthood ordinance each month for ten minutes to teach quorum members the proper procedures for exercising their priesthood. Use Appendix 1 of this study guide for guidelines.

Search These Commandments

D&C 1:37

Personal Study

Consecrate time for regular and prayerful study of the scriptures and words of the living prophets.

In 1983, the Church commenced a four-year cycle of studying each of the four standard works in successive years. This year we are encouraged to prayerfully read, ponder, and apply the teachings of the Doctrine and Covenants.

Elder Joseph Fielding Smith noted: "The Doctrine and Covenants is distinctively peculiar and interesting to all who believe in it. . . . it is the only book in existence which bears the honor of a preface given by the Lord himself" (*Church History and Modern Revelation,* 1:252).

1 The Value of the Doctrine and Covenants

Bearers of the priesthood should be familiar with the principles taught in the Doctrine and Covenants. The importance of this book of revelation was emphasized by President Joseph Fielding Smith:

"In my judgment there is no book on earth yet come to man as important as the book known as the *Doctrine and Covenants,* with all due respect to the *Book of Mormon,* and the *Pearl of Great Price,* which we say are our *standards in doctrine.* The book of *Doctrine and Covenants* to us stands in a peculiar position above them all.

"I am going to tell you why. When I say that, do not for a moment think I do not value the *Book of Mormon,* the *Bible,* and the *Pearl of Great Price,* just as much as any man that lives; I think I do. I do not know of anybody who has read them more, and I appreciate them; they are wonderful; they contain doctrine and revelation and commandments that we should heed; but the *Bible* is a history containing the doctrine and commandments given to the people anciently. That applies also to the *Book of*

1

Mormon. It is the doctrine and the history and the commandments of the people who dwelt upon this continent anciently.

"But this *Doctrine and Covenants* contains the word of God to those who dwell here *now. It is our book*. It belongs to the Latter-day Saints. More precious than gold, the Prophet says we should treasure it more than the riches of the whole earth. I wonder if we do? If we value it, understand it, and know what it contains, we will value it more than wealth; it is worth more to us than the riches of the earth" (*Doctrines of Salvation*, 3:198–99).

■ Explanatory Introduction (Doctrine and Covenants, 1981 edition). What are the purposes of the Doctrine and Covenants, and why is it important to you individually? _____

_____

■ D&C 1:37. What has the Lord said regarding the contents of the Doctrine and Covenants? _____

_____

■ The Lord's admonition to *search these commandments* received further emphasis in the following plea from President Heber J. Grant:

"I wish that I had the ability to impress upon the Latter-day Saints the necessity of searching the commandments of God, the revelations from the Lord, the Creator of heaven and earth, as contained in the Doctrine and Covenants. If we as a people would live up to those wonderful revelation that have come to us, we would be a bright and shining light to all the wide world" (in Conference Report, Oct. 1927, p. 4).

■ D&C 115:4–5. How can your becoming familiar with the word of the Lord in the Doctrine and Covenants help you to be a light and standard for others? _____

_____

2 Consecrate Time for Regular Scripture Study

Elder John A. Widtsoe observed:

"Faith in the gospel is much like a living organism. To be healthy and vigorous it must be fed. If starved, it sickens, weakens, and may die. Loss of faith may always be traced to neglect, mistreatment, or sin. "The food of faith is simple but imperative. Knowledge of the gospel must be maintained and increased by regular, continuous study. . . .

". . . It is an erroneous assumption . . . that knowledge of the gospel comes as it were, with breathing, while to secure academic knowledge requires toil and more toil" (as quoted in *Science and Your Faith in God*, compiled by P. R. Green, pp. 249–51).

- 2 Nephi 31:19–20. What does it mean to *feast* upon the words of Christ? Does it involve more than reading? _____

- To *feast* upon the scriptures implies more than a casual commitment to study. Elder Howard W. Hunter noted:

"Those who delve into the scriptural library . . . find that to understand requires more than casual reading or perusal—there must be concentrated study. It is certain that one who studies the scriptures every day accomplishes far more than one who devotes considerable time one day and then lets days go by before continuing. Not only should we study each day, but there should be a regular time set aside when we can concentrate without interference" (in Conference Report, Oct. 1979, p. 91; or *Ensign*, Nov. 1979, p. 64).

- What is your present schedule of uninterrupted scripture study? Have you consecrated a special time each day to feed your faith through scripture study? Consider the past week. How much time did you devote to scripture study? What can you do to improve?

- Elder Carlos E. Asay said:

"I fear that many of us rush about from day to day taking for granted the holy scriptures. We scramble to honor appointments with physicians, lawyers, and businessmen. Yet we think nothing of postponing interviews with Deity—postponing scripture study. Little wonder we develop anemic souls and lose our direction in living. How much better it would be if we planned and held sacred fifteen or twenty minutes a day for reading the scriptures. Such interviews with Deity would help us recognize his voice and enable us to receive guidance in all of our affairs" (in Conference Report, Oct. 1978, p. 79; or *Ensign,* Nov. 1978, pp. 53–54).

▪ How can daily reading of the scriptures be considered as *interviews* with the Lord? _____

_____

▪ If you maintain an appointment book, or otherwise plan your daily activities in advance, do you have time set aside (consecrated) for daily "interviews with Deity"?

What could you do to make time for daily scripture reading part of your regular schedule? _____

_____

Are there things that presently occupy your time that you could eliminate for more important matters, such as personal scripture study?

▪ Elder Hunter asked: "Where could there be more profitable use of time than reading from the scriptural library the literature that teaches us to know God and understand our relationship to him? Time is always precious to busy people, and we are robbed of its worth when hours are wasted in reading or viewing that which is frivolous and of little value" (in Conference Report, Oct. 1979, p. 91; or *Ensign,* Nov. 1979, p. 64).

▪ Just as the body can starve without proper nourishment, so can our spirits suffer without regular spiritual sustenance. President Harold B. Lee observed that "if we're not reading the scriptures daily, our testimonies are growing thinner, our spirituality isn't increasing in depth" (address at Regional Representatives' seminar, 12 Dec. 1970).

3 Study the Words of the Living Prophets

In addition to a study of the scriptures, we should be studying the words of the living prophets.

▪ D&C 21:1–5. What command did the Lord give us regarding the words of his prophet? _____

_____

- What promises are given to those who obey this commandment? _____

- On-going revelation to guide the Lord's Church comes through his divinely designated prophets. President Ezra Taft Benson cautioned that "one who rationalizes that he or she has a testimony of Jesus Christ but cannot accept direction and counsel from the leadership of His church is in a fundamentally unsound position and is in jeopardy of losing exaltation" (in Conference Report, Apr. 1982, p. 90; or *Ensign*, May 1982, p. 64).

- D&C 1:38. Why is it dangerous to reject the words of the Lord's prophet? _____

- How can one get a conviction that the words of the prophet are the words of the Lord? _____

Elder Marion G. Romney suggested that "those . . . who will through *mighty prayer and earnest study* inform themselves as to what these living prophets say, and *act* upon it, will be visited by the spirit of the Lord and know by the spirit of revelation that they speak the mind and will of the Father" (in Conference Report, Apr. 1945, pp. 89–90; emphasis added).

- Speaking of the Lord's Apostles and prophets, Elder Boyd K. Packer noted:

"It is not because of travel nor professional success that we ought to pay heed to them. Nor is it because they are nimble of mind or wise in years. These things are incidental only.

"We listen to them because they have been 'called of God, by prophecy, and by the laying on of hands, by those who are in authority to preach the gospel and administer in the ordinances thereof.' (Article of Faith 5.)" (in Conference Report, Oct. 1968, pp. 73–76).

- Why are Apostles and prophets not ordinary men? _____

Elder Mark E. Petersen counseled as follows:

"The people anciently were willing to accept the divine callings of their leaders, not regarding them any longer as mere fishermen or tentmakers, for those brethren were placed by the Lord into a new category as his divinely chosen servants. So we of today must look beyond the former occupations and personal activities of our modern leaders and see them as the servants of God that they are now. . . .

"God has now lifted them out of those familiar patterns and has given them a new status in life. He has summoned them to high callings in his ministry. A sacred mantle has descended upon them, the mantle of their divine commission, the mantle of prophecy!

"They speak with new voices; they are guided by a heavenly light. *They are ordinary no longer!* They are the anointed ones—the chosen ones—chosen by Almighty God!" (in Conference Report, Oct. 1981, pp. 89, 91; or *Ensign*, Nov. 1981, pp. 65, 66).

■ The importance of reading the words of living prophets was emphasized by President Ezra Taft Benson: "The words of the prophets, particularly the living President of the Church, are crucial reading and can give direction and comfort in an hour when one is down" (in Conference Report, Oct. 1974, p. 92; or *Ensign*, Nov. 1974, p. 66).

What have you read recently from the living prophet? _____

_____

Do you subscribe to and study the monthly *Ensign?* Do you regularly read the "First Presidency Message" contained in this magazine?

■ D&C 68:1–4. When the Lord's chosen servants speak "as moved upon by the Holy Ghost," how binding are their words?

_____

_____

It Will Make
A Difference!

The promise of the Apostle Paul that the scriptures "are able to make thee wise unto salvation through faith which is in Christ Jesus" (2 Timothy 3:15) is as valid today as it was when Paul wrote it centuries ago. (2 Timothy 3:15.)

A modern Apostle, Elder Hunter, said: "When we follow the counsel of our leaders to read and study the scriptures, benefits and blessings of many kinds come to us. This is the most profitable of all study in which we could engage" (in Conference Report, Oct. 1979, p. 91; or *Ensign*, Nov. 1979, p. 64).

Are you taking the time to reap the promised rewards and benefits?

Quorum Training Suggestions

Encourage the quorum members, by both invitation and example, to bring their scriptures to priesthood meeting each week. Use the scriptures each week in presenting your lessons, and invite quorum members to participate by reading or looking up the scriptures under discussion.

Set an example in scripture study by using and displaying the Latter-day Saint editions of the scriptures, published in 1979 and 1981.

Invite quorum members to turn to the Topical Guide headings of "Scriptures, Study of," and "Scriptures, Value of" to locate various scriptural statements about the importance of the scriptures. Read and discuss several of these passages.

- Assign a quorum member to give a brief (less than five-minute) presentation about some of the features of the 1981 edition of the Doctrine and Covenants.

- Introduce quorum members to the scripture study schedule on p. vi of the study guide and challenge them to make a commitment to complete the reading assignment for this year.

- Read Doctrine and Covenants 88:118–19, and discuss how organizing a regular scripture study program can help increase one's faith and spirituality.

- Invite several quorum members to share their ideas on how one can plan and maintain a regular time for scripture study each day. You might challenge each quorum member to select the plan that best fits his schedule and follow it during the coming week, and to be prepared to report on its success the following Sunday.

- Display a recent issue of the *Ensign* that has the conference talks (May and November). Briefly explain that at least two lessons during the coming year will be devoted to a discussion of the most recent general conference, in which the quorum will have an opportunity to study the words of the living prophets. Show them the two general conference inserts in this year's Melchizedek Priesthood Personal Study Guide.

■ Read Doctrine and Covenants 28:2, and point out that the President of the Church occupies the place Joseph Smith occupied at the time of this revelation—prophet, seer, and revelator of The Church of Jesus Christ of Latter-day Saints.

■ Read and discuss the following admonition from President Lee: "The President of the Church . . . alone has the right to declare new doctrine. . . . The President of the Church alone may declare the mind and will of God to His people. No officer nor any other church in the world has this high and lofty prerogative" (*Stand Ye In Holy Places*, pp. 109–10).

■ Check back issues of the *Ensign* or other official Church publications for examples of how individuals have been blessed through following the counsel of the Lord's servants and regularly reading and pondering the scriptures.

■ Read Doctrine and Covenants 18:27–36, and point out how reading the scriptures can give one the experience of *hearing* the voice of the Lord.

■ Read Doctrine and Covenants 68:1–4, and discuss how we are to receive the words of the Lord's servants. Point out the importance of our being in tune to receive the words of the prophets *as if* from the mouth of the Lord (see D&C 21:52).

■ Read and discuss the following quotation by Bishop J. Richard Clarke: "We are the beneficiaries of great sacrifice. What excuse do we have for not taking advantage of this? Brothers and sisters, you don't have to be a natural student to read the scriptures; you just need to love the Lord" (in Conference Report, Oct. 1982, pp. 18–19; or *Ensign*, Nov. 1982, p. 15).

Welcome Services Workshop: Caring for Self and Family

D&C 104:11–13

Personal Study

Familiarize yourself with basic welfare principles and set a personal and family preparedness goal.

The Lord revealed through the Prophet Joseph Smith principles that help families and communities achieve good will, harmony, and brotherhood and fill temporal as well as spiritual needs and wants. Obedience to these principles unites men in an order like that of the ancient Zion of Enoch's time, whose citizens became so righteous that they were translated to a higher spiritual realm.

Early Latter-day Saints longed to establish a Christ-like society, a New Jerusalem, with an order like that of the ancient city of Enoch—and the Lord gave them the principles upon which such a society must be based. We still have the principles the early Saints received through the Prophet Joseph Smith. Although we no longer use the united order, we do have a program through which we may practice some of the same principles of consecration and stewardship in a limited way for our improvement and ultimate perfection. This program includes the welfare plan, established to build character in the lives of the Latter-day Saints by honest work and generous giving. Today the welfare plan is perhaps better known as welfare services—those services we perform as individuals and as a Church for the well-being or welfare of others, of our families, and of ourselves.

---

1 Some Principles of Zion

- What are the principles upon which Zion rests?

- Consider the society of Enoch as described in Moses 7:18. What were the characteristics of this society? _____

- What are some other characteristics of a Christ-like people? _____

- Consider the traits we must develop to be a Christlike people as listed in the following scriptures:

1 John 4:7–11. What should be our attitude toward one another? _____

Mosiah 2:17. What is one way to serve God? _____

Genesis 3:19. What is Adam told he must do all his life? _____

D&C 104:17–18. If we love the Lord, what will we do with our means? _____

D&C 104:11–13. Upon what additional principles is Zion built? _____

Love, service, work, self-reliance, consecration, stewardship—we must live these principles if we are to become a people like the people of Enoch, who "were of one heart and one mind, and dwelt in righteousness; and there was no poor among them" (Moses 7:18).

2 Approach Zion through Personal and Family Preparedness

- In speaking of Zion, President Spencer W. Kimball said:

"This highest order of priesthood society is founded on the doctrines of love, service, work, self-reliance, and stewardship, all of which are circumscribed by the covenant of consecration.

"May I turn now to some of the activities and programs that represent ways to live these principles.

"As you know, in the recent past we have placed considerable emphasis on personal and family preparedness. I hope that each member of the Church is responding appropriately to this direction" (in Conference Report, Oct. 1977, p. 125; or *Ensign*, Nov. 1977, p. 78).

▪ Study carefully the six areas of personal and family preparedness.

1. Literacy and education
2. Career development
3. Financial and resource management
4. Home production and storage
5. Physical health
6. Spiritual and social-emotional strength

▪ Each of these six areas of personal and family preparedness is further explained below. As you consider each of these explanations, a response line is provided where you can write down a tentative goal in each area (see the list of some possible goals on pages 15–17). Where applicable, you should consider your goals with your wife and family. Might one or more of these goals become the basis of your progress toward personal and family preparedness this year?

Literacy and education. Standard: To the extent of his ability, a prepared person is able to read, write, and do basic mathematics. He regularly studies the scriptures and other good books. Parents teach these skills and habits to family members. Parents and children take advantage of educational opportunities.

What is a goal you might set in this area? _____

_____

Career development. Standard: Each young person should receive counsel to help in selection of a career that will satisfy personal and family economic needs and provide personal satisfaction (D&C 75:29). Each person should select a suitable vocation or profession and pursue appropriate training. Retraining or vocational counseling will sometimes be necessary later in life.

What is a goal you might set in this area? _____

_____

Financial and resource management. Standard: The prepared person should establish financial goals, pay tithes and offerings, avoid debt, pay obligations, wisely use and preserve family resources, and save during times of plenty for times of need.

What is a goal you might set in this area? _____

Home production and storage. Standard: As appropriate, each person and family should become self-sufficient by producing needed commodities through gardening, preserving foods, sewing, and making household items. Where legally permitted, each person or family should store a year's supply of food, clothing, and, where possible, fuel. If this is not possible, store what you can.

President Ezra Taft Benson suggested that "the revelation to produce and store food may be as essential to our temporal salvation today as boarding the ark was to the people in the days of Noah" (in Conference Report, Oct. 1980, p. 46; or *Ensign*, Nov. 1980, p. 33).

What is a goal you might set in this area? _____

Physical health. Standard: Every member should obey the Word of Wisdom and practice sound principles of nutrition, physical fitness, weight control, immunization, mother and child health care, accident prevention, dental health, and medical care. President Benson noted that "the condition of the physical body can affect the spirit" (in Conference Report, Oct. 1974, p. 9; or *Ensign*, Nov. 1974, p. 66). Members should live in a healthful and clean environment. In addition, each member should acquire appropriate skills in first aid, safety, home nursing, and food selection and preparation.

What is a goal you might set in this area? _____

Spiritual and social-emotional strength. Standard: Each person should build spiritual strength to meet life's challenges and stresses with confidence and stability by learning to love God and communicate with him in personal prayer, to love and serve his neighbor, and to love and respect himself through righteous living and self-mastery. Spiritual and social-emotional strength are increased by studying the scriptures and gospel doctrines and by living the principles of the gospel.

What is a goal you might set in this area? _____

_____

As we achieve personal and family preparedness goals, not only will we be preparing our families for future emergencies, but our day-to-day living will be more stable and enjoyable. Of this type of life, President Spencer W. Kimball said:

"I like the way the Relief Society teaches personal and family preparedness as 'provident living.' This implies the husbanding of our resources, the wise planning of financial matters, full provision for personal health, and adequate preparation for education and career development, giving appropriate attention to home production and storage as well as the development of emotional resiliency. . . .

" . . . Yes, we are laying up resources in store, but perhaps the greater good is contained in the lessons of life we learn as we *live providently* and extend to our children their pioneer heritage. . . .

"Let's do these things because they are right, because they are satisfying, and because we are obedient to the counsels of the Lord. In this spirit we will be prepared for most eventualities, and the Lord will prosper and comfort us. It is true that difficult times will come. . . . But if we live wisely and providently, we will be as safe as in the palm of His hand" (in Conference Report, Oct. 1977, pp. 125–26; or *Ensign*, Nov. 1977, p. 78).

_____

**It Will Make
a Difference**

Speaking of our need to understand and live the basic principles set forth in this lesson, President Kimball has said: "May we all learn, obey, and teach these principles. Leaders, teach them to your members; fathers, teach them to your families. Only as we apply these truths can we approach the ideal of Zion" (in Conference Report, Oct. 1977, p. 125; or *Ensign,* Nov. 1977, p. 78). Let us apply these principles in our lives as we set goals and work to achieve the standards of personal and family preparedness.

Quorum Training Suggestions

- This is the first lesson in a three-week workshop on welfare services. This lesson has two objectives; first, to teach quorum members the gospel principles underlying welfare services, and second, to encourage quorum members to set one or more personal and family preparedness goals this year and then work to achieve the goal or goals.

The second lesson in the workshop focuses on ways the Church helps the poor, needy, and distressed. The third lesson deals more especially with individual and quorum duties to provide rehabilitation of and compassionate service to those with special needs. It also provides a summary of member duties in welfare services.

Start the lesson by quoting and discussing the following statement by Bishop Victor L. Brown:

"I fear that many think the welfare services program was designed primarily for doomsday. This is not true. The principles of the welfare services program are designed to help us live providently each day and to cope successfully with serious problems as they come into our lives" (in Conference Report, Oct. 1982, p. 116; or *Ensign*, Nov. 1982, p. 78).

- You may wish to begin the workshop by reviewing the self-study materials. Invite your quorum members to share insights from their personal study by asking such questions as the following:

What vital qualities of the human character can be damaged or destroyed if we accept help from others without working to the extent of our ability to earn what we receive?

Why is what we do for family, quorum, and ward members an accurate index of our own spirituality?

What is the relationship between our living the principles underlying welfare services and the establishment of a Christlike people?

- Discuss Elder Gordon B. Hinckley's address, "Welfare Responsibilities of the Priesthood Quorum," found on pages 285–89 in Appendix 2 of this study guide.

■ You may wish to show the filmstrip *Personal and Family Preparedness* (OF259) and discuss the idea that when a family becomes self-sufficient its members will not need Church welfare assistance and will be in a position to help others.

■ You may wish to ask the quorum members to open their manuals to pages 15–17 and to write down tentative personal and family preparedness goals. Challenge the quorum members to discuss these goals with their wives and families (where applicable) and to establish one or more personal and family preparedness goals in their families for this year. As quorum leaders, you may also wish to encourage the brethren to seek assistance by working with their home teachers in meeting these goals and to report their progress to the quorum later in the year.

■ You may also wish to obtain sufficient copies of the booklet *Essentials of Home Production and Storage* (PGWE1125) and of the Personal and Family Preparedness Standards and Worksheet (PGWE1191) for the quorum members to use in their homes to set meaningful goals. Some ideas for possible goals from the worksheet are listed here:

Literacy and education

1. Obtain a copy of the standard works for each family member.

2. Study the scriptures regularly.

3. Read good books regularly.

4. Use the local public library and take advantage of special seminars, conferences and courses.

5. Take advantage of on-the-job training opportunities.

Career development

1. Improve your job skills.

2. Learn a trade or profession.

3. Outline and follow a plan to prepare for your career.

4. Plan to perform your job well.

5. Teach children useful skills and teach them to enjoy work.

Financial and resource management

1. Pay a full tithe, a generous fast offering, and other offerings.

2. Properly budget your money.

3. Live within your income.

4. Plan major purchases, avoiding credit purchases.

5. Work toward home ownership.

6. Get out of debt.

7. Have a savings plan.

8. Provide financial security for times of disability and advanced age.

9. Take better care of your possessions.

Home Production and storage

1. Plant and care for a garden.

2. Learn techniques of home canning, drying, and freezing foods.

3. Preserve home grown products.

4. Where legally permitted, store a one-year supply of basic food, clothing, and, where possible, fuel. Store an emergency supply of water. If this is difficult because of small living quarters, then store what you can.

Physical health

1. Observe the Word of Wisdom.

2. Maintain proper weight and endurance through regular exercise, adequate rest, and a balanced diet.

3. Improve or maintain personal and home sanitation regarding water, waste disposal, food, and other matters.

4. Practice preventive measures to preserve good health.

5. Learn and practice home health skills (such as first aid, home nursing, mother and child care).

Spiritual and social-emotional strength

1. Read the scriptures daily.

2. Have personal and family prayer morning and night.

3. Repent of wrongdoing.

4. Make a new friend.

5. Resolve a difference with a loved one or friend.

6. Share feelings with another.

7. Identify some of your individual strengths.

8. Attend Church meetings regularly and participate in Church activities.

9. Hold family home evening weekly.

10. Perform frequent acts of service to family members and others.

■ As quorum leaders, you may also wish to cosponsor with the Relief Society a "preparedness fair" on a week night. The fair might include workshops, demonstrations, and displays on each aspect of personal and family preparedness.

■ Consider the general conference talks on welfare services and the *Distribution Center Catalog* for additional ideas and materials on welfare services.

■ In preparation for this lesson, you may wish to study the following:

1. President Spencer W. Kimball, "Welfare Services: The Gospel in Action," *Ensign*, Nov. 1977, pp. 76–79; or Conference Report, Oct. 1977, pp. 121–26.

2. President Spencer W. Kimball, "Becoming the Pure in Heart," *Ensign*, May 1978, pp. 79–81; or Conference Report, Apr. 1978, pp. 119–24.

3. The *Ensign* for February 1979, which contains articles titled "Living the Principles of the Law of Consecration," "Thirteen Wards," "Welfare Services in Perspective," "Fast Offerings: A Place for the Second Mile," "Staying Prepared," and "Becoming a Zion Society: Six Principles." A selection of these articles also appears in the January 1980 international magazines.

Welfare Services Workshop: Caring for the Poor and Needy

Lesson 3

D&C 44:6

Personal Study

Support the storehouse resource system by accepting welfare services assignments and giving a generous fast offering.

Speaking of the welfare services plan of the Church, President Spencer W. Kimball said:

"As we travel and visit the people throughout the world, we recognize the great temporal needs of our people. And as we long to help them, we realize the vital importance of their learning this great lesson: that the highest achievement of spirituality comes as we conquer the flesh. We build character as we encourage people to care for their own needs.

"As givers gain control of their desires and properly see other needs in light of their own wants, then the powers of the gospel are released in their lives. They learn that by living the great law of consecration they insure not only temporal salvation but also spiritual sanctification.

"And as a recipient receives with thanksgiving, he rejoices in knowing that in its purest form—in the true Zion—one may partake of both temporal and spiritual salvation. Then they are motivated to become self-sustaining and able to share with others.

"Isn't the plan beautiful? Don't you thrill to this part of the gospel that causes Zion to put on her beautiful garments? When viewed in this light, we can see that Welfare Services is not a program, but the essence of the gospel. *It is the gospel in action*" (in Conference Report, Oct. 1977, p. 123; or *Ensign*, Nov. 1977, p. 77).

18

1 We Are to Care for the Poor and Needy

President Marion G. Romney emphasized the importance of our responsibility to the poor and the needy when he said:

"The caring for the poor and the handicapped and those who need our help is a main purpose and an absolute requirement in fulfilling the royal law of loving our neighbors as ourselves. You will remember the great sermon of Amulek on prayer, in which he tells the people to pray and tells them how often to pray—morning, night, and noon—and tells them where to pray and how to pray and what to pray for. He goes into great detail and then he says that 'after ye have done all these things, if ye turn away the needy, and the naked, and visit not the sick and afflicted, and impart of your substance, if ye have, to those who stand in need—I say unto you, if ye do not any of these things, behold your prayer is vain, and availeth you nothing, and ye are as hypocrites who do deny the faith' " (in Conference Report, Apr. 1978, p. 142; or *Ensign,* May 1978, p. 95).

▪ Alma 34:17–28. Why is it important that we assist those in need? _____

_____

▪ Mosiah 18:29. In what ways are we to assist the needy? _____

_____

▪ Mosiah 18:27–28. With what attitude are we to impart of our substance? _____

_____

2 The Storehouse Resource System Organizes Our Giving

The storehouse resource system is that group of resources provided by the Church and its members to assist those in need. This system is made up of the following elements:

1. Employment system

2. Bishops' storehouses

3. Production projects

4. LDS Social Services

5. Deseret Industries

6. Fast Offerings and other welfare resources

■ *Employment system.* To assist members who need jobs, local priesthood quorums should organize an employment system using ward and stake employment specialists to identify appropriate job opportunities for those in need. In areas where the Church population is large enough, employment centers staffed by professionals have been established.

■ *Bishops' storehouse.* A bishops' storehouse contains a supply of commodities produced in large part by Church members. Although these storehouses provide many of the same services as retail food stores, not one has a cash register. The only way a member may obtain commodities from a storehouse is through a bishop's requisition order.

■ *Production projects.* Where appropriate, each unit of the Church may participate in a project that produces food or nonfood commodities of high quality for the welfare services system. These projects include raising vegetables or sugar beets, processing tuna, and manufacturing household supplies.

■ *Social services.* Agencies of LDS Social Services help members with social and emotional problems. The two main types of help are licensed services (such as adoption, help for unwed parents, foster home care, and Indian student placement) and clinical services (including professional therapy for individuals and families).

■ *Deseret Industries.* Deseret Industries includes a number of nonprofit family thrift stores and work centers where members may buy new, refurbished, and "as-is" items. This program provides members with an opportunity to donate all types of new or used merchandise to help those in need. Deseret Industries provides workshops to help the elderly, the handicapped, and others reach their highest vocational capacities. Donated clothing, furniture, toys, and other items are collected through regular drives and are then repaired by Deseret Industries employees, many of whom are elderly or handicapped. Meaningful work helps these people build their skills, their self-esteem, and their confidence. Deseret Industries also serves as a bishops' storehouse from which a bishop may requisition nonfood commodities to provide for the needy.

■ *Fast offerings.* Through fast offering funds bishops are able to provide for needy members' cash needs.

■ *Other welfare services resources.* The bishop may call upon quorum members to share their individual resources and talents with those in need. In addition, missionaries with welfare service asssignments labor in many nations as resource persons to help local priesthood leaders apply and teach members the principles of caring for themselves, their families, and others.

■ Because of these resources provided by the Church and its members, "bishops may now provide clothing, shelter, food, medical assistance, employment, adoption and foster care services, and professional therapy for the emotionally afflicted" (J. Richard Clarke, in Conference Report, Apr. 1978, p. 125; or *Ensign*, May 1978, p. 83).

---

3 How We Can Support the Storehouse Resource System

■ An important part of our priesthood responsibilities is to accept assignments in the storehouse resource system. Such assignments may include helping with the quorum employment system, assisting in the cultivation of crops, working at a bishops' storehouse, or organizing a Deseret Industries drive. In this regard Elder Gordon B. Hinckley has said: "The quorum becomes a resource of organized and disciplined manpower available to the bishop and stake president in carrying forward the production and processing of welfare commodities. It is in the quorum that the strong hands of willing men are found to thin the beets, to haul the hay, to build the fences, and to carry forward the myriad requirements of our welfare projects" (*Ensign*, Nov. 1977, p. 86).

■ The attitude with which we give is as important as our giving, itself. A priesthood quorum member was once asked to hoe beets at a stake welfare farm. He took his young son with him, and the two of them started to work at one end of a very long field. As it grew later and later, the other men who were working in the field left one by one, until the father and his son were the last ones working. The son turned to his father and asked, "Dad, everyone else has gone. Why are we still here?" The father replied, "Son, some men come merely to hoe weeds. They come out of duty. Others come to help grow food for the needy. They come out of love. And some come because this is one of the highest ways of honoring the promises and covenants they made at baptism, to support one another and bear one another's burdens. When we finish this row, I think we will have done our part and for the right reasons."

■ Another way to care for the poor and needy is to give a generous fast offering.

■ Isaiah 58:5–11. What are some of the reasons for fasting? _____

_____

■ What blessings does the Lord promise to those who fast appropriately and for the right reasons? _____

_____

President Spencer W. Kimball has called upon Church members to increase their fast offering contributions:

"Each member should contribute a generous fast offering for the care of the poor and the needy. This offering should at least be the value of the two meals not eaten while fasting.

" 'Sometimes we have been a bit penurious and figured that we had for breakfast one egg and that cost so many cents and then we give that to the Lord. I think that when we are affluent, as many of us are, that we ought to be very, very generous. . . .

" 'I think we should . . . give, instead of the amount saved by our two meals of fasting, perhaps much, much more—ten times more when we are in a position to do it' [Conference Report, Oct. 1974, p. 184].

". . . If we give a generous fast offering, we shall increase our own prosperity both spiritually and temporally" (in Conference Report, Oct. 1977, p. 126; also *Ensign*, Nov. 1977, pp. 78–79).

■ Mosiah 18:8–11. When we accept welfare assignments willingly and pay generous fast offerings, how are we fulfilling these obligations of membership in the Lord's Church? _____

_____

Will It Make a Difference?

In our dispensation the Lord has commanded that his people shall be provided for. "But," he cautioned, "it must needs be

done in mine own way" (D&C 104:15–16). At the present time
the welfare services plan is the Lord's "own way" of caring for
the poor and the needy. By means of this plan we are able to
reach out to those in need—to the widow, the orphan, the
handicapped, and the distressed—as we have been commanded
(see D&C 44:6).

As we willingly accept welfare assignments and give a generous
fast offering, we play a vital part in the Lord's work. As we offer
both our time and our means, we develop "the pure love of
Christ" (Moroni 7:47) and thus qualify to "become the sons of
God" (Moroni 7:48).

Quorum Training Suggestions

■ This is the second lesson in a three-week quorum workshop on
welfare services. One of your obligations as quorum leaders is to
be certain that the members of your quorum understand how
important it is that they support the storehouse resource system
by accepting welfare services assignments and by giving a
generous fast offering. To help quorum members better
understand how the resources of the storehouse resource system
are allocated, describe how the ward welfare services committee
works on the local level to assist those in need.

■ To encourage individual study, invite the quorum members to
share insights from their personal study by asking questions
such as the following:

What is meant by the statement, "Welfare Services is not a
program, but the essence of the gospel"?

What benefits can be derived from the welfare services plan by
both the giver and the receiver?

What is the main reason for giving a generous fast offering?

■ You may wish to make a list of welfare assignments that might
be given to a quorum member and explain the purpose of each.

■ You could invite a member of the bishopric to outline on the
chalkboard the resources of the storehouse resource system
available to your Church unit and to explain how those
resources are used to help the needy.

■ You may want to show the sixteen-minute film *Welfare—
Another Perspective* (MP172). For non-English speaking areas, use

the filmstrip *Welfare Services, The Gospel in Action (Bermejillo)* (OF283). Both provide excellent background material and ideas for discussion. If you use a film, you may want to spend an extra week on this lesson.

▪ Encourage quorum members to review Isaiah 58:3–11 and to evaluate their own fast-offering contributions in light of section 3 of this lesson.

▪ You could invite the bishop or the appropriate high councilor to visit the quorum to explain the welfare production projects, if any, within the stake and the vital role that assigned labor plays in the success of such projects.

▪ Additional resources that you may wish to consult in preparing this lesson are the following:

J. Richard Clarke, "The Storehouse Resource System," *Ensign,* May 1978, pp. 82–84; also Conference Report, Apr. 1978, pp. 124–27

Gordon B. Hinckley, "Welfare Responsibilities of the Priesthood Quorums," *Ensign,* Nov. 1977, pp. 84–86 (see Appendix 2, pp. 285–89)

Victor L. Brown, "A Vision of the Law of the Fast," *Ensign,* Nov. 1977, pp. 82–84

The February 1979 issue of the *Ensign,* which contains several excellent articles on welfare services principles and the storehouse resource system, especially the article titled "Thirteen Wards"

The *Welfare Services Handbook*

Welfare Services Workshop: Helping Those with Special Needs

D&C 52:40

Personal Study

Reach out to assist those with special needs.

In one of his parables, the Savior said of those who will inherit the celestial kingdom:

"For I was an hungered, and ye gave me meat: I was thirsty, and ye gave me drink: I was a stranger, and ye took me in:

'Naked, and ye clothed me: I was sick and ye visited me: I was in prison, and ye came unto me.

"Then shall the righteous answer him, saying, Lord, when saw we thee an hungered, and fed thee? or thirsty, and gave thee drink?

"When saw we thee a stranger, and took thee in? or naked, and clothed thee? . . .

"And the King shall answer and say unto them, Verily I say unto you, Inasmuch as ye have done it unto one of the least of these my brethren, ye have done it unto me" (Matthew 25:35–40).

The Savior has made it clear that our salvation depends in large measure upon how we assist those in need. Some have needs that are easily met, such as a neighbor who needs help moving or who needs a meal provided at a time of illness or bereavement. Others have needs that are much more complex. The elderly, dependent children, those involved in deviant behavior, the sick and the bereaved, those with severe employment difficulties, and those in hospitals, prisons, or other institutions are only a few with very special needs.

Bishop Victor L. Brown, reporting in a welfare services session of general conference, revealed the following:

"The average ward has one blind child, four children with hearing problems, nine with speech difficulties, two with learning disabilities, two who are physically disabled, and five who are retarded. . . . Considering the adults who have problems, . . . the numbers are even higher" (*Ensign*, Apr. 1976, p. 14).

We have the primary responsibility for meeting our own needs, then the family is responsible, and then the Church. But beyond these guidelines there is a great need for sensitive, loving, personal service. Such service is an expression of Christlike compassion and understanding and a willingness to "bear one another's burdens, that they may be light" (Mosiah 18:8).

Study this material thoroughly and prayerfully, and consider how you and your family can apply these principles. Prepare to participate in the third quorum workshop.

---

1 I Will Ease the Burdens of Those in Need

■ Mosiah 18:8–10. What are the obligations of Church members toward the handicapped, the institutionalized, the elderly, or others with special needs? How is this kind of caring for others related to our willingness to "stand as witnesses of God at all times and in all things"?

■ Job 29:12–13, 15–17, 25. According to the Lord's own witness, Job was a perfect man (see Job 1:8). What do these verses describe about Job's love and care for the poor and the needy and the distressed? (Compare Deuteronomy 27:18–19.)

■ Matthew 25:33–40. What great blessings does the Lord promise to those who learn to serve as these verses prescribe?

The following guidelines should help us better understand brothers and sisters with handicaps, whether physical or emotional:

A person with a hearing disability. Face him when you speak, and do not turn or nod your head frequently. Let your facial expression support what you are saying and feeling. Speak naturally, avoid shouting, and speak distinctly at a moderate pace.

A person with a visual disability. Make your presence known by speaking and saying your name. Talk naturally about the things you see, and do not hesitate to use "seeing" words: "I'm glad to see you." "Come and see the new baby." Guide with your voice as well as with your hands. Let the person place his hands on your arm or shoulder. Prepare him for unexpected hazards, such as stairs. Physical contact—a handshake or a pat on the back—can take the place of smiles and facial expressions.

A person with another type of physical handicap. Many physically handicapped persons live alone and are unable to do certain necessary tasks, such as replacing light bulbs, shoveling walks, and mowing lawns. It is important, however, that you let a person with a physical handicap do what he can for himself. Do not obviously avoid looking at a deformity, but look the person in the face. Remember that even at the best of times, any person may not be entirely well; watch for signs that a handicapped person needs general encouragement as well as specific help.

A person with a mental handicap. Be friendly. In speaking with a person who has a mental handicap, use simple words and do not raise your voice. Make instructions simple, and give them one at a time. Show the person in addition to telling him. Peer group acceptance is as important to a mentally handicapped person as to anyone else, and his feelings are equally sensitive. With more emphasis on participation than on achievement, he should be encouraged to be involved in programs of the Church to the extent possible.

▪ A handicap in no way implies inferiority. A handicapped person does not need pity; he needs understanding and the knowledge that he has some control over his own life. We should help every member to be as independent as possible.

Do not assume that a member with special needs cannot serve. A handicapped person needs to be a giver as well as a receiver. He should have opportunities to give meaningful service, but he should not be given assignments beyond his capabilities, which can lead to frustration and embarrassment.

---

2 I Will Reach Out to the Lonely and Confined

▪ Alma 1:27–30. What do these verses tell us about the Church in Alma's day? What did this Book of Mormon people do for the sick and the afflicted? What can we give in addition to our substance?

Elder L. Tom Perry, in giving tribute to his father, has emphasized the rewards that come from reaching out and ministering to those with special needs:

"My father was a bishop. . . .

"I will always remember the dignity and patience he exhibited towards those in need. I particularly remember a little old man who had lost his wife and some of the soundness of his mind. My father not only filled the role of his bishop, but also that of his friend. To the family, however, this little old man was considered to be somewhat of a pest. When he would become lonely he would make his way to see my father. It didn't matter whether it was ten o'clock at night or five-thirty in the morning, Father would always welcome him into our home, give him some nourishment, and then he would drive him back to his place of residence.

"I remember at his passing seeing Father reading a letter addressed to 'My friend, Bishop Perry,' as a final thank-you for taking an interest in his life when he was an old man. I saw the tears roll down my father's cheeks as he read the letter. It was then I think I recognized for the first time an understanding of the rewards of gospel service" (*Ensign*, May 1977, p. 90).

3 I Will Comfort the Widow and the Orphan

Elder Gordon B. Hinckley has explained as follows why men in the priesthood need to serve the widows and the fatherless: "When the Relief Society was organized the Prophet Joseph said of the women of the Society: 'They will fly to the relief of the stranger; they will pour in the wine and the oil to the wounded heart of the distressed; they will dry up the tears of the orphan and make the widow's heart to rejoice.' (B. H. Roberts, *Comprehensive History of the Church*, 4:112.) I would hope that the same might be said of the men of the priesthood" (*Ensign*, Nov. 1977, p. 86).

■ D&C 44:6. What are the Saints commanded to do for those in need? Can the high requirement of this passage be met without personal involvement? Why is personal involvement often necessary?

■ James 1:27. How does James define the pure practice of
religion? How is this principle such an exact and revealing
measure of a man's religion and spirituality?

---

4 I Will Be a Friend to the Aged

The late President J. Reuben Clark, Jr., said:

"I honor and respect old age. I would not see it suffer from
want, nor from disease that can be helped. It is entitled to every
care, to every act of kindness, to every loving caress which a
grateful community and a devoted family can give.

"I have every sympathy with age. I know the difficulties which
age has. . . .

"Some plan must be devised to make certain that no aged
person shall be cold or go hungry or unclad. *But the prime
responsibility for supporting an aged parent rests upon his family, not
upon society. . . . The family which refuses to keep its own is not
meeting its duties.* When an aged parent has no family or when
the family is itself without means, then society must, as a matter
of merest humanity, come to the rescue. This is perfectly clear"
(as quoted by Marion G. Romney, in Conference Report, Apr.
1976, pp. 165–66; or *Ensign,* May 1976, p. 121; italics added).

About our responsibility to befriend and care for our parents
and others who are aged, President Kimball said:

"We hear reports from time to time of older men and women
who, in the sunset of their lives, are neglected by their families
and their neighbors. Those who are both poor and old often
suffer doubly. We hope family members, quorums, Relief
Society officers, bishops, and others using the Lord's own way,
will make certain that they are not inadvertently neglecting such
needy people. The ways the world has of helping the poor are
not often the Lord's way. We must render help in the Lord's
way, *but let us do it! . . .*

" . . . The ones about whom I am particularly speaking,
however, are those who will suffer in silence, because they are
proud or because they do not know what to do. Surely sensitive
home teachers, visiting teachers, quorum leaders, and bishops
can be more effective in both ascertaining and responding to the

needs of these individuals and meeting them" (address at
Regional Representatives' seminar, 29 Sept. 1978; italics added).

Quorum Training Suggestions

This lesson is the last part of a quorum workshop on welfare
services.

As quorum leader, you have a major responsibility for those
with special needs. All quorum members have the obligation
inherent in their ordination to reach out and care for those with
special needs. This last part of the quorum workshop on welfare
services should provide an excellent opportunity for you to teach
your quorum how to serve the poor, the needy, and the
distressed. The quorum members must realize that many people
would love to help but sometimes do not know who needs their
help. As President Spencer W. Kimball said: "I do not worry
about members of the Church being unresponsive when they
learn of the needy as much as I worry about our being unaware
of such needs" (address at Regional Representatives' seminar, 29
Sept. 1978, p. 2). Therefore, as a part of this quorum workshop
and as a regular part of quorum business (at least monthly), you
may wish to review briefly the individual circumstances of
quorum or ward members with special needs; you could then
encourage quorum members to serve these people quietly and
privately, by such services as helping members who are moving,
visiting the sick and the homebound, and providing
transportation for the aged. Of course, such services should not
conflict with care by the home teachers and others, nor should
delicate or confidential matters or needs that might cause
embarrassment be discussed openly in the quorum meeting. We
should coordinate, through the welfare services committee, our
Church efforts to help those in need. We should be wise and
sensitive in our private efforts.

■ If a member of your ward has had professional experience with
the handicapped, invite him to share with the quorum his
positive experiences in helping such persons.

■ You may wish to encourage members of the quorum to discuss
during a special family home evening the principles covered in
this lesson.

■ One of the most frequent failings in helping those with special
needs is inconstancy. A widow may receive a call that on

Saturday quorum members will come to clean and repair and replace. On Saturday, they come and do that and then leave. Sunday comes and goes, a week passes with no follow-up, and months and years go by with little further help or contact. Emphasize the need for constancy. Remind the quorum how long the days and weeks become to someone with special needs who is neglected.

■ President N. Eldon Tanner's address "Latter-day Samaritans" (*Ensign*, Nov. 1977, pp. 91–93; or Conference Report, Oct. 1977, pp. 118–21) contains insight on reaching out and caring for those with special needs. A quorum member could be assigned to discuss President Tanner's talk as part of this workshop. Bishop J. Richard Clarke's "Ministering to Needs through LDS Social Services" (*Ensign*, May 1977, pp. 85–87) and Sister Barbara B. Smith's "In the Time of Old Age" (*Ensign*, May 1978, pp. 85–86; also Conference Report, Apr. 1978, pp. 128–30) are excellent supporting resources for this workshop.

■ Because this is the final workshop of this series, you may wish to summarize and discuss the welfare services duties of members. Quorum members can provide for themselves, their families, and those in need by doing the following:

Learn and live gospel principles of love, service, work, self-reliance, consecration, and stewardship.

Achieve greater personal and family preparedness. Read and learn. Do good work and improve job skills. Use money and other resources wisely. Grow your own food and obtain a year's supply of food, clothing, and fuel (where possible). Exercise and eat properly. Learn to deal with life's problems in a spiritual way. (See 1 Timothy 5:8.)

Help the Church care for the poor, the needy, and the distressed. Give a generous fast offering. Help provide needed commodities or services (see D&C 52:40).

Care for your family and neighbors. Look after your parents and other family members (see 1 Timothy 5:8). Show concern for your neighbors. Care for the sick, the bereaved, the elderly, the orphaned, widows, those in hospitals or prisons, the handicapped, and others with special needs (see Mosiah 4:16–26; 18:8–9).

Let Every Man Learn His Duty

D&C 107

Personal Study

Learn the duties of the priesthood office you hold.

Elder Mark E. Petersen, has said the following regarding the importance of the Priesthood:

"The Holy Priesthood is the power by which mortal men may act in the name of God.

"Think of it! The power to act for God! Who can grasp the significance of such a delegation of authority? Who can measure such a privilege?

"The entire plan of salvation is embraced in priesthood functions. Without the priesthood there would be no salvation, for it is through the Church that the Lord saves his faithful people, and it is through the priesthood—men called of God as was Aaron—that the Church fulfills its divine destiny" (*Priesthood*, p. 48).

"What, then, are the duties related to the Holy Priesthood? asks Elder Petersen.

"They may be summarized as follows: (1) strengthening the established church; (2) preaching the gospel to the world; and (3) laboring for our dead.

"All three responsibilities require the exercise of priesthood, primarily that of the Melchizedek order" (*Priesthood,* p. 49).

It is a great honor to bear the sacred Melchizedek Priesthood and to serve as an elder or a seventy or a high priest. Do we understand the duties and responsibilities of the priesthood offices that we hold? Are we prepared to give an account to the Lord of what we have done with the sacred power and authority that he has entrusted to our care?

1 Priesthood Is the Power and Authority of God

▪ President Spencer W. Kimball said: "The priesthood is the power and authority of God delegated to man on earth to act in all things pertaining to the salvation of men. It is the means whereby the Lord acts through men to save souls. Without this priesthood power, men are lost" ("The Example of Abraham," *Ensign,* June 1975, p. 3).

▪ D&C 107:1–6, 18–20. There are in the Church two divisions of priesthood—the Melchizedek Priesthood and the Aaronic Priesthood. What do the scriptures say is the power and authority of the higher priesthood? _____

_____

What is the power and authority of the lesser priesthood? _____

_____

▪ What priesthood offices are there in the Melchizedek Priesthood?

D&C 107:7 _____

_____

D&C 107:25 _____

_____

D&C 68:19 _____

_____

D&C 124:91 _____

_____

D&C 107:23 _____

_____

▪ What priesthood offices are there in the Aaronic Priesthood?
D&C 20:57–59 _____

_____

D&C 20:53 _____

_____

D&C 20:46 _____

D&C 107:68 _____

■ D&C 124:143. Why has the Lord provided these priesthood offices? (Compare Ephesians 4:11–15.) _____

■ Elder Bruce R. McConkie said: "The priesthood is greater than any of its offices. No office adds any power, dignity, or authority to the priesthood. All offices derive their rights, virtues, and authorities from the priesthood" ("Tools to Help the Quorum Achieve Its Goals," address at Regional Representatives' seminar, 4 Oct. 1973). Since the priesthood is greater than any of its offices, why can't a high priest perform any greater service in the kingdom than an elder? _____

2 Act in the Office in Which You Are Appointed

■ What are offices or callings in the priesthood? Elder Bruce R. McConkie explained: "They are assignments to labor on the basis of primary responsibility in a specialized field of priesthood service. Service is essential to salvation. . . . We have to get outside of ourselves and do something for someone else, patterning our course after that of the Lord Jesus, if we are going to have an inheritance with him" ("Tools to Help the Quorum Achieve Its Goals").

■ Why do we have offices or callings in the priesthood? Elder McConkie said:

"So that brethren can become specialists in the performance of priesthood labors. . . .

" . . . In other words, the perfect system of priesthood correlation is for an elder to do the work of an elder, a seventy the work of a seventy, and a high priest the work of a high priest" ("Tools to Help the Quorum Achieve Its Goals").

■ D&C 20:38–45. What is the work of an elder? _____

What additional elements of the work of an elder are listed in these verses: D&C 42:12, 44; 107:11–12? _____

_____

What additional duties have been assigned to elders in the Church today by those who hold the keys to direct the work of the priesthood? _____

_____

■ D&C 107:25, 97. What is the work of a seventy? Seventies are elders with all the powers of elders, plus the additional call and ordination to do what? _____

_____

■ D&C 107:10, 12, 17. What is the work of a high priest? _____

_____

What additional elements of the work of a high priest are listed in these verses: D&C 102:1; 124:133–35? _____

_____

High priests are elders with all the powers of elders, plus the additional call and ordination to do what? _____

_____

■ D&C 84:109–10. What are the Lord's instructions to those who hold the various offices of the priesthood? _____

_____

■ D&C 107:99–100. What two things does the Lord expect of every priesthood bearer? _____

_____

Will It Make a Difference?

The Lord expects every priesthood bearer to learn his duty and to act diligently in his own calling. By studying carefully the scriptures in this lesson, we can learn more about the priesthood we bear and how to magnify our calling in it. We should study further to increase our understanding of the duties and opportunities of the priesthood office we hold. We should always remember that our labors in our priesthood office are subject to the presidency of our quorum leader. Let us learn our duties and strive diligently to act in the priesthood office to which we have been called.

Quorum Training Suggestions

As a quorum leader, you have a responsibility to preside over your quorum members, "and to sit in council with them, and to teach them according to the covenants" (see D&C 107:89). In this lesson you should help the quorum members understand what the priesthood is and help them learn how to perform the duties of the office they hold. Assign the quorum members to study the personal study guide material before coming to the quorum meeting so that they will be prepared to discuss the various offices and callings in the priesthood. As you plan the quorum training, you may wish to use some of the following ideas.

▪ To encourage individual study, invite the quorum members to share the answers they found to questions in the self-instruction portion of the lesson. You might ask the following questions:

What is the priesthood, and why is it important?

What are the offices in the two divisions of priesthood?

Why has the Lord provided these priesthood offices?

▪ Assign one or more quorum members to prepare before coming to quorum meeting to report briefly on Elder McConkie's address, "Only an Elder." This address was printed in *My Errand from the Lord: A Personal Study Guide for Melchizedek Priesthood Quorums 1976–77*, pages 239–49, and in the *Ensign*, June 1975, pages 66–69. (The principles discussed in this address apply also to seventies and high priests.)

▪ In order to emphasize the idea that every priesthood office is important, have a quorum member read this statement by President Joseph F. Smith:

"I hold to the doctrine that the duty of a teacher is as sacred as the duty of an apostle, in the sphere in which he is called to act. . . .

"A deacon in the Church should exercise the authority of that calling in the Priesthood, and honor that position as sincerely and faithfully as a high priest or apostle should his calling" (*Gospel Doctrine*, pp. 163, 168).

■ Discuss with the quorum members "the oath and covenant which belongeth to the priesthood" (see D&C 84:33–44). Ask such questions as these:

What does the Lord expect of us?

What blessings are promised to those who obtain the priesthood and magnify their calling?

What does it mean to magnify a calling? (See also Jacob 1:19; Ezekiel 3:17–21.)

As a priesthood bearer, what can I do to learn my duties? to keep them in mind? to magnify my calling better?

Provide paper and pencils to the quorum members, and encourage them to list what they personally need to do to learn their duty, to keep their duty in mind, and to magnify their calling better. You may need to offer some general suggestions, based on your understanding of the needs of quorum members. Challenge them to select one or two items from their lists to begin working on during the coming week.

■ Remind the quorum members that at least once each year the quorum leader will have a personal interview with each quorum member. Suggest to quorum members that they might prepare for these interviews by being ready to discuss such questions as these:

What do you understand your priesthood duties to be?

What plans do you have to learn and to better understand your priesthood duties?

How do you plan to magnify your priesthood calling? In what ways? Are your plans consistent with the principles of priesthood service as found in the Doctrine and Covenants? Does your quorum leader agree with how you plan to magnify your priesthood office, or with how you are magnifying it now?

■ Compile as a quorum a list of basic responsibilities shared by every priesthood bearer. This list might include personal worthiness, gospel study, service to others, missionary work, genealogical and temple work, personal and family preparedness, and citizenship and community involvement.

■ Ask the quorum members why some priesthood bearers do not learn or carry out their priesthood duties. As reasons are suggested, discuss ways to overcome the obstacles. For example, if lack of time seems to be a problem, you may need to spend some time discussing the principles of time management. Ask quorum members for reasons why some priesthood bearers do learn and carry out their priesthood duties. Discuss how these same practices could be adopted by everyone.

The Light of Christ

D&C 88:3–50

Personal Study

Seek to understand the roles of the Light of Christ and the Holy Ghost in your life.

The Lord is concerned about all of his children; he has not left us alone to grope in spiritual darkness. He has provided us with the means of distinguishing good from evil and has made available to all his children a basic spiritual sense that can eventually lead them to a full discovery of him and all righteousness.

President David O. McKay said: "Man is a spiritual being, a soul, and at some period of his life everyone is possessed with an irresistable desire to know his relationship to the Infinite. . . . There is something within him which urges him to rise above himself, to control his environment, to master the body and all things physical and live in a higher and more beautiful world" (*True to the Faith*, p. 244).

Do you sense in your own life that the Lord indeed is "not far from every one of us" (Acts 17:27)? We should always keep our lives in order so that we may feel the Spirit of the Lord with us. We should be anxiously working to attain a greater measure of light and truth.

1 What Is the Light of Christ?

■ D&C 88:6–13. What is the Light of Christ? _____

_____

What functions of the Light of Christ do you discover in the previous verses? _____

_____

"This Light of Christ is not a personage. It has no body. I do not know what it is as far as substance is concerned; but it fills the immensity of space and emanates from God. It is the light by which the worlds are controlled, by which they are made. It is the light of the sun and all other bodies. It is the light which gives life to vegetation. It quickens the understanding of men, and has these various functions as set forth in these verses.

"It is: 'The light which is in all things, which giveth life to all things, which is the law by which all things are governed, even the power of God who sitteth upon His throne, who is in the bosom of eternity, who is in the midst of all things.' (D&C 88:13.)

"This is our explanation in regard to the Spirit of Christ, or Light of Truth, which every man receives and is guided by. Unless a man had the blessings that come from this Spirit, his mind would not be quickened; there would be no vegetation [growing]; the worlds would not stay in their orbits; because it is through this Spirit of Truth, this Light of Truth, according to this revelation, that all these things are done" (Joseph Fielding Smith, *Doctrines of Salvation*, 1:52).

2 The Light of Christ Strives to Lead Mankind

■ John 1:6–9; Moroni 7:15–18; D&C 84:45–48. To whom is the Light of Christ given? _____

_____

What will result for those who hearken to the Light or Spirit of Jesus Christ? _____

_____

"If a man who has never heard the gospel will hearken to the teachings and manifestations of the Spirit of Christ, or the Light of Truth, which come to him, often spoken of as conscience— every man has a conscience and knows more or less when he does wrong, and the Spirit guides him if he will hearken to its whisperings—it will lead him eventually to the fulness of the gospel. That is, he is guided by the Light, and when the gospel comes he will be ready to receive it. This is what the Lord tells us in section 84 of the *Doctrine and Covenants*" (Joseph Fielding Smith, *Doctrines of Salvation*, 1:51).

Why is it not possible for one to truthfully say, "I have no way of knowing the truth of God or what is right"? _____

_____

"No person is, nor can he be, justified in rejecting these teachings and commandments, which have been revealed by the Lord, on the basis that he does not know they are true, because everything the Lord does or says has within itself the evidence of its own authenticity, and every person is divinely endowed with the means to discover that evidence and know for himself that it is true" (Marion G. Romney, in Conference Report, Apr. 1976, pp. 120–21; or *Ensign*, May 1976, p. 81).

■ Alma 10:1, 4–6. Have there been times in your life when you were "called" but "'would not hear"?

■ 2 Nephi 26:11; Ether 2:15; Alma 12:9–11. What happens when someone consistently and totally refuses to hearken to the influence of the Light of Christ? _____

_____

In summary, the Light of Christ is given to all and will brighten or dim in each of our lives according to how well we hearken to its promptings.

_____

3 The Light of Christ and the Holy Ghost

"The Holy Ghost should not be confused with the Spirit which fills the immensity of space and which is everywhere present. This other Spirit is impersonal and has no size, nor dimension; it proceeds forth from the presence of the Father and the Son and is in all things. We should speak of the Holy Ghost as a personage as 'he' and this other Spirit as 'it,' although when we speak of the power or gift of the Holy Ghost we may properly say 'it.' . . .

". . . The Holy Ghost, as we are taught in our modern revelation, is the third member in the Godhead and a personage of Spirit. These terms are used synonymously: Spirit of God, Spirit of the Lord, Spirit of Truth, Holy Spirit, Comforter; all having reference to the Holy Ghost. The same terms largely are used in relation to the Spirit of Jesus Christ, also called the Light of Truth, Light of Christ, Spirit of God, and Spirit of the Lord; and yet they are separate and distinct things. We have a great deal of confusion because we have not kept that clearly in our minds" (Joseph Fielding Smith, *Doctrines of Salvation*, 1:49–50).

"It is by the power of God that all things are made that have been made. It is by the power of Christ that all things are governed and kept in place that are governed and kept in place in the universe. It is the power which proceeds from the presence of the Son of God throughout all the works of his hands, that giveth light, energy, understanding, knowledge, and a degree of intelligence to all the children of men, strictly in accordance with the words in the Book of Job: 'There is a spirit in man; and the inspiration of the Almighty giveth them understanding.' It is this inspiration from God, proceeding throughout all his creations, that enlighteneth the children of men; and it is nothing more nor less than the spirit of Christ that enlighteneth the mind, that quickeneth the understanding, and that prompteth the children of men to do that which is good and to eschew that which is evil; which quickens the conscience of man and gives him intelligence to judge between good and evil, light and darkness, right and wrong.

"But the Holy Ghost, who bears record of the Father and the Son, who takes of the things of the Father and shows them unto men, who testifies of Jesus Christ, and of the everliving God, the Father of Jesus Christ, and who bears witness of the truth—this Spirit, this Intelligence, is not given unto all men until they repent of their sins and come into a state of worthiness before the Lord. Then they receive the gift of the Holy Ghost by the laying on of the hands of those who are authorized of God to bestow his blessings upon the heads of the children of men. . . .

"The question is often asked, Is there any difference between the Spirit of the Lord and the Holy Ghost? The terms are frequently used synonymously. We often say the Spirit of God when we mean the Holy Ghost; we likewise say the Holy Ghost when we mean the Spirit of God. The Holy Ghost is a personage in the Godhead, and is not that which lighteth every man that cometh into the world. It is the Spirit of God which proceeds through Christ to the world, that enlightens every man that comes into the world, and that strives with the children of men, and will continue to strive with them, until it brings them to a knowledge of the truth and the possession of the greater light and testimony of the Holy Ghost" (Joseph F. Smith, *Gospel Doctrine*, pp. 66–68).

"The person of the Holy Ghost can work through the Spirit of Christ that permeates everything, or he can work by personal contacts. The Holy Ghost can act through some other influence or force. This may be a crude illustration, and yet I think it answers our purpose. We have in this building a young lady sitting down at the switchboard. Someone on this floor wants to get in touch with someone on the second floor; somebody else in another part of the building wants to talk with someone in another building; and so on. They are all connected with the parties they want to talk to. In a similar way the Holy Ghost could speak to someone here, someone over there, and someone way off in some other part of the country, even in a foreign land, and each receive the message intended for him. That is not hard to understand when we think of telegraphy. They send several messages over a wire at the same time. Radio stations send messages of different wave lengths all over the earth" (Joseph Fielding Smith, *Doctrines of Salvation*, 1:54).

It Will Make a Difference

"The Old Testament prophets repeatedly foretold the great apostacy and referred to a darkness that would cover the earth and the people. From the scriptures . . . it is evident that only through the Spirit of Christ can we be enlightened and comprehend truth and that when the gospel was withdrawn from the earth, the progress of man was retarded. Since the restoration of the gospel, and the investiture once again of the power of God as given to man through the priesthood of God, it is remarkable to note the advances in all fields of learning. All truth is discerned through the Spirit of Truth or the Light of Christ" (N. Eldon Tanner, in *Conference Report*, Oct. 1977, pp. 75, 76).

▪ How can you make the Spirit of Christ more meaningful in your life? _____

Quorum Training Suggestions

■ Discuss in what sense the Lord is "not far from every one of us" (Acts 17:27).

■ Carefully read and discuss D&C 88:6–13, 41. List the various functions of the Light of Christ on the chalkboard. Ask: What would happen to the world, indeed to men and all living things, were the Light of Christ withdrawn (see Mosiah 2:20–22)?

■ Discuss the relationship of the Light of Christ and our accountability before the Lord. Can any who are accountable escape responsibility for the choices they make in life? Why?

■ Discuss the distinction between the Light of Christ and the gift of the Holy Ghost (see President Marion G. Romney's remarks in Conference Report, Apr. 1977, pp. 59–63; or *Ensign*, May 1977, pp. 43–45).

■ Read the following statement by President J. Reuben Clark, Jr. and discuss our responsibility to help unkindle the dimming lights of those who have slipped into inactivity or are following the ways of the world: "It is my hope and my belief that the Lord never permits the light of faith wholly to be extinguished in any human heart, however faint the light may glow. The Lord has provided that there shall still be there a spark which, with teaching, with the spirit of righteousness, with love, with tenderness, with example, with living the Gospel, shall brighten and glow again, however darkened the mind may have been. And if we shall fail so to reach those among us of our own whose faith has dwindled low, we shall fail in one of the main things which the Lord expects at our hands" (in Conference Report, Oct. 1936, p. 114).

■ Have quorum members look up references to the Light of Christ in the Topical Guide of the Latter-day Saint edition of the King James Bible.

■ Discuss the relationship of one's conscience to the Light of Christ.

■ Read and discuss the definition of the Light of Christ found on page 725 of the Bible Dictionary in the Latter-day Saint edition of the King James Bible.

■ Read and discuss the following statement by President Spencer W. Kimball: "The conscience whispers to us what is right and what is wrong. We cannot blame others or circumstances. We know what is right" (in Conference Report, Apr. 1974, pp. 125; or *Ensign*, May 1974, p. 87).

■ Read and discuss the following observation by Elder Boyd K. Packer: "It is critically important that you understand that you already know right from wrong, that you're innately, inherently, and intuitively good. When you say, 'I can't! I can't solve my problems!' I want to thunder out, 'Don't you realize who you are? Haven't you learned yet that you are a son or a daughter of Almighty God? Do you not know that there are powerful resources inherited from Him that you can call upon to give you steadiness and courage and great power?' " ("Self Reliance," *Speeches of the Year,* 1975, Provo, Utah, Brigham Young University Press, p. 355).

Male and Female Created He Them

D&C 38:27

Personal Study

Understand the divine callings of men and women.

President Spencer W. Kimball, speaking of the creation of Adam and Eve, said:

"As they completed this magnificent creation, they looked it over and pronounced it 'good, very good'—something that isn't to be improved upon by our modern intellectuals; the male to till the ground, support the family, to give proper leadership; the woman to cooperate, to bear children, and to rear and teach them. It was 'good, very good.'

"And that's the way the Lord organized it. This wasn't an experiment. He knew what he was doing" ("The Blessings and Responsibilities of Womanhood," *Ensign*, March 1976, p. 71).

Why is there confusion in the world today about the proper callings of men and women? Do you understand what the gospel teaches about these callings? Can you find security and peace in fulfilling your calling?

1 The Man Is to Preside, Provide, and Protect

■ Genesis 3:16–19. What is the calling the Lord gave to the man?

President Spencer W. Kimball commented: "I have a question about the word *rule*. It gives the wrong impression. I would prefer to use the word *preside* because that's what he does. A righteous husband presides over his wife and family" ("The Blessings and Responsibilities of Womanhood," p. 72). How should a husband preside over his wife and children? _____

■ 1 Timothy 5:8. What does this verse say man is to do? Can a man justifiably reject the responsibility to provide for his family or transfer it to government, to the Church, or to his wife? Why? _____

_____

■ Of a man's duty to provide for his wife, President David O. McKay said, "Woman's mission and throne is the family, and if anything is withheld that would make her more efficient, useful, or happy in that sphere, she is wronged and has not her rights" (*Church News*, 24 Jan. 1970, p. 2). How can a man lighten his wife's load? With what should he provide her? _____

_____

■ Ephesians 5:25. How can you love your wife as required in this verse? _____

_____

President Kimball said:

"Can you think of how [Christ] loved the Church? Its every breath was important to him. Its every growth, its every individual, was precious to him. He gave to those people all his energy, all his power, all his interest. He gave his life—and what more could one give? . . .

"When the husband is ready to treat his household in that manner, not only his wife but also his children will respond to his loving and exemplary leadership. It will be automatic. He won't need to demand it" (*Men of Example*, address to religious educators [published by the Church Educational System], 12 Sept. 1975, p. 5).

How can you provide for and protect your wife and your family in this manner? _____

_____

How much of your life are you giving to them now? _____

_____

■ Elder Bruce R. McConkie wrote: "[Husbands] must . . . love their wives, sacrifice for their well-being and salvation, and guide them in holiness until they are cleansed, sanctified, and perfected, until they are prepared for exaltation in that glorious heaven where the family unit continues. Husbands thus become in effect the saviors of their wives" (*Doctrinal New Testament*

Commentary, 2:519). How can a man guide his wife and children in holiness? What personal attributes must he possess if he is to do so? _____

_____

■ What should be our priorities? Elder L. Tom Perry said:

"Brethren, your first and most responsible role in life and in the eternities is to be a righteous husband.

"Second only to the title of husband is that of father" ("Father—Your role, Your Responsibility," in Conference Report, Oct. 1977, p. 96; or *Ensign,* Nov. 1977, p. 63).

2 Woman Is to Be a Wife and a Mother

■ Genesis 2:18; 3:16. What is the calling the Lord gave to the woman? _____

_____

Meet means *suitable* or *proper*. What does it mean to be a help *meet*, or *suitable*, for man? _____

_____

■ D&C 25:5. What instruction did the Lord give to Emma Smith?

_____

Can this same instruction apply to all wives? _____

_____

President Kimball said: "Women are expected to earn the living only in emergencies, and . . . many are the broken homes resulting when women leave their posts at home. You see, if both husband and wife are working away from home and come home tired, it is very easy for unpleasantness and misunderstandings to arise" (*Faith Precedes the Miracle,* p. 129).

■ Moses 4:26. In addition to being a wife, which is a woman's foremost calling, she is also a mother. President N. Eldon Tanner said, "The happiest women I know are those whose families would rather be home than any place else; whose children come bounding in after school to look for Mother to tell her about their activities of the day; who share the sorrows and joys and successes of those children and rejoice in their accomplishments" ("Happiness Is Home Centered," *Ensign*, June 1978, p. 2). How much of the responsibility of creating a home where children want to be belongs to the father? _____

What kinds of things can a father do to help? _____

■ "What good is the big picture window and the lavish appointments and the priceless decor in a home if there is no mother there? The mother as a mother, not a breadwinner, is an essential figure in this battle against immorality and wickedness. I would also go back to the family where children were accountable and where father was the head of the family. Would you think me naive if I were to propose that this battle ultimately will be won on such simple grounds as the children coming in after school to homemade bread and jam with Mama there? Or on such grounds as Daddy and Mama taking their youngsters to sacrament meeting? Or that tender hug as they are put to bed and Daddy or Mama saying, 'We need you in this family. You are part of us, and no matter what your troubles are, you can come home'? Would you think me naive to believe that ultimately on the home ground, this battle will be won?" (Boyd K. Packer, address to Seminaries and Institutes faculty, 14 July 1958, pp. 6–7).

What can a husband do to create this kind of home? _____

If a man is married to a woman who is not doing her part to make home a heavenly place, how can he encourage her? _____

How could meeting together at a regular time each week to discuss ways of improving help the family solve this problem?

3 The Two Shall Become One

■ Genesis 2:24; 5:1–2. What are the man and the woman to become? _____

Why were the man and the woman both called Adam? _____

How can this ideal be achieved by every married couple? _____

■ President Marion G. Romney said:

"[Husbands and wives] . . . should be one in harmony, respect, and mutual consideration. Neither should plan or follow an independent course of action. They should consult, pray, and decide together.

"In the management of their homes and families, husbands and wives should counsel with each other in kindness, love, patience, and understanding" ("In the Image of God," *Ensign*, March 1978, p. 2; compare Moses 5:12, first sentence of 16).

■ What are the husband and wife expected to do? _____

In what spirit are they to do it? _____

■ President Kimball said:

"There must be a great unselfishness, forgetting self and . . . subjugating self.

" . . . There must be continued courting and expressions of affection, kindness, and consideration to keep love alive and growing.

" . . . There must be a complete living of the commandments of the Lord as defined in the gospel of Jesus Christ" (*1976 Devotional Speeches of the Year* [Provo, Utah: Brigham Young University Press, 1977], p. 147).

If all husbands and wives heeded this counsel, would marital unhappiness, misunderstandings, or divorces occur? How well are you applying this counsel in your own marriage? When was the last time you expressed your affection and appreciation to your wife? Has she done anything to make your life fulfilled? Have you told her so?

Will It Make a Difference?

President Kimball issued this challenge: "And so we plead with you fathers to return to your little kingdoms and, with kindness, justice, proper discipline, and love, to inspire your family. We appeal to mothers to help create that happy family relationship. We desire that our people strengthen their families" (*Men of Example*, p. 5).

Quorum Training Suggestions

This lesson may generate much discussion. Many members of the quorum may have strong feelings about the ideas discussed. It will be important for you to make sure that the quorum members understand the basic callings of men and women as given in the scriptures and as taught by modern prophets.

- To encourage individual study of the self-instruction materials, use questions such as these to begin the quorum discussion: How should a man treat his wife and his children? In what ways can a husband encourage his wife to magnify her calling as a wife and a mother? What must a husband and wife do to become one?

- Encourage quorum members to sit down with their wives during a quiet hour to study the self-instruction materials together.

- List on the chalkboard the many aspects of the callings of a man and a woman. Under the title *Man*, for example, you might list *husband*, *father*, *provider*, and *protector*. Under *Woman*, you might list *wife*, *mother*, and *homemaker*.

- Discuss the ways a righteous husband should preside over his family. Use D&C 38:27 and 121:41–44 in the discussion. Refer also to President Marion G. Romney, "In the Image of God" (*Ensign*, March 1978, pp. 2–4); and Elder Bruce R. McConkie, "Our Sisters from the Beginning" (*Ensign*, Jan 1979, pp. 61–63).

- Caution the quorum members to avoid judging their wives or their children and to develop an attitude of helpfulness and love. Use Matthew 7:1–5 and the following statements of President Harold B. Lee and Elder Marvin J. Ashton in your discussion. President Lee observed: "Someone has said that a shoddy housekeeper is more often than not the evidence of an unsuccessful manager of her household. And may I add, so often is it the reflection of the kind of treatment she gets from her husband" ("Be Loyal to the Royal within You," *Speeches of the Year*, 1973 [Provo, Utah: Brigham Young University Press, 1974], p. 92). Elder Ashton stated, "To the husband who says his wife is the poorest money manager in the world, I would say, 'Look in the mirror and meet the world's poorest teacher-trainer' " ("One for the Money," *Ensign*, July 1975, p. 73).

■ Show the filmstrip *Father, Consider Your Ways* (OF090; 10 minutes).

■ Use the posters "Why the Family?" (IP069 or IS069) and "The Goal: Family Exaltation" (IP079 or IS079).

■ Consider this statement by President Kimball: "Let us create a climate in which we encourage the sisters of the Church to have a program of personal improvement. It ought to be a practical and realistic program . . . it ought to cause them to reach new levels of achievement . . . to find real self-fulfillment through wise self-development in the pursuit of righteous and worthy endeavors" ("Privileges and Responsibilities of Sisters," *Ensign*, Nov. 1978, p. 104). Ask such questions as these: "Why is it important for women to learn and achieve if they are to be effective wives and mothers? How can a husband encourage his wife to pursue a program of personal improvement?"

■ Check recent conference issues of the *Ensign* (May and November) for current statements by the Brethren about male and female roles.

Why You Are Free to Choose

D&C 29:39

Personal Study

Realize that you are free to choose eternal life or spiritual death because of the Atonement.

We were all involved in a great conflict in the premortal world. Our eternal happiness was at stake.

▪ Moses 4:3. What was the basic issue over which this conflict was waged? _____

_____

How crucial did the Lord consider our agency to be to our eternal growth?

Consider the words of President Joseph F. Smith:

"God has given to all men an agency and has granted to us the privilege to serve him or serve him not, to do that which is right or that which is wrong, and this privilege is given to all men irrespective of creed, color or condition. The wealthy have this agency, the poor have this agency, and no man is deprived by any power of God from exercising it in the fullest and in the freest manner. This agency has been given to all. This is a blessing that God has bestowed upon the world of mankind, upon all his children alike" (*Gospel Doctrine*, p. 49).

▪ How much do you prize this God-given agency? Why is it crucial to your happiness? How is your agency made possible in mortality? What responsibility do you have as a priesthood bearer in connection with your agency?

1 Why Is Freedom of Choice Necessary?

■ Moses 7:32. When did man receive his agency on the earth?

_____

Who gave man his agency? _____

_____

■ Why is your agency so vital? Consider the words of President David O. McKay:

"Next to the bestowal of life itself, the right to direct that life is God's greatest gift to man. Among the immediate obligations and duties resting upon members of the Church today, and one of the most urgent and pressing for attention and action of all liberty-loving people, is the preservation of individual liberty. Freedom of choice is more to be treasured than any possession earth can give. . . .

"Free agency is the impelling source of the soul's progress. It is the purpose of the Lord that man become like him. In order for man to achieve this it was necessary for the Creator first to make him free" (in _Conference Report_, Apr. 1950, p. 32).

"Man's greatest endowment in mortal life is the power of choice—the divine gift of free agency. No true character was ever developed without a sense of soul freedom" (_Man May Know for Himself_, p. 80).

■ D&C 121:37. What happens when a priesthood bearer attempts to exercise control over others unrighteously? _____

_____

Why is coercion so detrimental? _____

_____

■ D&C 121:46. What does the Lord promise to those who use their agency and priesthood righteously? _____

_____

Why could you not achieve the same blessing by compulsion?

_____

2 Why Are You Free to Choose during Mortality?

Identify from the following passages some conditions that make it possible for you to exercise your agency.

■ 2 Nephi 2:16. On what condition are you free to act for yourself? _____

_____

■ Helaman 14:30–31. What does verse 30 say must be present before you can exercise your agency? _____

_____

According to verse 31, what kind of knowledge is necessary for the use of agency? _____

_____

You are free to choose between good and evil, between eternal life and spiritual captivity. But how did eternal life become a real choice for you? _____

_____

■ 2 Nephi 9:8–9. What ultimate "choice" would you have had if the Savior had made no atonement? _____

_____

Can you see that if there had been no atonement you really would not have been free to choose eternal life?

■ 2 Nephi 2:26–29. According to Lehi, what are your basic choices in mortality (see also 2 Nephi 10:23)? _____

_____

Again, why is eternal life a real possibility for you? _____

_____

■ Alma 42:27. Although the Lord makes available the gift of eternal life, and even entices you to seek it, what will he not do? _____

_____

Who then is responsible for what you ultimately receive and become? _____

_____

3 Why Exercise Your Agency Wisely?

When you make a choice, you also choose its consequences. Examine some consequences of bad choices.

■ Moses 5:23. What was the word of the Lord to Cain regarding his choices? _____

_____

■ 1 Samuel 16:12–13; 2 Samuel 11; D&C 132:39. Faithful young David became the great king of ancient Israel but committed grievous sins and lost his eternal inheritance. The Prophet Joseph Smith said:

"No murderer hath eternal life. Even David must wait for those times of refreshing, before he can come forth and his sins be blotted out. For Peter, speaking of him says, 'David hath not yet ascended into heaven, for his sepulchre is with us to this day.' His remains were then in the tomb. Now, we read that many bodies of the Saints arose at Christ's resurrection, probably all the Saints, but it seems that David did not. Why? Because he had been a murderer. . . . The prayers of all the ministers in the world can never close the gates of hell against a murderer" (*Teachings of the Prophet Joseph Smith*, pp. 188–89).

"David sought repentance at the hand of God carefully with tears, for the murder of Uriah; but he could only get it through hell: he got a promise that his soul would not be left in hell" (*Teachings*, p. 339).

As you ponder this tragic episode involving David, what can you learn? Why is David not free (see D&C 88:86)? _____

_____

■ What effect does sinning have upon you? upon your use of the priesthood? _____

_____

■ Consider, for example, how these sins affect you: dishonesty; irreverence; selfishness; lust; pornography; sexual immorality; the use of tobacco, drugs, or alcohol; profanity; idleness; hate; jealousy; indifference. Can you give examples of how one or more of these robs one of "freedom in Christ"? _____

_____

Consider now what results when you use your agency wisely to make righteous choices.

■ John 8:31–32, 36. What two things does Jesus say one must do to be his disciple? _____

_____

If you use your agency wisely and follow the Savior, what will result? _____

_____

Do you see that you have freedom to choose additional freedom (freedom in Christ) or slavery (spiritual captivity)?

■ What does choosing the following virtues free you *from* and *for*? Honesty, reverence, gratitude, kindness, considerateness, prayer, faith, purity, love. What results as you adopt these qualities in your life? _____

_____

How does seeking righteousness affect your ability to magnify your priesthood? Are you able to be a better Saint, a better husband or father, a better priesthood man? Why? _____

_____

■ Ponder the case of Joseph who was sold into Egypt (see Genesis 39). He resisted the advances of Potiphar's wife and was imprisoned falsely because of the woman's accusations. How did Joseph enjoy liberty in Christ even though he was imprisoned physically? Why was the Lord able to use Joseph as an instrument in building his kingdom? _____

_____

■ Alma 41:1–10, especially verses 3–6. In speaking of restoration in the resurrection, what reason does Alma give for exercising your agency properly? _____

_____

**Will It Make
a Difference?**

In our day the Lord has counseled: "Abide ye in the liberty wherewith ye are made free; entangle not yourselves in sin, but let your hands be clean, until the Lord comes" (D&C 88:86).

In ancient times Joshua led the people of Israel across the Jordan river into their promised land, and through the mercy of God, the land was delivered to them. The cities, lands, and vineyards were distributed among the tribes of Israel according to their families as an *inheritance* from the Lord. After Joshua finished his work and concluded a great exhortation to Israel in which he declared, "Choose you this day whom ye will serve." The record says, "Joshua let the people depart, every man unto his *inheritance*" (Joshua 24:15, 28; italics added).

You have a choise of your inheritance also, made possible by the Savior's atonement. What *inheritance* will you receive after this life? Choose your course wisely and be a powerful priesthood instrument in the hands of the Lord.

Quorum Training Suggestions

■ Encourage the quorum members to bring their scriptures to quorum meeting. Follow suggestions and directions of your quorum leaders as you prayerfully adapt your teachings of this lesson to the special needs of your quorum members. Avoid discussion of quorum members' personal problems as you relate their needs to the subject.

■ Briefly review with the quorum the reason for the war in the premortal world. Ask why agency is so crucial to our eternal happiness and growth.

■ Have a quorum member read 2 Nephi 2:27–29. Discuss what basic choices we have in mortality. Give some specific examples of choices that seem to fall into the categories Lehi describes.

■ Ask the question, "What does your agency have to do with your use of the priesthood?" Ask the brethren how they might become effective or ineffective in their use of their priesthood. Seek for personal comments and specific examples.

■ Raise the question, "What conditions must exist in order for you to be free to make moral choices?" Emphasize the fact, as stressed in part 2, that without the atonement of Christ, our only possible end would be physical and spiritual death (see 2 Nephi 9:8–9; 2:26).

■ Discuss the fact that we have as a gift from Christ the agency to choose freedom in Christ or captivity (spiritual death) (see 2 Nephi 2:27). You may wish to discuss as a quorum some of the questions in part 3 regarding how sin enslaves or binds us, or how following Christ frees us. Ask the members to give examples, using the scriptures in the discussion. You may introduce the discussion by having one member read Moses 3:17 and another read John 8:31–32, 36. Then ask the quorum the difference between the freedoms spoken of.

▪ Ask a quorum member in advance to briefly discuss what ultimate consequences flow from pure or impure thoughts, thoughtful or selfish deeds, noble or immoral acts. How do these living patterns affect our ability to magnify our priesthood?

▪ Read Doctrine and Covenants 58:26–29, and discuss the relationship of agency to self-motivated acts of service and compassion.

▪ Have a quorum member read Doctrine and Covenants 29:36–40. Discuss how in yielding to temptation we become subject to the devil.

Receive the Servants of the Lord Sent to You

D&C 20:47

Personal Study

Receive the servants of the Lord sent to you.

John was discouraged. He felt weighted down by the responsibilities of being a husband, father, provider, Church worker, neighbor, and citizen. He and his wife, Sally, had five children, three of them teenagers. His oldest son, Bill, was hesitating about a mission. Another son, Jim, was having difficulty in school. Liza was dating a nonmember. John had wanted to prepare the twins well for baptism, but now, with their eighth birthday just next week, it was too late, and John was disgusted with himself. He and Sally had not completed their genealogy commitments, and despite all his good intentions their "year's supply" would only last for a few months. In addition to all this, John had not paid tithing on his wages for two months earlier in the year, and he was worried about being able to make it up in time for tithing settlement. Every time he heard Church leaders advise the members to set their houses in order, John felt upset and afraid.

Have you ever felt like John? Do your many responsibilities ever seem impossible to fulfill? Are you weighted down by the thought that you are accountable to God for each of these responsibilities? Did you know that God has provided channels through which you may receive help and counsel?

---

1 God Reveals through His Servants All Things Necessary for Perfecting the Saints

■ D&C 28:11; compare D&C 42:88. Hiram Page had a serious problem. The Lord directed Oliver Cowdery to meet with Hiram and to help him. In what kind of setting was Oliver's help to be offered? _____

_____

Why would Hiram be most comfortable receiving counsel in that kind of setting? _____

_____

Did his meeting with Oliver constitute a channel through which Hiram could receive the help he needed?

■ In recent years a decline of moral principles, an increase of divorce, the philosophies of men, and the movement for population control have combined to threaten the institution of marriage and the divinely appointed family unit. Of these and other challenges, President Harold B. Lee quoted a revelation of the Lord to President John Taylor: "Let not your hearts be troubled. . . . Fear not and observe my laws and I will reveal unto you, from time to time, through the channels that I have appointed . . . (I want you to mark that) . . . *through the channels that I have appointed*, everything that shall be necessary for the future development and perfection of my Church" (in Conference Report, Oct. 1962, p. 80; or *Improvement Era*, Dec. 1962, p. 940). What did President Harold B. Lee emphasize when he quoted this revelation? _____

_____

What did the Lord say would be revealed through appointed channels? _____

_____

Can we ever hope to solve our problems or perfect our lives if we reject the counsel revealed to us through appointed channels? Why? _____

_____

■ D&C 8:2; 9:8–9. What is one of the channels through which we can receive help and counsel for solving our problems? Is this channel reserved only for those who have already solved all their problems and become perfect in their lives? What, according to these verses, must we do to receive help and counsel through this channel? (Compare D&C 42:61; 46:7.) _____

_____

■ D&C 46:15–16, 27. How could the power to discern the gifts described in these passages enable the bishop to give individual help and direction to each member of his ward? _____

_____

After we have done all we can to solve our own problems and perhaps arrived at solutions that we feel to be confirmed by the Spirit, why might it still be wise to visit with our bishop? _____

_____

■ D&C 107:85–89. What are the special duties of a quorum president? _____

_____

Are these duties to be discharged only in quorum meeting? _____

_____

Could we receive specific direction and help from our quorum president as we meet with him on other occasions? What preparations and attitudes would be necessary on our part to enable us to benefit from this channel?

---

2 **We May Receive Specific Counsel and Help through Our Home Teachers**

■ Ephesians 4:11–13. What are some of the officers the Lord has appointed to serve him? _____

_____

We can have a personal interview with some of these officers, our home teachers, as often as we need. Why did the Lord appoint teachers and other officers, according to verse 12? _____

_____

Was this ministry to be only a general one, or was it to reach each individual, all members, according to verse 13? _____

_____

Why would much of this help and direction be most effective when given individually? _____

_____

■ Elder Boyd K. Packer said:

"It's interesting to apply a principle or two of wiring to our responsibility in the Church. The Lord has always commenced at the source of the power and run the lines out from there to reach every soul. . . .

" . . . If we are going to deliver the power to the individual, particularly to the youth, it must come through the parents, through the father. . . .

"In the past after some little effort, if we couldn't get the power through we'd just change the diagram and wire past him. Perhaps with a little more patience, a little long suffering, by waiting it out for awhile, or by increasing the power from above, we might have had that circuit opened. . . .

" . . . The source of power for the father is in his priesthood quorum. That power is to be transmitted on signal from the bishop through the priesthood home teachers" ("Priesthood Home Teaching," address at Regional Representatives' seminar, 12 Dec. 1970).

■ D&C 20:53–55. How completely do these passages describe the home teacher's opportunities for service? Over eighty years ago, Elder Matthias F. Cowley said:

"The teachers . . . ought to be men endowed with the spirit of revelation from God. They ought to study the principles of the Gospel, and to so live that they may enjoy the inspiration of the Holy Ghost in their instructions, so that their instructions may be understood and be attractive to the children; that they should not go simply to carry out a routine, to ask certain questions, just to be able to say that they have made their monthly visit" (in Conference Report, Apr. 1902, pp. 38–39).

Who would avoid seeking counsel from such men as Elder Cowley described? _____

_____

What could such men give to the father who prepared himself to seek, receive, and accept their counsel? _____

_____

■ What could happen if a father failed to recognize the important place of the home teachers? _____

_____

Are home teachers expected to impose themselves and their counsel upon the father in the home? _____

_____

Or should the father be the one to make his needs known to them and to humbly and actively seek their direction and counsel? _____

_____

Why? _____

_____

Who could be held responsible if the family suffers from difficulties that home teachers could have helped solve if they had known about them? _____

_____

What power or assistance could the father be denying himself and his family if he never seeks to make his home teachers welcome and acquainted with his needs?

_____

3 Seek the Counsel and Direction of Your Home Teachers

▪ John 13:20. What are we actually doing when we receive those the Lord sends to us? _____

_____

▪ D&C 84:35–39. What do we pledge to do when we take upon ourselves the covenants of the holy priesthood? _____

_____

Abraham was greatly blessed because he sought humbly and diligently to receive the servants of the Lord who were sent to him. Abraham had been promised by the Lord that he would be the father of many nations and that his wife Sarah would be the mother of many nations. But for many years Sarah had been unable to bear children. Abraham and Sarah were both "well stricken in age; and it ceased to be with Sarah after the manner of women" (Genesis 18:11). Abraham must have yearned to know how the promised blessings could come. Then one afternoon the Lord sent three of his mortal servants, three men, to visit Abraham (see Joseph Fielding Smith, *Doctrines of Salvation*, 1:16–17).

▪ Genesis 18:1–2. How did Abraham react when he first recognized these servants that the Lord had sent to him? _____

How, according to the customs of the day, did he honor them as he greeted them? _____

Why do you think Abraham was so eager to see and to welcome these servants? _____

▪ Genesis 18:3–5; carefully consider verse 5. How do we know that Abraham was not anxious for these servants to leave? _____

Was Abraham content knowing that perhaps the only benefit of this visit would be his opportunity to show the Lord how highly he regarded the servants the Lord sent to him? _____

▪ Genesis 18:6–8. What is conveyed by the words "hastened" and "ran"? _____

What is intended by the words that "he stood by them" while they ate? _____

Do you suppose Abraham would have received the Lord himself any differently than he received the Lord's servants (compare Genesis 19:1–2)? _____

▪ Genesis 18:9–11. What blessing did these servants of the Lord leave with Abraham and Sarah? _____

What great honor would come to Sarah because she, too, "judged him faithful who had promised" (Hebrews 11:11)? _____

Do you think the Lord would have given Abraham the promised blessing if Abraham had rejected or dishonored these servants of the Lord? _____

_____

Why? _____

_____

■ Matthew 10:40–42; 25:40. Some men, even though they need blessings desperately, are reluctant to receive their home teachers the same way Abraham received the servants of the Lord. Could it be because they lack Abraham's humility and spiritual maturity? Because they do not yet understand the teachings and functions of the Church? Could it be because of their failure to live the commandments? Have they perhaps been offended by someone? Are they simply reluctant to become involved? Or could it be because they think their home teachers are not acknowledged experts in the field in which they need help? About this last objection, President Spencer W. Kimball said many years ago: "The Lord . . . has, in many cases, found His better-trained people unresponsive to the spiritual, and has had to use spiritual giants with less training to carry on His work" ("Education for Eternity," address at Brigham Young University, in *Speeches of the Year*, 1967–68 [Provo, Utah: Brigham Young University Press, 1968], p. 5).

■ Matthew 25:45. Why would it take humility and meekness for a priesthood bearer to ask his home teacher for help and counsel with his problems? _____

_____

Of course, it should be remembered that some serious problems are more appropriately discussed with the bishop or quorum leader than with the home teachers.

**Will It Make
a Difference?**

President Joseph F. Smith said: "May all the people open their doors, call in the members of their families, and respect the visit of the teachers to their homes, and join with them in striving to bring about a better condition, if possible, in the home than ordinarily exists. If you can advance, try to aid the teachers to help you make that advancement" (*Gospel Doctrine*, p. 189).

Quorum Training Suggestions

As quorum leaders you are in a unique position for counseling your brethren about the principles in this lesson. This is not a lesson on home teaching. Rather, it is a lesson on how to properly receive the servants of the Lord and the great blessings that can result. Ward and quorum leaders are responsible to see that every father and family has someone to whom they can turn for help. But the responsibility to seek and accept the help available rests upon the father in the home.

■ To encourage individual study, invite quorum members to share insights from their personal study by asking such questions as these: What channels of help are available to me as I seek to sanctify and perfect my life? What responsibilty do we have to our home teachers even if at the time we do not see the need for any particular blessing from them? Why is the way we treat our home teachers a partial index of our love and regard for the Lord? (See Matthew 10:40–42 and 25:40.)

■ There are several lessons about home teaching in previous Melchizedek Priesthood personal study guides. You may wish to refer the quorum to those lessons (see the entries under "Home Teaching" in the index).

■ Carefully consider in light of Doctrine and Covenants 88:33 the need for fathers to receive the Lord's servants.

■ Discuss the father's responsibility for what the home teachers do in his home. How does receiving the Lord's servants enhance the father's ability to accomplish what he needs to accomplish in his home? Discuss how a father might call on his home teachers for assistance, or work through the home teachers to obtain special help with such responsibilities as genealogy, preparing a son for a mission, solving many kinds of family problems, budgeting and finance, and others.

■ Read and discuss Ephesians 4:11–13. Perhaps the most important factor in any priesthood holder's progress toward perfection is his personal worthiness. How could a trusting relationship between the father and his home teacher help with this matter?

• Review recent conference talks, as found in the May and November *Ensign*, for statements about home teaching that could be used in this lesson.

• Discuss the following statement by Elder L. Tom Perry: "Home Teachers . . . are called to represent the quorum president and, through the quorum president, the bishop. Thus, they are priesthood representatives called to assist the quorum leaders in watching over and strengthening the quorum members, including fathers and their families" (in Conference Report, Oct. 1982, p. 42; or *Ensign*, Nov. 1982, p. 31).

Building the Kingdom of God

D&C 39:13

Personal Study

Strive with increased effort to build up the kingdom of God.

In the main lobby of the Church Office Building in Salt Lake City is a painting that portrays Christ giving final instructions to the Twelve just before his ascension. Of that scene, President Spencer W. Kimball said:

"Perhaps he is thinking: 'Go with a faith like that of Moses, that the impossible can happen.' . . . He is saying, 'Go ye into all the world and preach the gospel to every creature.' Perhaps he is thinking of Yugoslavia and Iran and India and Greece and Czechoslavakia and Russia, that will come into being after his crucifixion and ascension, with closed doors which will need to be opened. . . . He IS saying without all of the explanations of the hows and whys, 'Go ye into all the world and preach the gospel to every creature' " ("Lengthening Our Stride," address at Regional Representatives' seminar, 3 Oct. 1974).

What must Church members do to fulfill the Savior's command? Will present levels of performance be sufficient to establish the gospel throughout the earth? Will increased proselyting be adequate if personal worthiness, obedience, sacrifice, and service do not keep pace?

1 **The Church Is the Stone Cut Out of the Mountain without Hands**

■ Daniel 2:28–45. What day and age was the king's dream about? What is the stone cut without hands? How will it fill the whole earth? _____

_____

What is the kingdom that will stand forever? _____

What does this teach about the destiny of the Church in the last days? _____

_____

■ President Kimball explained the interpretation of Daniel in this way:

"Daniel said to the king that his dream was a portrayal of the history of the world. . . .

"Nebuchadnezzar represented the king of kings, a world power, representing the head of gold.

"Another kingdom would arise and take over world dominion.

"The interpretation included the domination of other kingdoms. Cyrus the great, with his Medes and Persians, would be replaced by the Greek or Macedonian kingdom under Philip and Alexander; and that world power would be replaced by the Roman Empire; and Rome would be replaced by a group of nations of Europe represented by the toes of the image. . . .

"And it was in the days of these kings that power would not be given to men, but the God of heaven would set up a kingdom—the kingdom of God upon the earth, which should never be destroyed nor left to other people.

"The Church of Jesus Christ of Latter-day Saints was restored in 1830 . . . and this is the kingdom, set up by the God of heaven, that would never be destroyed nor superseded, and the stone cut out of the mountain without hands that would become a great mountain and would fill the whole earth" (in Conference Report, Apr. 1976, pp. 9–10; or *Ensign*, May 1976, pp. 8–9).

■ D&C 65:1–6. What was committed unto men on the earth? What is the prophesied destiny of the Church, as described in these passages? _____

_____

What are some of the members' responsibilities in bringing about the fulfillment of the prophecy described in these passages? _____

_____

2 This Church Shall Roll Forward Until It Shall Fill the Whole Earth

■ Mosiah 18:9. In how many aspects of life are we expected to stand as witnesses of the truth that we have received? _____

What other ways may we stand as witnesses besides our necessary participation in the important missionary work? _____

■ President Brigham Young declared: "This kingdom will continue to increase and to grow, and . . . become more wonderful and conspicuous to the nations, until it fills the whole earth" (as cited by Spencer W. Kimball in "When the World Shall Be Converted," *Ensign*, Oct. 1974, p. 13).

■ Jeremiah 31:31–34. How many of the Lord's people shall know the Lord according to these passages? _____ _____

How extensively will the knowledge of the Lord be established in the earth? _____

Is there any reason for the Saints to become discouraged?

■ Moses 7:62. How will righteousness and truth sweep the earth like a flood? _____

How does this passage describe the conditions that will prevail in the last days when the kingdom of God begins to "sweep the earth"? _____

President Kimball said: "This spreading of the gospel will occur, therefore, in a time of great iniquity; righteousness and evil will exist side by side. We must not, therefore, fail to do our part to help the gospel cover the earth, even though circumstances around us may be very difficult and trying" (address at Regional Representatives' seminar, 3 Oct. 1974).

3 **We Must Do the Very Best We Can in Our Assigned Responsibility**

■ Alma 39:11. Why wouldn't the Zoramites accept Alma's testimony? _____

Is there a relationship between the example we set and the willingness of the world to accept our message? Why? _____

■ Have you ever "almost" done your best in one of your responsibilities? The *almost* attitude of King Agrippa (see Acts 26:24–28) did not bring him salvation. Elder James E. Faust said:

"Almost. What a heartbreaking sound the word *almost* has. *Almost* some of our good members keep the Word of Wisdom; *almost* some go to priesthood meeting and sacrament meeting; *almost* some hold family home evening. Some of us *almost,* but not quite, pay our tithing" (*To Reach Even unto You,* p. 125).

What *almosts* are presently cluttering your life and keeping you from doing and being your best? _____

■ D&C 9:5, 10–11; see also Matthew 25:14–46. How would we feel if the Lord had to say these things to us concerning the tasks for which we have been made responsible? What appears to be the blessing bestowed upon us if we do well in the particular duties assigned to us? What shall be the result if we do not?

■ Why must we improve daily if we are to do our best? In speaking of the members of the First Presidency, Elder Loren C. Dunn said: "In looking at the life of a President [Joseph Fielding] Smith or a President [Harold B.] Lee or a President [N. Eldon] Tanner, we see nothing instantaneous. Their success is the application of principles of truth and righteousness over a lifetime, day in and day out—offering the prayers, having the faith, meeting the trials. It is a gradual process, and it requires not only the application of the principles of truth and righteousness but also the passage of time" ("Read, Ponder, Pray," *Brigham Young University Speeches of the Year,* 7 March 1972 [Provo, Utah: Brigham Young University Press, 1972], pp. 3–4).

■ At one of his first speaking assignments as a new Apostle, Elder Spencer W. Kimball expressed concern that such a high calling should come to one such as he. He said: "Brothers and Sisters: I don't know exactly why the Lord has called me, but I do have one talent to offer. My father taught me how to work; and if the Lord can use a worker, I'm available" (see Robert L. Simpson, in Conference Report, Oct. 1975, p. 18; or *Ensign*, Nov. 1975, p. 13). Why is the principle of hard work such an important one in aiding the rolling forth of the kingdom? _____

Why is it a demonstration of integrity for a man to work to the best of his ability in an assignment even though that assignment may not be one that commands public attention or acclaim? ____

4 Let Us Strive to Do Our Best in Our Present Responsibilities

As the Church increases in size and in stature among the nations, and as the opposition increases against truth and personal holiness, can we not draw comfort and courage from the life and example of the Prophet Joseph Smith? Can we not allow the spirit of his conviction and love for the work to thrill us and inspire us with the determination to do our best, as he said:

"Brethren, shall we not go on in so great a cause? Go forward and not backward. Courage, brethren; and on, on to the victory! Let your hearts rejoice, and be exceedingly glad. . . .

" . . . And again I say, how glorious is the voice we hear from heaven, proclaiming in our ears, glory, and salvation, and honor, and immortality, and eternal life; kingdoms, principalities, and powers!" (D&C 128:22–23).

Will It Make a Difference?

President Harold B. Lee said: "You cannot lift another soul until you are standing on higher ground that he is. You must be sure, if you would rescue the man, that you yourself are setting the example of what you would have him be. You cannot light a fire in another soul unless it is burning in your own soul"

(Conference Report, Apr. 1973, p. 178; or *Ensign*, July 1973, p. 123).

Quorum Training Suggestions

As you contemplate the great prospects and opportunities for service that confront members of the Church, it will be obvious that a large measure of the responsibility for teaching and encouraging priesthood holders to do their best will rest upon you as quorum leaders. You know the members of your quorum, and you should know whether they are doing the best they can in the responsibilities to which they have been assigned. Of course the most direct and effective means to help the brethren in your quorum is through substantive and meaningful personal priesthood interviews with the senior home teacher who has the responsibility to meet regularly with the father of the family. As you work through this effective channel and as you teach and sit in council with your brethren in quorum meeting, you should lead and encourage them to lengthen their stride in all their assigned areas of accountability.

Assign quorum members to study the preceding material so that they will be prepared to discuss ways to increase their efforts and effectiveness.

▪ To encourage individual study, allot a few moments to reviewing the self-study portion of the lesson:

What did Daniel mean when he said that the stone cut without hands would fill the whole earth?

How can the enemies of the kingdom of God decrease when the power of Satan is so real in the world?

How can we as fathers ensure that our children are prepared to be Church members who will reach out and make a difference in the world?

▪ Present these statements and discuss the questions: The Prophet Joseph Smith said: "We ought to have the building up of Zion as our greatest object" (*Teachings*, p. 160). On another occasion he said: "I calculate to be one of the instruments of setting up the kingdom of Daniel by the word of the Lord, and I intend to lay a foundation that will revolutionize the whole world" (*History of The Church of Jesus Christ of Latter-day Saints*, 6:365).

What is meant by the statement in Daniel 2:44 that "the kingdom shall not be left to other people"?

Do we have any guarantee that we will be part of the Lord's program in the last days simply because we are members of the Church?

■ One of the following may be helpful in demonstrating the need for men in the priesthood to strive to do better:

Filmstrip, *It All Started with Thad* (OF056, 15 min.), which tells the story of how a small boy causes his whole family to become enthusiastic about missionary work, and of the success they have.

Motion picture, *Go Ye into All the World* (MP162, 30 min.), in which President Kimball shows how we must respond to the challenges facing us to spread the gospel throughout the earth.

■ Study Joseph Smith, *History of The Church of Jesus Christ of Latter-day Saints,* vol. 1, pp. XXXIV-XL, for an understanding of Daniel's interpretation of Nebuchadnezzar's dream.

■ Present and discuss this case study.

Brent was concerned because he had been in the ward for a long time, and still it seemed that he was always passed over for the assignments that he considered to be significant. Finally, in an interview with his quorum president, he blurted out his justification for not doing well in his home teaching and other quorum assignments. "President, it seems that I could do this job forever and no one would ever notice or care. I have to feel like the work I am doing matters a little."

Are there any such things as "little" assignments in the Church? Will the breadth or duration of our assignments in the kingdom matter in eternity, or is it the quality of our service that matters? Refer to Doctrine and Covenants 18:15 in your discussion.

Should the nature of our assignments have any effect upon our determination to do the very best that we can?

Can we ever hope or expect to be responsible for larger matters if we cannot manage smaller and less prominent matters? Refer to Matthew 25:24–30 in your discussion.

Do you convey an attitude of loyalty and support for the Church leaders as you lead and guide the members of your quorum?

Have you personally lengthened your stride, and are you trying to do the very best you can in your assigned responsibilities?

■ Challenge quorum members: If this is an area of concern for you, if you feel you are not working as hard as you should and could for the building up of the kingdom, consider these questions:

What can you do in your assigned responsibilities to express to our Father in Heaven that you desire to be more diligent?

What is preventing you from doing as well as you would like?

Can you commit yourself now to do better and begin now to plan how you will do it?

The Way to Perfection

D&C 93:1

Personal Study

Learn to consider your life from an eternal perspective.

You may know of a story similar to the following: "I received a phone call late one night. My neighbor, Bill, had died unexpectedly from a heart attack. His wife tearfully asked, 'Would you help us with the funeral? Bill thought so much of you.' The day of the funeral was cold and wet. Not many people attended. I felt the gloom of the day settle over me as I thought of Bill. He had had good parents, and he had been raised in the Church, but he had never been able to really grasp the meaning of the gospel. He had never been able to really look beyond this life and focus on eternal values. As the funeral progressed, I couldn't help but notice Bill's wife. She had wanted so much to have Bill take their family to the temple to be sealed. I had tried to encourage Bill, only to have him reply, 'Someday I'll get around to Church things, but I have too much to do right now.' I recalled the day that Bill's oldest boy had been ordained a deacon. How he had wanted his dad to do it, but his dad hadn't seemed to care—'I'll have to be out of town that week'—and so the bishop performed the ordinance. The way is straight and narrow, but too many times we begin to believe that it is broad and unrestricted. I wondered if Bill had felt that way."

Does it appear that Bill made his decisions with an awareness of his eternal destiny? How can a knowledge of the plan of salvation help us to understand the importance of our probation in this world? Do we understand the significance of our premortal life? Do we know the purpose of our life here? Do we make our decisions in this world with an awareness of eternal things?

1 We Participated in the Councils of the Premortal World

■ Acts 17:29; D&C 93:38; see also Alma 13:2–12. Who is the father of the spirits of all men? _____

_____

What do these passages suggest were the consequences of our probation in the premortal world? _____

_____

■ D&C 93:36; 130:18–21; Abraham 3:18–19, 22. What is the "glory of God"? _____

_____

What do these passages say we must do to acquire this? _____

_____

Had all of the spirit children of God acquired the same amount of glory by the end of the premortal probation? _____

_____

Why? _____

_____

■ President Joseph Fielding Smith said: "*The spirits of men were not equal. They may have had an equal start,* and we know they were all innocent in the beginning; but the right of free agency which was given to them enabled some to outstrip others, and thus, through the eons of immortal existence, to become more intelligent, more faithful, for they were free to act for themselves, to think for themselves, to receive the truth or rebel against it" (*Doctrines of Salvation*, 1:59).

■ Job 38:4–7. What part did we play in the premortal councils?

_____

_____

President Joseph F. Smith said: "Our spirits . . . were in the councils of the heavens before the foundations of the earth were laid. We were there. We sang together with the heavenly hosts for joy when the foundations of the earth were laid, and when the plan of our existence upon this earth and redemption were mapped out. We were there; we were interested, and we took a part in this great preparation. . . . We were vitally concerned in the carrying out of these great plans and purposes, we understood them, and it was for our sakes they were decreed, and are to be consummated" (*Gospel Doctrine*, pp. 93–94).

■ Revelation 12:7–9; D&C 76:25–29. What was the result of Lucifer's rebellion? _____

_____

Did we participate in this conflict? _____

_____

Whom did we follow? _____

_____

What are some of the blessings that we receive because of our loyalty? _____

_____

_____

2 We Are Here to Prove Ourselves

■ Abraham 3:24–26. What did the Lord say would be the purpose of life? _____

_____

How many of the words of God are we accountable to accept?

_____

Who delivers the commands of God in our stake? in our ward? What should be our relationship to these men? _____

_____

■ Hebrews 12:1; Mosiah 3:19. Should you be unduly concerned to compare that particular "race that is set" before you with the course of life that God has designed to prove and purify someone else? _____

_____

What should our attitude be with respect to the things that we cannot change? _____

_____

Could we say that one of the greatest purposes of life in the mortal world is to learn to submit our will to the will and designs of God? _____

_____

Why? _____

_____

Elder Rex D. Pinegar observed:

"We may feel that life is cruel and unfair to us, that we would like to retreat into our own shelter and never have to venture forth into the world. To do so, however, would be to deny ourselves the opportunities for growth which life and its experiences are designed to bring to us" (in Conference Report, Oct. 1982, p. 34; or *Ensign*, Nov. 1982, p. 25).

■ Alma 34:32–34. What is the message of these verses? President Joseph Fielding Smith said: "This mortal probation . . . would either give to those who received it the blessing of eternal life, which is the greatest gift of God, and thus qualify them for godhood as sons and daughters of our Eternal Father, or, if they rebelled and refused to comply with the laws and ordinances which were provided for their salvation, it would deny them the great gift and they would be assigned, after the resurrection, to some inferior sphere according to their works. *This life is the most vital period in our eternal existence*" (*Doctrines of Salvation*, 1:69).

---

3 We Will Receive a Final Judgment and Live Forever in the Kingdom We Merit

■ 1 Corinthians 15:40–41. Has the Lord made provision in eternity for the varying degrees of obedience and righteousness in men? _____

_____

Why is this necessary? _____

_____

What determines the degree of glory we are assigned to? _____

_____

■ D&C 76:81–90, 98–106. Who are those who inherit the telestial glory? _____

_____

Why do they have to suffer? _____

_____

When will they be redeemed? _____

_____

■ D&C 76:71–80. What are the requirements for the terrestrial kingdom? _____

_____

Will any members of the Church be found there? _____

Why could not the people in this kingdom be assigned to the celestial kingdom instead? _____

_____

■ D&C 76:50–70, 92–96. What do these passages teach us about the requirements for celestial glory? _____

_____

■ President George Albert Smith said:

"When the time comes for that resurrection, if we are worthy . . . we will be quickened celestial bodies, and from then on, we will dwell in the celestial kingdom, the highest of all kingdoms. But [the Lord] has taught us also that there are other places where we may go. If we don't want to go to the celestial kingdom, by being less careful and particular about keeping the commandments of God, we may go into the terrestrial kingdom, and if we are still more careless, we may find our way into the telestial kingdom, which is the least of the kingdoms of glory.

"There are some people who have supposed that if we are quickened telestial bodies that eventually, throughout the ages of eternity, we will continue to progress until we will find our place in the celestial kingdom, but the scriptures and revelations of God have said that those who are quickened telestial bodies cannot come where God and Christ dwell, worlds without end" (in Conference Report, Oct. 1945, p. 172).

■ D&C 76:112; 131:4; 132:17. What do these passages say about the duration of the judgment that shall be pronounced at the end of the world? _____

_____

President Spencer W. Kimball said: "After a person has been assigned to his place in the kingdom, either in the telestial, the terrestrial or the celestial, or to his exaltation, he will never advance from his assigned glory to another glory. That is eternal! That is why we must make our decisions early in life and why it is imperative that such decisions be right" (*The Miracle of Forgiveness.* pp. 243–44).

**It Will Make
a Difference!**

President Joseph Fielding Smith declared:

"There was a time before we ever came into this world when we dwelt in his [God's] presence. We knew what kind of a being he is. One thing we saw was how glorious he is. Another thing, how great was his wisdom, his understanding, how wonderful was his power and his inspiration. And we wanted to be like him. . . .

"If we will just be true and faithful to every covenant, to every principle of truth that he has given us, then after the resurrection we would come back into his presence and we would be just like he is. We would have the same kind of bodies—bodies that would shine like the sun" (*Take Heed to Yourselves!*, p. 345).

Quorum Training Suggestions

As a quorum presidency, you conduct personal priesthood interviews. You participate in quorum socials, projects, and assignments, and you fellowship the members of your quorum in many ways. You spend time in their homes, and you pray for them. What can you do to help them consider the blessings and challenges of life from an eternal perspective? How can you lead them to live for eternity? As you plan the quorum instruction, some of the following instructional alternatives may be useful to you:

■ Assign quorum members to study carefully the preceding material so they will be prepared to participate in this quorum training on learning to look at this life from an eternal perspective.

■ To encourage individual study, invite quorum members to briefly share their insights from their study of the self-instructional material. You might also ask the following questions:

To what extent were we involved in the premortal councils? Why were we involved?

What is the purpose of mortal life? What are we expected to do here?

Why do we speak of the judgment as the "final judgment"?

■ You may wish to show the filmstrip *Man's Search for Happiness* (OF034, 14 min.).

■ Discuss ways that we can keep an eternal perspective for ourselves and for the members of our family. Your discussion might include such suggestions as these:

Display pictures in the home that portray eternal themes, such as pictures of temples.

Display in the home or periodically review family pictures that show parents and loved ones in various stages of growth and progress. Notice how quickly it will seem that the years have passed.

Visit old family homesites or the cemeteries where ancestors and other loved ones may be buried. Discuss the places and people of years gone by that are only memories now.

Recall the birth of children, and discuss how in just a few short months someone we knew nothing about has been born into our family and has grown to become so vital a part of the family that we cannot imagine what life would be like without him.

■ Display and discuss the meetinghouse library poster "The Purpose of Life" (IQ031).

■ Divide the quorum into three discussion groups, with a member of the quorum presidency leading each group. Discuss how we as priesthood holders could help our inactive and nonmember friends and neighbors to see the purpose of life and the reality of eternity. Your discussion might include such suggestions as these:

Simply bearing testimony to others about how we feel about eternal things.

Holding a neighborhood fireside at which the film *Man's Search for Happiness* could be shown and discussed.

■ Bring a piano into the quorum meeting room, and sing the hymn "O My Father" (*Hymns*, no. 139).

- Discuss the following chalkboard illustration and questions:

		Past	Present	Future
God's eternal perspective		Past	Present	Future
Man's limited perspective		Past	Present	Future

How could a knowledge of the eternal nature of man give greater perspective to life and its purposes in the following situations?

A young married couple lost their firstborn child.

A teenage boy attempts suicide because he thinks that life is worthless.

A young girl wonders if staying chaste will really make a difference in her life.

A couple have marital difficulties and wonder if it is worth it to them to solve the problems.

Thou Shalt Not Commit Adultery

D&C 42:24

Personal Study

Revere the sacred vows of the marriage covenant.

A young stake high councilor returned home late one evening sober and shaken. A court had been convened for a man he knew and admired. The charge was adultery. The accused had offered no defense. Instead, he had explained the traveling required by his job and the loneliness of frequent separations from his wife and children. He described reading material that he had never permitted in his home but that he had acquired to "pass the time" when he was away. He told of frequent dinners and other business associations that had led to the crumbling of defenses that he had once believed could not be shaken. He broke down frequently as he related the events that had led, step by step, to the adulterous act and then sobbed uncontrollably as he described the weight that had settled upon him, robbing him of even a moment's peace from the time of the transgression to his appointment with the court. He welcomed excommunication as some relief from sorrow and anguish too heavy to bear.

Reflecting on what he had heard and felt during the evening, the young high councilor thought, "I hope that my wife and our home and our family always seem as precious and dear to me as they do at this moment." He felt chastened and humbled as he realized how vulnerable all men are to temptation. He wakened his wife and, without explanation, held her close and silently pled with the Lord for strength to continue to be true and faithful so that such a tragedy as he had witnessed would never enter his life.

1 The Sin Next to Murder

- Exodus 20:14. What is the Lord's command with respect to fidelity in marriage? _____

Has it ever been revoked? Suspended? Modified? Has it been overthrown by the so-called sexual revolution or replaced by a "new morality"? _____

- Concerning the unchanging nature of God and his commandments, President Spencer W. Kimball said: "We do not believe in situation-itis; we do not go with the people who think that this is a different age, this is a different time, these people are more enlightened, that was for the old times. Always the Lord will hold to his statements that he has given through the ages, and he will expect men to respect themselves, to respect their wives, and the wives to respect their husbands" (in Conference Report, Apr. 1975, p. 162; or *Ensign*, May 1975, p. 109).

- Alma 39:3–5, 9; D&C 19:25. How serious is the sin of sexual immorality? _____

Why is it that the taking of life and the abuse of the powers of creating life should be numbered among the most grievous of all sins? _____

Can you see that murder and improper sexual involvement are both unauthorized uses of the power of life and as such are more serious than all other sins except the sin against spiritual life, the denial of the Holy Ghost?

- Leviticus 20:10. What was the penalty for adultery in the days of ancient Israel? _____

What is the penalty today for him who "repenteth not" (see D&C 42:24). _____

What does it mean to be cast out? _____

■ Nowhere is the destructive power of sexual sin better illustrated than in the Old Testament account of David, one of the greatest of Israel's kings. Of him Elder Dean L. Larsen said:

"As a young man, David demonstrated a courage and a strength and a power that likely has not been equaled in all of the great characters of the scriptures. He fought with wild beasts and overcame them, defeated the giant Goliath virtually with his hands, and then served through many years as the leader of Israel and demonstrated in the process tremendous control, tremendous discipline. The greatest enemy he had, perhaps, through most of these years—at least the greatest threat to his existence—was the man Saul. Yet on several occasions when David could have removed this threat by taking the life of Saul, who was in his hands, he withheld and controlled those impulses. That demonstrated tremendous power and control. Then later in his life, as a mature man with all the strength that kind of life had brought him, David was unwise. It was not because David was weak that he fell. He was unwise. I suspect that David had reached the point where he felt he was strong enough to indulge the entertainment of some enticing possibilities. On the day he stood on his rooftop and observed the wife of one of his officers, instead of taking himself by the nape of the neck, so to speak, and saying, 'David, get out of here!' David remained. David thought about the possibilities, and those thoughts overcame David and eventually controlled him. One of the saddest entries in all of our scripture, I think, is that which the Lord gave the Prophet Joseph Smith in section 132 of the Doctrine and Covenants. Speaking of David's situation today, he said, 'For he hath fallen from his exaltation, and received his portion' (D&C 132:39). . . . David, King David, one of the great and powerful men of the Old Testament times, could have been today among the gods if he had controlled his thoughts" (*Speeches of the Year* [Provo, Utah: Brigham Young University Press, 1976], pp. 121–22).

The tragic sequence of David's loss of exaltation was, first, his failure to control his thoughts; second, his adultery; and, third, his murder of Uriah to cover up his unrepented actions.

■ Genesis 39:7–12. In marked contrast to the transgression of David is the story of Joseph as a servant in the household of Potiphar. President Harold B. Lee describes Joseph as "a handsome, good looking lad and 'well-favored,' and just [at] the age when temptations are strongest, he was far removed from the restraining influences of home and family" (*Decisions for Successful Living*, p. 78). Moreover, he was subjected, as President Spencer W. Kimball has written, to "the wiles of a wicked, voluptuous woman, displaying all her advantages of high station, beauty, and political power. . . .

"When all else failed she attempted force and intimidation and blackmail. But Joseph stood his ground. He refused to yield to her pleadings. Her clothing, or lack of it, her perfumes, her sexy advances, her pleadings—all these bombarded a clean young man willing to suffer any penalty in order to keep his virtue" (*The Miracle of Forgiveness*, pp. 70–71).

How could a similar resolve prepare us to respond to temptation? _____

_____

■ Jacob 2:31–35. How does Jacob describe the innocent victims of sexual sin? _____

_____

How important to you are the tender and delicate feelings of your companion? _____

_____

Why could marital unfaithfulness cause children to lose confidence in their fathers? _____

_____

What do you think Jacob meant when he said, "many hearts died, pierced with deep wounds"? _____

_____

_____

2 Avoid Even the Thought

■ Jacob 2:5; Matthew 5:27–28. What, according to Jacob, was the beginning of sin? _____

_____

Can we acknowledge the evil of actual physical adultery and yet believe that the thought of adultery is harmless or trifling? _____

Why? _____

■ Proverbs 6:23–29. How is "lusting after beauty" like treading on hot coals? _____

What will often be the result? _____

President Kimball wrote: "The final act of adultery is not the only sin. For any man or woman to begin to share affection or romantic interest with any other than the spouse is an *almost certain approach to ultimate adultery*" (*The Miracle of Forgiveness*, p. 70; italics added). On another occasion he deplored the pervasiveness of infidelity and warned:

"Infidelity is one of the great sins of our generation. The movies, the books, the magazine stories all seem to glamorize the faithlessness of husbands and wives. *Nothing is holy*, not even marriage vows. . . .

"The adversary is subtle; he is cunning, he knows that he cannot induce good men and women immediately to do major evils so he moves slyly, whispering half truths until he has his intended victims following him, and finally he clamps his chains upon them and fetters them tight, and then he laughs at . . . their misery" (in Conference Report, Oct. 1962, p. 56; or *Improvement Era*, Dec. 1962, p. 928).

■ Ephesians 5:3–5. What effect can "filthiness," "foolish talking," or "jesting" about sacred matters have on a man who is constantly exposed to it and does nothing about it? _____

Could foolish talking refer to so-called "harmless" flirtations? Have you been offended in the presence of those who seem obsessed with sexual matters or who delight in joking about sacred things? How are these things destructive to the marriage relationship? _____

■ Consider the counsel of Elder James E. Faust:

"Our loyalty to our eternal companion should not be merely physical, but mental and spiritual as well. Since there are no harmless flirtations and no place for jealousy after marriage, it is best to avoid the very appearance of evil by shunning any questionable contact with another to whom we are not married" (in Conference Report, Oct. 1977, p. 14; or *Ensign*, Nov. 1977, p. 10).

3 Spouse and None Else

■ D&C 42:22. What does it mean to "love thy wife with all thy heart"? President Kimball elaborated:

"And, when the Lord says *all* thy heart, it allows for no sharing nor dividing nor depriving. And, to the woman it is paraphrased: 'Thou shalt love thy husband with *all* thy heart and shalt cleave unto him and none else.'

"The words *none else* eliminate everyone and everything. The spouse becomes preeminent in the life of the husband or wife, and neither social life nor occupational life nor political life nor any other interest nor person nor thing shall ever take precedence over the companion spouse. We sometimes find women who absorb and hover over the children at the expense of the husband, sometimes even estranging them from him.

"The Lord says to them: 'Thou shalt cleave unto *him* and none else.'

"Marriage presupposes total allegiance and total fidelity. . . . all the heart, strength, loyalty, honor, and affection, with all dignity. Any divergence is sin; any sharing the heart is transgression. . . . We should . . . have an eye, an ear, a heart single to the marriage and the spouse and family" (*Faith Precedes the Miracle*, pp. 142–43).

■ Ephesians 5:28–29, 33. How do these verses instruct men to love their wives? _____

Would a man who nourishes and cherishes his companion as he does himself seek sexual favors that are offensive to his wife? Would he even consider any sexual activity outside of the marriage relationship?

▪ To those who are considering divorce or who have permitted their marriages to become common or stale and have thus become vulnerable to unholy influences, Elder Faust counseled that one of the reasons for divorce "is the lack of a constant enrichment in marriage. It is an absence of that something extra which makes it precious, special, and wonderful, when it is also drudgery, difficult, and dull. . . .

"We build our marriages with endless friendship, confidence, integrity, and by administering and sustaining each other in our difficulties" (in Conference Report, Oct. 1977, p. 13; or *Ensign,* Nov. 1977, p. 10).

4 Hope for Those Who Repent

▪ Matthew 12:31–32. Is it possible to repent of sexual transgressions? _____

President Harold B. Lee gave the following counsel:

"Now some of you have made mistakes and have no doubt sinned. Satan, that master of lies, would try to make you believe that because you have made a mistake, all is lost. He will try to persuade you to continue to live the life of sin. This is a great falsehood. All sins, except the unpardonable sin, which is the sin against the Holy Ghost, can be repented of, and through the power of redemption and the gospel of Jesus Christ all sins may be remitted, but they cannot be remitted until we who have sinned, as the prophets have taught, have done all we can to make right that which we have done which was wrong in the sight of God" ("Strengthening the Home," pp. 5–6).

▪ D&C 58:43. What is required of a man in order to truly repent? _____

▪ D&C 107:71–73. Who has the Lord designated to hear the confessions of transgressors in his church? _____

▪ The importance of a sinner's confession to the proper priesthood leader was emphasized by Elder Spencer W. Kimball: "The confession of his major sins to a proper Church authority is one of those requirements made by the Lord. These sins include adultery, fornication, other sexual transgression, and other sins of comparable seriousnes" (*The Miracle of Forgiveness*, p. 179).

The advantage of such a confession, beyond the fact that it is a requirement for the Lord's forgiveness, was stressed by Elder Kimball: "Confession is not only the revealing of errors to proper authorities, but the sharing of burdens to lighten them. One lifts at least part of his burden and places it on other shoulders which are able and willing to help carry the load" (*The Miracle of Forgiveness*, p. 187).

■ D&C 58:42; Isaiah 1:18. What promises does the Lord make to those who properly repent? _____

_____

You Can Make a Difference

Do imaginings or speculations concerning anyone other than our wife occupy your thoughts? Banish them! Do you have a relationship with anyone of the opposite sex that is characterized by teasing or flirtation or in which confidences or sympathies are exchanged? End it! Is there any appetite or influence in your life that interferes with total commitment to your wife and children? Subdue it! President J. Reuben Clark has said: "Our very civilization itself is based upon chastity, the sanctity of marriage and the holiness of home. Destroy these and Christian man becomes a brute" (in Conference Report, Oct. 1938, p. 137).

Give heed to the counsel of President Gordon B. Hinckley: "Brethren, keep your affections within your homes. Regard as your most precious possession in time or eternity she with whom you joined hands over the altar in the House of the Lord and to whom you pledged your love and loyalty and affection for time and all eternity" (in Conference Report, Apr. 1983, p. 68; or *Ensign*, May 1983, p. 52).

Quorum Training Suggestions

Quorum members who have reviewed this study guide should come to the quorum hour with some sense of the importance that the Lord attaches to the law of chastity and should have reflected on their sacred commitment to their wives. This discussion should focus on how that commitment may be strengthened and how temptation may be avoided.

▪ To encourage individual study, review the personal study guide by asking such questions as these: Why is chastity a fundamental law of marriage? What is the process by which Satan can enslave and destroy even the best of men? How can the bonds between husband and wife become unbreakable?

▪ Ask the quorum members to think about their feelings toward their wives in the days of courtship and early marriage. Review some ways in which those feelings can be retained or, if necessary, renewed.

▪ Invite the quorum members to share positive, uplifting ideas for keeping a marriage fresh, alive, and holy.

▪ President Spencer W. Kimball has counseled priesthood holders to "follow what Paul said when he urged Timothy to 'intreat . . . the elder women as mothers; the younger as sisters, with all purity.' (1 Timothy 5:1–2)." (in Conference Report, Oct. 1978, p. 62; or *Ensign*, Nov. 1978, p. 43). How could our adopting this attitude contribute to our keeping the law of chastity?

▪ In the same address President Kimball interpreted the obligation of priesthood men to provide for their households as including an obligation to provide "affectional security" as well as economic security. Discuss some ways in which this might be done.

▪ What is the connection between partaking of things forbidden by the Word of Wisdom and breaking the law of chastity? Why does the indulgence of one appetite make it easier to indulge another? How does the bridling of passions help us to be filled with love? (See Alma 38:12.)

▪ Lead quorum members in a review of selected scriptures listed in the Topical Guide under the headings of *Adulterer, Chastity,* and *Self-Mastery.*

▪ Discuss the importance of surrounding ourselves with worthy literature, music, and all art forms in helping us avoid taking steps that can lead to tragic consequences.

■ Using Doctrine and Covenants 87:8 as a reference point, discuss ways in which we can "stand in holy places" and avoid the sin of unchastity.

The Gospel of Love in Action

D&C 112:11

Personal Study

Recognize opportunities to share the gospel with love.

President George Albert Smith was widely known for his great love for all mankind. A later President of the Church said of him: "President George Albert Smith was a disciple of friendship and love. He was indeed a friend to everyone. My gaze at his likeness seemed to give me a warmth of that radiance which made every man his friend" (Harold B. Lee, in Conference Report, Oct. 1972, p. 19; also *Ensign*, Jan. 1973, p. 24).

An example of President Smith's generosity and benevolence is his statement to a Protestant minister in England: "Keep all the glorious truths that you have acquired in your churches, that you have absorbed from your scriptures, keep all that, keep all the fine training that you have received in your educational institutions, all the knowledge and truth that you have gained from every source, keep it all. . . . Then let us sit down and share with you some of the things that have not yet come into your lives that have enriched our lives and made us happy. We offer it to you without money and without price. All we ask you to do is hear what we have to say, and if it appeals to you, accept it freely. If it does not, then we will go our way to somebody else" (*Sharing the Gospel with Others*, pp. 218–19).

There are many good people in the world, men and women "who are only kept from the truth because they know not where to find it" (D&C 123:12). Do we love these people, some of whom may be our neighbors, friends, or relatives? Are we willing to share with them in a spirit of love and kindness that which enriches our lives and makes us happy? How far should our love extend? (See D&C 112:11.)

1 Our Responsibility to Share the Gospel with Love

■ Matthew 22:35–40. What are the first and second great commandments? What are some ways you can show your love for your neighbor? _____

_____

President Heber J. Grant said, "The best way in the world to show our love for our neighbor is to go forth and proclaim the gospel of the Lord Jesus Christ, of which he has given us an absolute knowledge concerning its divinity" (in Conference Report, Apr. 1927, p. 176).

■ Mosiah 28:3; Alma 31:34–35. What seems to have motivated the great missionaries we read of in the Book of Mormon? Do we feel the same concern for the welfare of our neighbors?

■ President N. Eldon Tanner noted that in order to be successful in teaching others "one must show love and actually feel love for the person he is trying to instruct. No power is as motivating as the power of love" (*New Era,* June 1977, p. 5).

■ What do the following scriptures teach us about our responsibility to share the gospel?

D&C 38:40–41 _____

_____

D&C 63:37 _____

_____

D&C 88:81 _____

_____

D&C 133:8 _____

_____

■ President Spencer W. Kimball posed the following questions: "Let us assume for a moment that the roles were reversed—that you were not a member of the Church but that your present nonmember neighbor was a Latter-day Saint. Would you want him or her to share the gospel with you? Would you then rejoice in the new truths you had learned? Would your love and respect increase for your neighbor who had shared these truths with you?" (*Ensign*, Oct. 1977, p. 3). What would our answers to these questions be? Do we love our neighbors, friends, relatives, and associates enough to share the gospel with them?

▪ President Ezra Taft Benson has reminded us that "This is our first interest as a Church—to save and exalt the souls of the children of men" (in Conference Report, Apr. 1974, p. 151; or *Ensign*, May 1974, p. 104).

2 The Blessings of Sharing the Gospel

▪ D&C 18:10–16. How precious are souls in the sight of God? What blessing will be ours if we bring souls to him? _____

▪ D&C 84:61. What promise does the Lord make here? _____

Elder William R. Bradford has pointed out that "the two-fold nature of the purpose of missionary work [is] first, to sanctify the missionary himself, and second, to bring converts to a knowledge of the truths of the restored gospel of Jesus Christ and to baptism into His Church—which is the sure and natural product of a missionary who is in the process of sanctification" (in Conference Report, Oct. 1981, p. 71; or *Ensign*, Nov. 1981, p. 49).

3 How Can We Share the Gospel with Others?

There are many ways to share the gospel. If we are motivated by love and a desire to serve God, we will be able to find ways to share the gospel. Consider the following.

▪ Elder David B. Haight has counseled: "If you will involve your whole family—pray as a family for success; select a family to fellowship; set goals and dates for accomplishment; commit yourselves to do whatever is appropriate; then fast and pray, and then pray and fast—I promise you that your warning voice will be heard. This is the day when the harvest is ripe, the press is full. The Lord will bless your efforts. You will witness friends enter the waters of baptism" (in Conference Report, Oct. 1976, pp. 28–29; or *Ensign*, Nov. 1976, p. 23).

Why is it important to prayerfully select a family? Does the Lord know who is ready to accept the gospel? Why is the timing that may result from prayerfully selecting a family so important?

■ President Spencer W. Kimball said:

"Our goal should be to identify as soon as possible which of our Father's children are spiritually prepared to proceed all the way to baptism into the kingdom. One of the best ways to find out is to expose your friends, relatives, neighbors, and acquaintances to the full-time missionaries as soon as possible. Don't wait for long fellowshipping nor for the precise, perfect moment. . . .

"If they won't listen and their hearts are hardened with skepticism or negative comments, they are not ready. In this case, keep loving them and fellowshipping them and wait for the next opportunity to find out if they are ready. You will not lose their friendship. They will still respect you" (*Ensign*, Oct. 1977, p. 6).

Why is it important to continue being a genuine friend even to those who are not interested in hearing the gospel? _____

■ D&C 11:21. Personal testimony is also important in sharing the gospel with others. What two responsibilities do we have? Why is it important to remember that the Holy Ghost does the converting? _____

Your Love Can Make a Difference

President George Albert Smith testified: "The gospel of Jesus Christ . . . is a gospel of love and kindness. It will cause us, if we are living as we should, to love our neighbors as ourselves, and go out of our way, if possible, to help them understand better the purpose of life" (in Conference Report, Oct. 1948, pp. 167–68). What can you do to show you really love your neighbors? How will your willingness to share the gospel of love influence your friends and neighbors?

Quorum Training Suggestions

As quorum leaders you do have opportunities to teach and train
the members of the quorum to share the gospel with others.
Frequently quorum members may want to share the gospel but
are not sure how to do it. Your concern here is not to develop
some minutely prescribed program which may or may not fit the
peculiar circumstances of the members of your quorum. Rather,
your concern is to help quorum members to recognize the broad
range of opportunities that occur in daily life and to respond to
these opportunities when they occur.

■ To encourage individual study, allow the brethren to share
their thoughts from their personal study. You might also ask the
following questions:

Why is "sharing the gospel" such an appropriate expression of
what we are expected to do?

Why is *every* church member (see D&C 38:40) expected by the
Lord to share the gospel with his neighbors and not leave that
responsibility only with the missionaries?

Why is it true that a person who is not living the gospel as he
should and has some reservations in his testimony could hardly
succeed in sharing the gospel regardless of the procedures or
techniques he may employ?

Why are love and sincerity so important in our efforts to share
the gospel with others?

■ Show the film *Go Ye into All the World* (MP162, 28 min.), which
features President Kimball's vision of missionary work.

■ Have the quorum divide into three or four groups to discuss
ways that members of the Church can support the missionary
effort. List on the chalkboard or compile into a handout the
ideas suggested. Some examples might include the following:

Be a model of righteousness, an example of the believers (see
1 Timothy 4:12).

Fast and pray that doors, both of nations and of the hearts of
men, will be opened.

Support and encourage the stake and full-time missionaries.

Prepare and encourage sons to serve full-time missions.

Provide financial assistance to missionaries by contributing to family, quorum, or ward missionary funds or to the General Missionary Fund.

Share copies of the Book of Mormon with nonmembers.

Share subscriptions to the Church magainzes with nonmembers.

Discuss how each of these suggestions could be applied in your own area.

■ Present these situations, and discuss how each could have been turned into a possible opportunity to share the gospel:

John works in an assembly plant. He goes out to the parking lot each noon to eat his lunch alone because he does not like the smoke and the language that are common in the company lunchroom.

Bill buys gasoline for his car at one service station even though he realizes that his nonmember neighbor operates a service station just a few blocks farther down the street.

When Sister Johnson received a phone call from nonmember neighbors inviting her and her husband to a party where she knew liquor would be served, she simply gave as an excuse that she and her husband would be busy that evening and made no further effort to contact her nonmember neighbors.

■ Read Mosiah 18:9, and explain that this verse lists some of the promises we make at the time of baptism. Ask: "What do the phrases 'at all times and in all things, and in all places that ye may be in' mean?" Make an extensive list of the kinds of ordinary situations that occur from day to day that could be used to share the gospel. Analyze each situation to see how it could be turned into an opportunity to share the gospel.

■ Present this case study, and discuss the questions that follow it: Dan and Ed were neighbors. Dan was not a member, and Ed decided that he would try to become close to Dan. Gradually, over the weeks, a friendship began to grow. They found they had some things in common, and within a few years, they were very close friends. One day it occurred to Ed that the purpose for which he had commenced this friendship with Dan was to try to introduce him to the Church. So he arranged a get-together between families and made a point to explain to Dan that they would discuss the Church. They did, and Dan and his family were not interested. However, Ed continued to enjoy his friendship with Dan. Many years passed, and one day Dan approached Ed and said: "Over all these years, I have learned to cherish our friendship. You have been loyal and good to me and my family. We have admired the way you and your family live, and have decided that we would like to believe as you believe and worship as you worship. How can we join The Church of Jesus Christ of Latter-day Saints?"

Why is a desire to join the Church not always an immediate thing?

What did Ed and his family do that contributed so much to Dan's conversion?

Be careful not to discount those who may have an immediate interest in joining the Church. Sometimes we can prolong a person's not joining the Church because of our not being sensitive to his interest.

Multiply and Fill the Earth

D&C 132:63

Personal Study

Understand the obligations and blessings of parenthood.

Elder James E. Talmage said:

"What is man in this boundless setting of sublime splendor? I answer you: Potentially now, actually to be, he is greater and grander, more precious according to the arithmetic of God, than all the planets and suns of space. For him were they created; they are the handiwork of God; man is His son! In this world man is given dominion over a few things; it is his privilege to achieve supremacy over many things" ("The Earth to be Redeemed," *Sunday Night Talks by Radio;* as cited by Joseph Anderson, in Conference Report, Apr. 1978, pp. 106–07; or *Ensign,* May 1978, p. 70).

Church leaders have stated clearly that children are the heritage of the Lord. Any unrighteous interference with the fountains of life is a grievous sin. Thus, the Church speaks with a clear voice on such issues as birth control, abortion, and the "population explosion."

1 The Command to Multiply and Fill the Earth Is Still in Force

■ Genesis 9:1; Moses 2:28. What was the first commandment given by the Lord to Adam and Eve? _____

Is it still in force? President Ezra Taft Benson has declared: "The first commandment given to man was to multiply and replenish the earth with children. That commandment has never been altered, modified, or canceled" (in Conference Report, Apr. 1969, p. 12; or *Improvement Era,* June 1969, p. 44).

■ D&C 49:15–17. What has the Lord said of these things in the present dispensation? _____

_____

It is significant that those who enter into the covenant of eternal marriage are commanded, like Adam and Eve, to multiply and replenish the earth. "The Lord has told us that it is the duty of every husband and wife to obey the command given to Adam to multiply and replenish the earth" (First Presidency [Heber J. Grant; J. Reuben Clark, Jr; David O. McKay], in Conference Report, Oct. 1942, p. 12).

■ One important reason for marriage is the bearing and rearing of children, although it is not the only reason. Elder Parley P. Pratt wrote:

"The object of the union of the sexes is . . . procreation; also for mutual affection, and cultivation of . . . charity and benevolence, which are inspired by the Eternal Spirit; also for mutual comfort and assistance in this world of toil and sorrow, and for mutual duties towards their offspring. . . .

". . . To marry and multiply is a positive command of Almighty God, binding on all . . . who are circumstanced and conditioned to fulfil the same. To marry, propagate our species, do our duty to them, and to educate them in the light of truth, are among the chief objects of our existence on the earth. To neglect these duties, is to fail to answer the end of our creation, and is a very great sin" (*Key to the Science of Theology*, pp. 164–65).

■ In fulfilling the command of God we need to constantly remember that their first consideration is their wives. The prophets have made this clear:

"We seriously regret that there should exist a sentiment or feeling among any members of the Church to curtail the birth of their children. We have been commanded to multiply and replenish the earth that we may have joy and rejoicing in our posterity.

"Where husband and wife enjoy health and vigor and are free from impurities that would be entailed upon their posterity, it is contrary to the teachings of the Church artificially to curtail or prevent the birth of children. We believe that those who practice birth control will reap disappointment by and by.

"However, we feel that men must be considerate of their wives who bear the greater responsibility not only of bearing children, but of caring for them. . . . To this end the mother's health and strength should be conserved and the husband's consideration for his wife is his first duty, and self-control a dominant factor in all their relationships" (letter from the First Presidency [David O. McKay, Hugh B. Brown, N. Eldon Tanner,] 14 Apr. 1969).

■ Those who cannot have children through no choice of their own? _____

President Harold B. Lee declared: "Wives and mothers who have been denied the blessings of wifehood or motherhood in this life—who say in their heart, if I could have done, I would have done, or I would give if I had, but I cannot for I have not—the Lord will bless you as though you had done, and the world to come will compensate for those who desire in their hearts the righteous blessings that they were not able to have because of no fault of their own" (*Ye Are the Light of the World,* p. 292).

2 Providing for Children Both Physically and Spiritually

The responsibility of parenthood involves more than giving birth to children. It also involves nurturing and teaching those children and providing them with all physical necessities. Wise parents will establish warm relationships with their children; they will listen to their children's problems and attempt to respond lovingly to their physical and spiritual needs. Parents are especially obligated to teach gospel principles in their homes—by precept, by love, and by example. A home environment in which parents provide for both physical and spiritual needs will help shape a child's character. But a parent's concern should not end when a son or daughter leaves home to go to school, to work, to serve a mission, or to marry. While the relationship will be altered, it should never end.

■ Moses 6:57–58. What was Adam commanded to do? _____

■ Mosiah 4:14–15. What great responsibilities do parents have concerning their children? _____

_____

■ D&C 68:25–28. What is one way parents today are commanded to fulfill their responsibilities for their children? _____

_____

How can parents help children come to Christ and be born again? _____

_____

■ D&C 93:40. What does the Lord require of parents? Elder ElRay L. Christiansen said:

"Parenthood is a sacred trust. It is an approach to the divine—a God-given privilege that, with its never-ending responsibilities, brings rich and lasting rewards" (Conference Report, Apr. 1972, p. 42; or *Ensign*, July 1972, p. 54).

■ President Joseph F. Smith said, "The man, and the woman who are the agents, in the providence of God, to bring living souls into the world, are made before God and the heavens, as responsible for these acts as is God himself responsible for the works of his own hands" (*Gospel Doctrine*, p. 273).

■ Genesis 18:19. President Spencer W. Kimball has said of this passage:

"Abraham's desire to do God's will in all things led him to preside over his family in righteousness. Despite all his other responsibilities, he knew that if he failed to teach and exemplify the gospel to his children he would have failed to fulfill the most important stewardship he had received. . . . As we are told in the pamphlet *Father, Consider Your Ways:*

" 'Fatherhood is leadership. . . . Father, with the assistance and counsel and encouragement of your eternal companion, you preside in the home. It is not a matter of whether you are most worthy or best qualified, but it is a matter of law and appointment. . . . As a leader in your home you plan and sacrifice to achieve the blessing of a unified and happy family. To do all of this requires that you live a family-centered life' " (*Ensign*, June 1975, p. 5).

■ President Brigham Young said of mothers: "The duty of the mother is to watch over her children and give them their early education, for impressions received in infancy are lasting. . . . Children have all confidence in their mothers; and if mothers would take proper pains, they can instill into the hearts of their children what they please" (*Discourses of Brigham Young*, p. 201).

3 Finding Joy and Rejoicing through Posterity

■ Psalm 127:3–5. What is a great avenue to happiness? _____

_____

Many of God's greatest blessings come through children.

■ Moses 5:10–12. What caused Adam and Eve to rejoice? _____

_____

■ 1 Nephi 8:10–12. With whom did Lehi desire to share his joy?

_____

Why? _____

_____

■ 2 Samuel 18:33. How much did David love his son Absalom?

_____

■ Alma 36–42 (note chapter headings; see particularly Alma 38:2–3). How do we know that Alma received both great joy and great sorrow through his children?

■ Elder Boyd K. Packer said:

"Someday you will hold a little boy or a little girl in your arms and know that two of you have acted in partnership with our Heavenly Father in the creation of life. Because the youngster belongs to you, you may then come to love someone more than you love yourself. . . .

"Through this loving one more than you love yourself, you become truly Christian. Then you know, as few others know, what the word *Father* means when it is spoken of in the scriptures" (in Conference Report, Apr. 1972, p. 139; or *Ensign*, July 1972, p. 113.)

Honor, Understand, and Uphold as Sacred the Command to Have and Rear Children

Jesus allowed the little children to come to him, and he blessed them (see Matthew 19:13–15). Latter-day Saints should be anxious to bring children into their homes and to bless them with the gospel. As they do, joy will come to them.

Suggestions for Quorum Training

Quorum instruction will need to be given with sensitivity. The principle is that the Saints are commanded to be willing to marry and to have and rear children in righteousness within the sacred bonds of marriage. How this principle is to be carried out must finally be determined by each husband and wife, as they counsel with the Lord.

■ Encourage individual study by asking such questions as these: Is it optional to bring children into our homes under the new and everlasting covenant of marriage? What are two primary reasons for the physical expression of love in marriage? What should be a man's first consideration with regard to having children? Why?

■ Elder S. Dilworth Young has given a beautiful account of the genealogy of President Harold B. Lee in "Having Been Born of Goodly Parents" (*Ensign,* Jan. 1973, pp. 122–23; also Conference Report, Oct. 1972, pp. 159–62). It teaches obedience and sacrifice in obeying the command of God relating to parentage for Heavenly Father's children. Discuss ways in which husbands can fulfill the counsel of the First Presidency to show consideration to their wives regarding childbirth. Possibilities may include giving priesthood blessings, helping with the children, providing conveniences around the home, counseling and praying with her concerning the bearing and raising of children, and spending more time at home.

■ The following could aid in discussion:

"True motherhood is the noblest calling in the world, and we look with sorrow upon the practice . . . of limiting families, a tendency creeping into our own church.

"Some young couples enter into marriage and procrastinate the bringing of children into their homes. They are running a great risk. Marriage is for the purpose of rearing a family, and youth is the time to do it" (David O. McKay, *Church News*, 11 June 1952, p. 3).

■ Some Latter-day Saints, concerned about a population explosion, feel that this commandment of God should be altered. President Ezra Taft Benson has spoken on this subject. See Conference Report, Apr. 1969, p. 12; or *Improvement Era*, June 1969, pp. 43–44. For a refutation of the arguments of those who fear a "population explosion," see Philip F. Low, "Realities of the Population Explosion," in *Ensign*, May 1971, pp. 18–27.

■ The 16mm film *In This Holy Place* (MP034, approximately 20 minutes), shows the eternal nature of the family and the incomparable value of children.

Prepare Yourself to Teach the Gospel with Power

Lesson 15

D&C 42:11–14; 50:13–19

Personal Study

Qualify to become sensitive to the workings of the Spirit in order to teach the gospel with power and authority.

"Wherefore, I the Lord ask you this question—unto what were ye ordained?

"To preach my gospel by the Spirit, even the Comforter which was sent forth to teach the truth" (D&C 50:13–14).

All of us are teachers. As fathers, we teach, consciously or unconsciously. In advising a friend, setting family rules for children, or counseling with our wives, we are teachers. If one serves as a quorum leader, auxiliary teacher, or Aaronic Priesthood adviser, he is also a teacher. All our teaching should be by the Spirit and from the scriptures so that those whom we teach might say, as did the two disciples of Christ on the road to Emmaus, "Did not our heart burn within us, while he talked with us by the way, and while he opened to us the scriptures?" (Luke 24:32).

1 Teach by the Spirit

■ D&C 63:64. How do we receive the Spirit in order to teach sacred things? _____

_____

■ D&C 50:17–18. Note that we are not even to preach truth without the Spirit.

Through prayerful preparation, a teacher may feel an enlargement of his abilities. He may experience flashes of inspired thought and receive other manifestations of the Spirit in his teaching.

109

• D&C 42:14. If one does not receive the Spirit, what then? _____

Elder Joseph Fielding Smith said, "How necessary it is that we should be in possession of the Spirit of God that we may teach. If we do not have that spirit we should not attempt to teach until, in the spirit of repentance, prayer and faith we may obtain the guidance of the Holy Ghost" (in Roy W. Doxey, *The Latter-day Prophets and the Doctrine and Covenants*, 2:175–76).

2 Receive the Spirit through Prayer, Study, and Righteous Living

• Alma 17:2–3. According to this example, what things must we do in order to teach with the power and authority of God? _____

• D&C 42:14. How do we receive the Spirit? _____

Of course, to present the will of the Lord and to teach sound doctrine by his Spirit, we should study his doctrines and make them a part of our lives.

• D&C 52:9; 42:12. Which writings are we to study and use when we teach? _____

• D&C 11:20–21; 84:85. What are we promised if we study these doctrines and live righteously? _____

"A teacher should not be called primarily because of his schooling, or educational attainments, without taking into consideration his humility, his faith and his integrity to the cause of truth which he is supposed to represent. This training does not come through the study of science, art or literature, but through prayer and faith and the promptings of the Spirit of the Lord. It cannot be stated too forcefully that the man or the woman without faith in the gospel as it has been revealed in the day in which we live should not teach. The Lord has made it very emphatic" (Joseph Fielding Smith, *Doctrines of Salvation*, 1:312–13).

3 Teaching by the Spirit Brings Conviction and Changes Lives

▪ We are all gospel teachers—either by appointment or by the Lord's invitation (see D&C 38:40–41; 4:2–5).

▪ Alma 17:4. If the gospel teacher meets the requirements necessary to teach with power and authority of God, what effects can his teaching have? _____

▪ Teaching with power and conviction through the Spirit is illustrated by this event from the life of Elder Boyd K. Packer:

"Near the end of the course work for my doctorate, I was enrolled in an educational philosophy class with three other students. Two of us were completing our doctorates; the other two were just beginning their graduate work. An issue arose between me and the other doctoral candidate. It had to do with whether or not man is left totally to himself. Is he sufficient to himself, or are there external sources of intelligence to which he can appeal? . . .

"As the debate became more intense, the other two students took sides, one on each. So there we were, two contestants, each with a 'second.' The issue grew more important, and each day I left the class feeling more a failure. Why should this concern me? It concerned me because I was right and he was wrong, and I knew it and I thought he knew it; yet he was able to best me in every discussion.

"Each day I felt more inadequate, more foolish, and more tempted to capitulate. I spent much time in the library, searched out references, and studied at least as hard as my opponent. Nevertheless, each encounter saw me that much more defeated.

"Then one day one of the most important experiences of my entire education occurred. As we were leaving class, his 'second' commented, 'You're losing, aren't you.'

"There was no pride left to prevent me from consenting to the obvious, 'Yes, I'm losing.'

" 'Do you want to know what's the matter with you?' he asked.

"Interested, I answered, 'Yes, I would very much like to know.'

" 'The trouble with you,' he said, 'is that you're fighting out of context.' I asked him what he meant. I didn't know, and he didn't explain it. He just said, 'You are fighting out of context.'

"That night I thought continuously about his comment. It wasn't the grade or the credit I would win in this class—it was much bigger than that. I was being beaten and humiliated in my efforts to defend a principle that was true. His statement stayed in my mind, and finally, in my humiliation, I went before the Lord in prayer. Then I knew!

"The next day when we returned to class, I stayed in context. When the debate was renewed, instead of mumbling some stilted, sophisticated, educational jargon calculated to show I was conversant with philosophical terminology, I used the words the Lord used on the subject. Instead of saying, 'The *a priori* acquisition of intelligence as though from some external source of enlightenment,' I said plainly, 'Revelation from God!' I talked about the spiritual in the terms that described the spiritual. Suddenly the tables were turned. I was rescued from defeat, and I learned a lesson I shall not soon forget.

"The points I had been pressing with so little effect those several weeks suddenly became clear and compelling. I abandoned the foolish process of skirting around spiritual terms in favor of academic jargon.

"I stand in debt to that unassuming student from whose remark I learned so much. I will never forget it and would urge everyone who teaches in the Church to teach as the Lord taught, with the tools that He has provided, and not to be drawn out of context. Teach with the Spirit!" (*Teach Ye Diligently*, pp. 281–83).

■ Teaching by the Spirit includes bearing a personal witness of the truthfulness of gospel principles when moved upon by the Holy Ghost. Of this, President Joseph F. Smith said:

"One cannot give his testimony to another, yet he is able to aid his earnest brother in gaining a true testimony for himself. . . .

"A gift from God, if neglected, or unworthily used, is in time withdrawn; the testimony of the truth will not remain with one who, having received, uses not the sacred gift in the cause of individual and general advancement" (*Gospel Doctrine*, p. 206).

• President Harold B. Lee noted, "We have a right to gain the Spirit by which our words and our teachings, though they may be humble, will be carried and burned into the hearts of those whom we teach so that they will feel an impression and an understanding that otherwise would not be theirs" (*Ye Are the Light of the World*, p. 97).

In all our teaching, we should follow the example of Alma, who concluded a gospel discussion by declaring:

"Behold, I testify unto you that I do know that these things whereof I have spoken are true. And how do you suppose that I know of their surety?

"Behold, I say unto you they are made known unto me by the Holy Spirit of God. Behold, I have fasted and prayed many days that I might know these things of myself. And now I do know of myself that they are true; for the Lord God hath made them manifest unto me by his Holy Spirit; and this is the spirit of revelation which is in me" (Alma 5:45–46).

Will It Make a Difference?

Elder Spencer W. Kimball warned:

"If one cannot accept and teach the program of the Church in an orthodox way without reservations, *he should not teach*. It would be the part of honor to resign his position. Not only would he be dishonest and deceitful, but he is also actually under condemnation, for the Savior said that it were better that a millstone were hanged about his neck and he be cast into the sea than that he should lead astray doctrinally or betray the cause or give offense, destroying the faith of one of 'these little ones' who believe in him. And remember that this means not only the small children, it includes even adults who believe and trust in God" (in Conference Report, Apr. 1948, p. 109).

Suggestions for Quorum Training

• Sing and discuss the meaning of "Go, Ye Messengers of Glory," *Hymns*, no. 247.

• Discuss what it means to teach by the Spirit.

- How sensitive is the Holy Spirit? Can he ratify the actions of someone who willfully attempts to use his influence in any degree of unrighteousness? (See D&C 121:36–37.)

- Can the Spirit attend the preaching of someone who has not attempted to find out what the Lord has revealed on the concepts to be considered (see D&C 11:21–22)?

- Ask some of the brethren to relate experiences of teaching by the Spirit during family home evenings, at the dinner table, or while counseling with a child.

- Ask the brethren to discuss their experiences in getting and keeping the Spirit.

- What kind of gospel study is outlined by the Lord in Doctrine and Covenants 84:85?

- Invite a quorum member to report on the concepts outlined by the Prophet Joseph Smith in the *Teachings of the Prophet Joseph Smith*, pp. 242–48.

- Discuss the following statement by President Ezra Taft Benson: "The most important part of your teaching preparation is that you are guided by the Spirit" (*The Gospel Teacher and His Message*, [pamphlet, PUSIO574], p. 6).

- Discuss the importance of living by the Spirit in order to teach by the Spirit. Cite President Heber J. Grant's observation that "No man can teach the Gospel of Jesus Christ under the inspiration of the Living God and with power from on high unless he is living it" (in Conference Report, Apr. 1941, p. 3).

Being Faithful in Times of Adversity

D&C 121, 122, 123

Personal Study

Endure your afflictions patiently.

It was 5 June 1976. It appeared to be a peaceful Saturday morning in Idaho. Then, with very little warning, the Teton Dam broke and spilled 250,000 acre-feet of water that became a rushing, crashing wall of destruction. Whole communities were destroyed, and homes, farms, buildings, businesses, machinery, and automobiles washed away—the flood left a trail of devastation. Seven thousand people lost their homes and possessions.

Why would God allow such a tragedy? Why such immense destruction? Shortly after the disaster, Elder Ezra Taft Benson visited the area. The waters had subsided. The residents, the great majority of them Latter-day Saints, were now faced with the monumental task of rebuilding. Elder Benson said to the Saints:

"I'm a better man for having been with you today and for having witnessed how beautifully you have responded to this disaster. This is probably the worst disaster that I have seen in the United States and it parallels what I saw in Germany immediately after the Second World War.

"I want you to know, and I promise you in the name of the Lord, that good will come from this disaster" (David Mitchell, "Thousands of Saints Left Homeless by Idaho Flood," *Ensign*, Aug. 1976, p. 74).

Do we understand that adversity may come even to the righteous? Do we understand the purpose of adversity? Have we taken the time to reflect on the good that might come from adversity?

1 Adversity May Come to the Righteous

Problems are not always a punishment for sin. We often experience adversity even when we are righteous.

▪ D&C 122:5–7. Did the Prophet Joseph Smith deserve to suffer all these things? Can all adversity be eliminated by living the gospel of Jesus Christ? Why? _____

_____

▪ President Marion G. Romney said:

"Latter-day Saints know that much of pain and suffering would be avoided if the people would accept and follow the Savior. Our mission, as a church, is to bring people to a knowledge of Christ and thus avoid all unnecessary suffering. We are aware, however, that should all men accept and live his teachings, adversity and affliction would still abound. . . .

" . . . We all knew when we elected to come into mortality, that we would here be proved in the crucible of adversity and affliction" (in Conference Report, Oct. 1969, p. 57; also *Improvement Era*, Dec. 1969, p. 66).

▪ Job 2:1–3, 9–10. Had Job given any cause to deserve the affliction that came to him? Elder Boyd K. Packer spoke of the Teton disaster and related "that he had heard someone ask, 'What did we do wrong to deserve such a disaster?' 'The answer is,' he said, 'probably nothing. If you attach tragedy or suffering or disaster to sin only, how do you explain the suffering of Christ? Fine people, living worthily, can be subject to disasters such as you have faced here. The difference will be in how you face it' " (Mitchell, p. 70).

2 What Is the Purpose of Adversity?

What is adversity designed to do? We need to understand the vital part that adversity plays in bringing us closer to perfection.

▪ 1 Peter 2:19–23. Why do good people who are struggling to live the gospel have to experience adversity? _____

_____

Elder Marion G. Romney taught:

"Just as Jesus had to endure affliction to prove himself, so must all men endure affliction to prove themselves. . . .

" ' . . . all the Saints . . . prophets and apostles, have had to come up through great tribulation . . . ' (Joseph Fielding Smith, *Teachings of the Prophet Joseph Smith*, 1938 ed., pp. 260–61)" (in Conference Report, Oct. 1969, p. 58; or *Improvement Era*, Dec. 1969, p. 67).

▪ Job 23:10, 14. What did Job say was the object of his being tested? _____

_____

What great blessing came to Job because he was willing to accept the course that God had appointed for him? _____

_____

▪ D&C 121:1–6. How hard was it for the Prophet Joseph to bear his confinement in Liberty Jail? _____

_____

The Prophet described his suffering in these words:

"We have been taken prisoners charged falsely with every kind of evil, and thrown into prison, enclosed with strong walls, surrounded with a strong guard, who continually watch day and night as indefatigable as the devil. . . .

" . . . We are compelled to hear nothing but blasphemous oaths, and witness a scene of blasphemy, and drunkeness and hypocrisy, and debaucheries of every description" (*History of The Church of Jesus Christ of Latter-day Saints*, 3:290).

▪ What great blessings came to the Prophet and the Church because he endured so well his suffering in Liberty Jail? _____

_____

▪ What great revelations came because the Prophet proved so valiant in the burdens of that confinement? _____

_____

▪ D&C 121:6–10; 122:7. What reasons does the Lord give for the anguish that the Prophet suffered? _____

_____

- Could the Lord prevent the trials that come to us? President Spencer W. Kimball has said:

"Yes. The Lord is omnipotent, with all power to control our lives, save us pain, prevent all accidents, drive all planes and cars, feed us, protect us, save us from labor, effort, sickness, even from death, if he will. But he will not.

"We should be able to understand this, because we can realize how unwise it would be for us to shield our children from all effort, from disappointments, temptations, sorrows, and suffering. . . .

" . . . Suffering can make saints of people as they learn patience, longsuffering, and self-mastery" (*Faith Precedes the Miracle*, pp. 96, 98).

- D&C 127:2. Why did the Prophet Joseph glory in tribulations?

_____

_____

Did he understand that even the righteous would suffer? Did he understand the purpose of adversity? Would he have said, "Why does it always happen to me?" or "'It seems like just one thing after another!'"? Why is this attitude so completely wrong?

_____

3 What Can We Do to Endure Adversity Well?

- Moses 6:31; see also Ether 12:23–27. Much of the adversity that we suffer in this life is caused by personal limitations beyond our control. What benefits may come if we learn to respond in the way we should? _____

_____

- D&C 122:4, 9. Has the Lord established limits and boundaries for the afflictions that come to us? What does the Lord mean when he says that the bounds of affliction are set? _____

_____

What comfort does this give to us as we struggle to endure adversity? _____

_____

■ Mosiah 2:17; Jacob 2:17. What benefits can come from serving others when we are in the midst of our own trials? _____

_____

When you are facing adversity in your life and one or two Saints show concern, does this help you carry your burden? Would a whole quorum's concern help to lighten the load even more?

_____

■ Why would listening to great music strengthen one in times of adversity? _____

_____

4 Seek to Grow by Responding Properly to Your Adversity

President Marion G. Romney said:

"I have seen the remorse and despair in the lives of men who, in the hour of trial, have cursed God and died spiritually. And I have seen people rise to great heights from what seemed to be unbearable burdens.

"Finally, I have sought the Lord in my own extremities and learned for myself that my soul has made its greatest growth as I have been driven to my knees by adversity and affliction" (in Conference Report, Oct. 1969, p. 60; or *Improvement Era*, Dec. 1969, p. 69).

Will It Make a Difference?

■ Elder Boyd K. Packer said, "I know there are times when you would want to give up, or to weep, or to yield, but you have got to stand steady as an example to others" (Mitchell, p. 70). How will it help us endure well if we know that other people are watching us and depending upon our example?

Quorum Training Suggestions

As quorum leaders, you know many of the trials and afflictions your quorum members are going through. Although some may not be opposed to sharing their experiences with the quorum, others would prefer to keep their trials to themselves. You should take every care to see that no confidences are broken. Your duty as a quorum leader is to teach this principle effectively but in a general way so that the quorum members may take comfort and apply the principles to their own situation. Ask that quorum members prepare for this quorum hour by studying carefully the preceding material on understanding the purpose of affliction. There may also be other materials that you may wish to suggest. As you plan the quorum training, you may wish to use some of the following ideas:

■ To encourage individual study, ask the quorum members to briefly share their answers to questions from the self-study portion of the lesson. You may wish to ask:

Why must good people who are struggling to live the gospel encounter adversity?

How can we benefit from the adversity that may come because of personal limitations beyond our control?

■ A poster could be made up with the newspaper headlines of different kinds of adversity: automobile accidents, floods, typhoons, robbery, drought, and others. This could serve as a springboard for a discussion of the fact that adversity may come even to the righteous. Discuss these questions:

Do you think the people affected by these events were evil?

How many of these events do you think could not have been avoided?

How many of these people were good and innocent?

Since you know the members of your quorum, you may ask someone in advance to bear his testimony of the growth he has experienced during trials in his life. Be absolutely sure that he feels comfortable doing this and is not doing so because he feels compelled.

■ Discuss: "What can quorum members do for individuals among their brethren who may currently be burdened with adversity?" To begin the discussion, you may have two members of the quorum role-play the following conversation:

BILL: John, I was sorry to hear that you have multiple sclerosis.

JOHN: Well, I'm doing the best I can.

BILL: I can't understand why it should happen to you. You're so young and have always been so active.

What is wrong with this conversation? Point out that John received no help in carrying his burden. Have the two quorum members role-play the situation again. This time Bill should give John some moral support, saying, "John, I want you to know that you have been such an inspiration to me and my family. It's been marvelous to see the way that you have handled your trials. It gives us the strength to handle our problems in a more constructive way."

■ Discuss how the following activities can be helpful or harmful, depending on the sincerity and good sense of the person seeking to help:

Expressions of concern

Visiting

Offering prayers

Seeking to anonymously help and encourage

The activities mentioned in James 1:27

■ Read and discuss D&C 136:31. These comments and questions may be helpful:

Lorenzo Snow said: "It is necessary we suffer in all things, that we may be qualified and worthy to rule and govern all things" (*Millennial Star*, 1 Dec. 1851, p. 363).

What are some of the trials likely to come to us? Why?

■ Discuss Mosiah 18:8–9. Is it easier to bear a burden if someone shares it with us? Remember that, as a quorum leader, you should help your quorum members understand that they cannot take another's burden away, but they can help others carry their burdens.

■ Display and discuss these posters depicting the trials of the early Saints: "Martin Handcart Co.—Bitter Creek, Wyoming, 1856" (OQ554); "Exodus from Nauvoo" (OQ233).

Obedience Is the First Law of Heaven

D&C 130:20–21

Personal Study

Learn why obedience is the first law of heaven.

"How was the fireside, John?" inquired a father of his teenage son, noticing an expression that usually meant frustration or resentment or both.

"It was just another one of those 'keep the commandments' lectures, Dad," John replied. "I get so tired of being constantly told to obey, to stay on the straight and narrow, to do this or not to do that. It's like no one trusts me to think for myself."

Father looked at son thoughtfully. "You feel hemmed in and restricted," he said quietly. "Perhaps it seems that if you always strictly obey, you must give up some of your freedom and miss out on some interesting experiences. I've had those feelings myself."

"Something like that, Dad," replied John, surprised at his father's understanding. "I don't want to be just like everyone else. Don't you think the Church stresses obedience so much just to keep everyone in line?"

Have you ever chafed, like John, at the requirements of gospel living? How can you convince a person with an inquiring mind of the value of foregoing some immediate satisfactions for the sake of keeping God's commandments? What are the blessings of obedience?

1 Obedience Is the Cardinal Commandment

■ President Charles W. Penrose, speaking in a sacrament meeting many years ago, gave some wise counsel. He chided the bishop for placing a sign in the chapel that said: "Order is the first law of heaven." President Penrose said this was incorrect because obedience is that first law. He pointed out that only through *obedience* could *order* be established (see *Church News*, 25 Apr. 1970, p. 14).

■ At the time of his appointment as President of the Church, Harold B. Lee said that the most important message he could give would be to keep the commandments of God: "The safety of the Church lies in the members keeping the commandments. There is nothing more important that I could say. As they keep the commandments, blessings will come" (*Church News*, 15 July 1972, p. 3).

■ Elder Marvin J. Ashton said:

"Only through obedience may we have permanent and lasting joy. I ask all of us this day to have the courage to be obedient. If we love God, we will keep his commandments. . . .

"One of the greatest blessings man has in his possession today is the opportunity to be obedient. All of our blessings flow from obedience. Obedience is a cardinal law of heaven. Righteousness and individual growth rest upon obedience. Obedience is an eternal principle available for the benefit and progress of mankind" (in Conference Report, Munich Germany Area Conference 1973, p. 22).

■ Genesis 22:1–3. In what sense did God "tempt" Abraham (the Joseph Smith Translation replaces *tempt* with *try* in this verse)?

_____

How did Abraham respond? _____

_____

When did he respond? _____

_____

■ 1 Samuel 15:3, 9–11, 22–24. What was the commandment of the Lord to Saul? Why did Saul say he had transgressed? For what other reasons do men disobey?

■ Abraham 3:25–26. For what purpose was the earth created? What probation did the Creator have in mind for those who would come to earth? _____

_____

What does the word *all* mean? _____

_____

Will obedience still be required of those who keep their second estate? President Joseph F. Smith said that when we assumed membership in the kingdom, we agreed "that we would obey the commandments of God. . . . even unto the end of our days. And when is the end of our days? . . . We shall never see the day . . . when it will not be a pleasure as well as a duty for us, as his children, to obey all the commandments of the Lord throughout the endless ages of eternity" (*Gospel Doctrine*, p. 210).

■ Mosiah 3:19. What are the inclinations of the "natural man"? How can these inclinations be put off? To whom do we turn in times of difficulty? How do affliction and suffering encourage meekness and submissiveness?

■ D&C 21:4–5. What is one source of "words" and commandments that we must obey? Why is it so important to learn and to keep God's commandments? The Prophet Joseph Smith said, "We cannot keep all the commandments without first knowing them, and we cannot expect to know all, or more than we now know unless we comply with or keep those we have already received" (*Teachings*, p. 256).

■ Men in all ages have been required to learn obedience. The Prophet Joseph Smith taught, "If a man gets a fullness of the priesthood of God he has to get it in the same way that Jesus Christ obtained it, and that was by keeping all the commandments and obeying all the ordinances of the house of the Lord" (*Teachings*, p. 308).

2 Obedience Is the Key to Light and Truth

■ D&C 93:36. What is the glory of God? _____

_____

How does the Lord define intelligence? How do knowledge and the capacity to *understand* truth differ from intelligence, which *is* light and truth? _____

_____

President Joseph Fielding Smith makes this distinction: "From the Lord's definition of intelligence we discover that there is a vast difference between the meaning of intelligence and that of knowledge. The former, while it includes the latter, is more potent and has a greater significance. Intelligence is more than the capacity to understand and communicate truth. The *intelligent man glories in righteousness;* not only does he *know* truth, but wisely *applies* it in all his actions" (*The Way to Perfection,* p. 227). What does obedience have to do with obtaining this kind of intelligence?

▪ D&C 131:6. With an understanding that intelligence is another term for light, truth, or the spirit and power and glory of God (see D&C 84:45), what kind of knowledge must a man gain in order to be saved? _____

_____

Compare Psalm 111:10. How does a man begin to acquire this kind of knowledge? _____

_____

▪ D&C 50:24. As a man obtains knowledge of saving principles through his obedience, what does he receive? _____

_____

If he "continueth in God," what more is given? _____

_____

How do we grow in knowledge, truth, and light (compare D&C 84:44–46)? _____

_____

And, if we persist, what will we eventually receive (compare D&C 93:20)?

▪ D&C 130:18–21. How lasting and valuable is the intelligence we obtain in this life? _____

_____

Are knowledge and the power to properly apply knowledge blessings from God? _____

_____

How are these and every blessing obtained? _____

_____

125

▪ 1 John 3:1–2. If, through revelation and by obedience, we obtain a fulness and "are glorified in truth" (D&C 93:28), what shall we be called? _____

_____

What shall we be like? _____

_____

Of these blessings promised to those who keep the commandments, President Joseph Fielding Smith wrote: "If we will be true and faithful to every covenant, to every principle of truth that he has given us, then after the resurrection we would come back into his presence and we would be just like he is. We would have the same kind of bodies—bodies that would shine like the sun. Moreover, if we are faithful and true while we are here, we would be his sons and his daughters" (*Take Heed to Yourselves!*, p. 345). Do you see how obedience to principles of light and truth will help us to grow in intelligence and to be glorified in the Savior as he is glorified in the Father?

3 Righteous Obedience Brings Blessings

▪ Of those who seek the blessings of obedience without actually obeying the law, the Prophet Joseph Smith said, "Everything that God gives us is lawful and right; and it is proper that we should enjoy His gifts and blessings whenever and wherever he is disposed to bestow; but if we should seize upon those same blessings and enjoyments without law, without revelation, without commandment, those blessings and enjoyments would prove cursings and vexations in the end" (*Teachings*, p. 256).

▪ In contrast, the Prophet Joseph Smith also said of righteous obedience, "In obedience there is joy and peace . . . and as God has designed our happiness . . . He never has—He never will institute an ordinance or give a commandment to His people that is not calculated in its nature to promote that happiness which He has designed" (*Teachings*, p. 256).

▪ President Joseph F. Smith spoke of the power that comes from obeying gospel ordinances: "The man or woman in this Church who desires to enrich his or her faith to the highest possible degree will desire to observe every rite and ordinance in the Church in conformity to the law of obedience to the will of God.

In these things, and through them, man gains a more perfect knowledge of God's purposes in the world. An enriched faith means an enlarged power, and though man may not have in this life an occasion to exercise all the powers that come to him through the enrichment of his faith, those powers may be exercised in their fulness in eternity, if not in time" (*Gospel Doctrine*, pp. 212–13).

▪ John 8:31–32. Of our duty to find out God's will and then obey it, President Joseph F. Smith said: "If we . . . ever become worthy to inherit the kingdom of God, we will do so on the principle of eternal truth. The truth is what will make us free; free from error, prejudice, selfishness, ignorance, contention, the power of the adversary of our souls, free from the power of death and hell; free to inherit the fulness of the everlasting gospel" (*Gospel Doctrine*, p. 214).

▪ Genesis 22:15–18. What blessings were promised to Abraham?

Compare Genesis 26:1–5. How did he merit those blessings? ____

How are we made partakers of them? _____

**It Will
Make a Difference**

True love of God is measured by obedience and service. Elder Marvin J. Ashton said: "A worthy prayer for all of us today, brothers and sisters, could be, 'Help me, Oh Lord, to obey promptly.' Obedience increases personal stature. Obedience increases personal capacity. Obedience helps mankind to know and become like God" (in Conference Report, Munich Germany Area Conference 1973, p. 23).

Suggestions for Quorum Training

It is your duty and opportunity as quorum leaders to assess the spiritual growth of your quorum members. How often is that growth slowed or even prevented because of a failure to obey? The quorum discussion should focus on the need for personal discipline so that complete obedience to the Lord's commandments can eventually be given. Emphasize freedom, peace, and confidence as the important blessings that follow obedience.

■ To encourage individual study, briefly review the personal study guide by asking such questions as these: Why is obedience referred to as a "cardinal" law of heaven and as "the most important message for the membership"? Is obedience a requirement of mortality only? How long will we be subject to the laws and commandments of God? How are obedience and the obtaining of intelligence related? Through what process may we eventually become like God and receive of his fulness?

■ Elder Delbert L. Stapley suggested that we discuss these questions in order "to determine where we presently stand in relation to the fundamental law of the celestial kingdom—the law of obedience:

"1. Do I study and ponder the scriptures in an effort to know the will of God and understand His commandments regarding His children?

"2. Do I follow the counsel of God's living prophet, or do I merely select those things with which I agree, disregarding the others?

"3. Do I seek the advice and counsel of my bishop and stake president on matters of concern to me and my family?

"4. Am I earnestly striving to discipline myself, placing my physical appetites under the subjection of my will?

"5. Am I making every effort to repent of past or present wrongdoings and correct them by doing right?

"6. Do I have an attitude of faith in God even though I experience trials, adversity, and affliction? And do I bear my burden without a complaining spirit?" (in Conference Report, Oct. 1977, p. 29; or *Ensign*, Nov. 1977, pp. 20–21).

■ Discuss the reasons why a man might refuse or be afraid to obey God's commandments. What are your feelings about a man who claims that he is unable to obey and, in effect, says: "That's just the way I am. I could never live that!" Are there men who would deliberately choose disobedience, knowing the consequences will be unhappiness and sorrow? Why?

■ D&C 95:1; 105:3–6. Review these passages and discuss the reasons why the Lord sometimes chastens his people by allowing them to suffer trials. Quorum leaders or members may have had humbling and difficult experiences that caused them to acknowledge their dependence on the Lord and to be more obedient and submissive. They may be willing to share testimonies of their spiritual growth.

Prophets Testified of Joseph Smith's Mission

D&C 135:3

Personal Study

Increase your appreciation for the divine calling and mission of Joseph Smith.

President Heber J. Grant has said: "In many places I have met people who have studied our faith. Some of them would say: 'I could accept everything that you people teach were it not for this man Joseph Smith. If you would only eliminate him!' " (*Gospel Standards*, p. 3).

If this happened to you, how would you respond? Can Joseph Smith be eliminated from the message and work of the restored gospel?

▪ D&C 122:1–2. Why do you think the Lord spoke as he did to the Prophet Joseph? How do you feel about Joseph Smith? Do you have a clear understanding of his calling? Have you received, and do you now have, a living witness of his divinely appointed mission?

---

1 **When Was Joseph Smith Selected for His Mission?**

▪ Abraham 3:22–23. How do you interpret this passage in relation to Joseph Smith? _____

▪ President Joseph F. Smith said:

"The Prophet Joseph Smith, and . . . Hyrum Smith, Brigham Young, John Taylor, Wilford Woodruff, and other choice spirits who were reserved to come forth in the fulness of times to take part in laying the foundations of the great Latter-day work, . . . were also among the noble and great ones who were chosen in the beginning to be rulers in the Church of God. Even before they were born, they, with many others, received their first lessons in the world of spirits, and were prepared to come forth in the due time of the Lord to labor in his vineyard for the salvation of the souls of men" (*Gospel Doctrine*, p. 475).

■ The Prophet Joseph himself once said: "Every man who has a calling to minister to the inhabitants of the world was ordained to that very purpose in the Grand Council of heaven before this world was. I suppose I was ordained to this very office in that Grand Council" (*Teachings of the Prophet Joseph Smith*, p. 365).

2 What Have Ancient Prophets Said about Joseph Smith and His Mission?

Numerous ancient prophets prophesied concerning both Joseph Smith and his mission.

■ Moses 1:41. When was the Lord to raise up a modern prophet "like unto Moses"? _____

_____

How is this verse referring to Joseph Smith (see D&C 28:2; 107:91)? _____

_____

■ 2 Nephi 3:6–15. Lehi, in speaking to a son named Joseph, cites the prophecy of Joseph who was sold into Egypt, who prophesied of a choice seer to be raised up out of his loins "in the latter days."

What was this seer's name to be (see verse 15)? _____

_____

What was to be the name of the seer's father (see verse 15)? _____

_____

What work was this seer, "great like unto Moses," to do (see verse 7)? _____

_____

Who is the seer spoken of? _____

_____

■ Isaiah 29:9–14 (see also 2 Nephi 27:4–26; JS—H 1:63–65). Isaiah is referring to the coming forth of the Book of Mormon. Who is the person to whom the book would come forth who would say, "I am not learned"? _____

What role did Joseph Smith have in the events here described?
_____

■ Isaiah 11. This is one of the chapters Moroni quoted to Joseph Smith when he appeared in 1823 (see JS—H 1:40). What is the significance of Moroni's quoting this chapter (compare especially Isaiah 11:1 with D&C 113:1–6)? _____

In summary, it is evident that the mission of Joseph Smith was of such magnitude that several of the ancients were privileged to see it and prophesy concerning it.

3 What Was Joseph Called to Do?

Several of the passages already cited have spoken of Joseph Smith's mission. Consider the following which clarify further his great calling:

■ Brigham Young commented: "It was decreed in the counsels of eternity, long before the foundations of the earth were laid, that he, Joseph Smith, should be the man, in the last dispensation of this world, to bring forth the word of God to the people, and receive the fulness of the keys and power of the Priesthood of the Son of God. . . . He was fore-ordained in eternity to preside over this last dispensation" (*Discourses of Brigham Young*, p. 108).

■ D&C 128:18–21. Which mighty prophets of old mentioned here communicated with Joseph Smith? _____

Why did they communicate with Joseph (see especially verses 18 and 21)? _____

What is significant about this dispensation, over which Joseph was called to preside? _____

■ President John Taylor spoke further concerning those who conferred keys or knowledge on Joseph:

"When Joseph Smith was raised up as a Prophet of God, Mormon, Moroni, Nephi and others of the ancient Prophets who formerly lived on this Continent, and Peter and John and others who lived on the Asiatic Continent, came to him and communicated to him certain principles pertaining to the Gospel of the Son of God. Why? Because they held the keys of the various dispensations, and conferred them upon him, and he upon us" (*Journal of Discourses*, 17:374–75).

"The principles which he [Joseph Smith] had, placed him in communication with the Lord, and not only with the Lord, but with the ancient apostles and prophets; such men, for instance, as Abraham, Isaac, Jacob, Noah, Adam, Seth, Enoch, and Jesus and the Father, and the apostles that lived on this continent as well as those who lived on the Asiatic continent. He seemed to be as familiar with these people as we are with one another. Why? Because he had to introduce a dispensation which was called the dispensation of the fulness of times, and it was known as such by the ancient servants of God" (*Journal of Discourses*, 21:94).

■ Joseph Smith's mission did not end with his death. President Brigham Young stated:

"Joseph Smith holds the keys of this last dispensation, and is now engaged behind the vail [sic] in the great work of the last days. . . . No man or woman in this dispensation will ever enter into the celestial kingdom of God without the consent of Joseph Smith. . . . He holds the keys of that kingdom for the last dispensation—the keys to rule in the spirit-world; and he rules there triumphantly. . . . He was foreordained in eternity to preside over this last dispensation" (*Journal of Discourses*, 7:289–90).

Do you sense the magnitude of Joseph's calling? It is evident that the Lord selected one of his most noble sons to preside over this dispensation.

4 Of What Value Is Joseph's Work to You?

■ D&C 135:3. List some of the specific, inspired contributions Joseph made to your life. _____

In light of these contributions, is it clear why many of the prophets have commented, as did Wilford Woodruff: "No greater prophet than Joseph Smith ever lived on the face of the earth save Jesus Christ" (*Journal of Discourses*, 21:317)?

■ D&C 1:17–30. List some further contributions or blessings made possible by the divine calling of Joseph Smith. _____

Which of these have you personally been blessed by? _____

■ D&C 21:1–6. What role was Joseph (and his prophet successors) to have in our lives? What blessings are made available when we receive their words "in all patience and faith"?

It Will Make a Difference!

"Two great truths must be accepted by mankind if they shall save themselves: first, that Jesus is the Christ, the Messiah, the Only Begotten, the very Son of God, whose atoning blood and resurrection save us from the physical and spiritual death brought to us by the fall; and next, that God has restored to the earth, in these last days, through the Prophet Joseph Smith, His holy Priesthood with all the fulness of the everlasting Gospel, for the salvation of all men on the earth. Without these truths man may not hope for the riches of the life hereafter" (message from the First Presidency [Heber J. Grant; J. Reuben Clark, Jr. David O. McKay], *Improvement Era*, Apr. 1935, pp. 204–05).

Ideas for Quorum Discussion

■ Encourage the quorum members to bring their scriptures to quorum meeting. Follow suggestions and directions of your quorum leaders as you prayerfully adapt your teaching of this lesson to the special needs of your quorum members. Avoid discussions of quorum members' personal problems as you relate their needs to the subject.

▪ You may begin the discussion by quoting President Grant's statement in the introduction. Why can we not eliminate Joseph Smith?

▪ Latter-day Saints are sometimes accused of worshiping Joseph Smith. You may wish to seek quorum members' comments on this criticism. You might use the discussion to draw comments concerning Joseph and the magnitude of his calling.

▪ President Harold B. Lee, quoting President George Albert Smith, said: " 'Many have belittled Joseph Smith, but those who have will be forgotten in the remains of mother earth, and the odor of their infamy will ever be with them, but honor, majesty, and fidelity to God, exemplified by Joseph Smith and attached to his name, will never die.' No truer words were ever spoken" (in *Conference Report,* Oct. 1973, p. 166; or *Ensign,* Jan. 1974, p. 126).

Ask quorum members to comment on this statement. Why will neither his name nor his work ever die? Draw from scriptures in part 3 for the discussion.

▪ You may wish to discuss in some detail the prophecies in part 2 concerning Joseph and his mission. Quorum members might be assigned before quorum meeting to report on one or more of the passages cited.

▪ Ask quorum members to suggest what blessings have been made available in their lives by the mission of Joseph Smith. List these on the chalkboard. Use the scriptures in part 4 for help.

▪ Challenge the brethren to seek to obtain or renew a witness of the divine mission of Joseph Smith. Conclude with testimony bearing.

▪ Review recent conference reports for testimonies by modren prophets regarding Joseph Smith's divine calling.

Discipline Your Children in the Home

D&C 121:34–46

Personal Study

Discipline your children righteously in the home.

Two young men were pedaling their bicycles toward work one day. It was raining lightly, and, as young people sometimes do, they were talking about home. One said: "I remember, I guess I was about twelve the last time my father spanked me. I had disobeyed him. When he found out about it, he asked me why. Instead of using my head, I smarted off a little, and so he told me he would meet me downstairs in ten minutes. I went downstairs, but I was sure I was too old to spank. After what seemed like a long time, Dad came downstairs. He was upset that I didn't seem to care. He used his hand and gave me a hard spanking. He gave me his handkerchief when he was through and said he was sorry he'd had to do that. He put his arm around me and hugged me and told me he loved me. There was deep feeling in his voice, and I knew he cared. Later that night, he tousled my hair and said quietly, 'Let's never again have to have the kind of trouble we did tonight.' "

"Did you ever have any more trouble?" the other asked.

"Oh, I'm sure I acted up again," the first responded, "but the thing I remember best was not the spanking. It was the feeling of hurt and love that I saw in my father's face. Always before when I'd seen that look, I'd thought he was mad. But that night I found out that he wasn't mad, he was hurt. I don't think I'll ever forget that."

"You must have a great dad," the second said as they pedaled along through the rain.

"I sure do!" came the reply.

1 Discipline as an Expression of Love

Discipline is teaching and correcting. Other lessons in this and previous study guides have been concerned with what and how to teach children. The material here is concerned with how to correct children.

■ Hebrews 12:11. What may be the benefits of discipline correctly administered? _____

_____

Most fathers want to be loved. Some fathers seek to court that love by indulging and giving broad license to their children. When such a child comes of age, he may then begin to ignore his father and even come to resent him. Such a son would have neither the benefits of training in restraint and discipline, nor respect for his father.

■ Proverbs 22:15; 29:15. What priesthood father would not prefer to be respected by a righteous son who had been brought to righteousness by correction than loved by a wayward son who had been left to do as he pleased? What may become of children who are left to learn of the evils in the world by their own experience and judgment? _____

_____

Elder Orson Pratt, an early Apostle, said: "Be familiar with your children that they may delight themselves in your society, and look upon you as a kind and tender parent whom they delight to obey. Obedience inspired by love, and obedience inspired by fear, are entirely different in their nature; the former will be permanent and enduring, while the latter only waits to have the object of fear removed, and it vanishes like a dream" (*The Seer*, pp. 185–6).

■ Hebrews 12:5–9. How does God deal with his children? _____

_____

How is this an expression of his love? _____

_____

■ 1 Nephi 8:37. Can anyone teach a child with more care and concern for his welfare than a parent?

- The First Presidency once stated that "the home is the basis of a righteous life and no other instrumentality can take its place nor fulfill its essential functions" (as cited by Harold B. Lee, in Conference Report, Oct. 1962, p. 72; also *Improvement Era*, Dec. 1962, p. 936). What makes the home a unique place to train children? _____

_____

President David O. McKay said: "Unhappiness in the child's life, as in the adult life, springs largely from nonconformity to natural and social laws. The home is the best place in which to develop obedience, which nature and society will later demand" (*Gospel Ideals*, p. 488). Why is the home the best place to teach obedience? _____

_____

What elements for teaching children are found in a righteous home and nowhere else? _____

_____

2 What Are Some Guiding Principles of Righteous Discipline?

There are many factors in appropriate and righteous discipline. Only a few of them may be considered here.

- D&C 58:26–28. How much initiative for governing the family is given to a father? _____

_____

- D&C 121:34–38. How tolerant are the powers of heaven with someone in a position of authority when that person presumes to use his authority in any degree of unrighteousness? _____

_____

Could the powers of heaven approve unrighteous dominion practiced by a father any more than they could approve of the same practiced by any other priesthood officer? _____

_____

- D&C 121:39–40. Do children have agency? _____

_____

Who is preeminently responsible to train children to use their agency properly? _____

Could such training be successful if a parent did not allow children any latitude whatsoever? _____

Why would that training fail if parents allowed their children unlimited freedom during their early years? _____

▪ D&C 121:41–42. How should a father take the lead in the home and in all family matters? _____

Why will family members begin to harbor resentments and bitterness when a father gives as the only reason for his directions to his family that he is the head of the house and that he should be obeyed? _____

Why would family members be less inclined to begrudge the position of the father if he attempted to lead according to the qualities described in these verses? _____

▪ D&C 121:43–44. When some family member is in serious error and resistant to counsel, and discipline is necessary, what does this passage say should be done first, under the guidance of the Holy Ghost? _____

What should be done next? _____

How will this procedure serve to help the erring family member be more open to correction and counsel? _____

▪ Colossians 3:21. If no love or gentleness is demonstrated after the discipline, how might the child be affected? _____

• D&C 121:45–46. How will the qualities described in these verses make it easier for a father to win the respect of family members? _____

_____

If a father has charity for the household of faith but has no charity for the rest of men, why will it be more difficult for his children to respect him? _____

_____

If a father has charity for mankind, but is critical and even cynical about leaders and members in the household of faith, will he have difficulty commanding the respect of family members? _____

_____

What great promises are given to those who strive to follow the counsel of these passages? _____

_____

Will It Make a Difference?

A priesthood-holding father and a loving mother, prayerfully counseling together, will hardly find a family problem that they cannot solve. As you study and review the principles and suggestions in this lesson, consider carefully how they may apply to you and your family.

Quorum Training Suggestions

As a perceptive quorum leader, you will know if members of your quorum have problems with discipline at home. The self-study portion of this lesson deals with fundamental principles of corrective discipline. Your purpose in the quorum meeting may be to teach and train your quorum members to understand and use those principles. Therefore, your plan for the quorum meeting should be to help your quorum members discipline their children righteously in the home. As you plan together as quorum leaders, the following suggestions may be of help to you. However, you should not try to assert your authority in the home of a quorum member. That would be inappropriate.

■ To encourage individual study, invite the quorum members to share their answers to three or four of the important questions of the self-study portion of the lesson, such as:

Why is it wrong to court the love of your children by giving them broad license and unlimited privileges?

What principles for teaching children will be followed in a righteous home?

■ Counsel the quorum members about where they should go to learn principles of corrective discipline. Parents with discipline problems and other challenges of parenthood frequently ask: "Where can I get help? Who can tell me what to do?" The Lord has revealed many principles through the prophets and the scriptures. The Lord expects us to apply these *general* principles to our *particular* situation. When the approach or remedies suggested by the Church leaders contradict the views of authorities in the world, the counsel of the Church leaders should of course take precedence. Where the counsel advanced by Church leaders and secular authorities is identical or similar, it is preferable to quote the Church leaders. Only where Church leaders have suggested broad guidelines and have left to others the details of application should material from secular authorities be included, and then only insofar as that detailed material may correspond to the spirit and direction of guidelines suggested by Church leaders.

■ Using the principles found in Doctrine and Covenants 121:34–46, analyze and discuss this case study:

John and Bill were young boys who usually spent a lot of time together. One afternoon, John said, "I'd better hurry home and feed the dog before my father gets home."

Bill replied, "Will he yell at you if you haven't?"

"No," John answered, "but he'll ask me if I did it, and if I didn't do it, he'll ask me why. And if I don't have a good reason, he might punish me. Even if he doesn't, I know he'll be disappointed in me, and I'll feel dumb."

"Why are you so sure he'll ask you?" Bill asked.

"He always asks me about anything he's assigned me to do. I can always count on that," John replied.

"My dad doesn't do that," Bill said. "He usually forgets what he's asked me to do. And if he does remember, and I haven't done it, he'll just yell at me and say I'm not responsible and won't ever do any good."

Which child was held accountable in the above situation?

What are some of the ways his father taught him accountability?

Why is each of these elements so important?

Why would the approach of the second father be undesirable?

What should the second father do if he really wants to teach his children to be accountable for what they do?

▪ Divide the quorum into three groups: fathers of children ages eleven and younger, fathers of children ages twelve to eighteen, and fathers of children ages eighteen and older. Have the members of the quorum presidency serve as the small-group leaders. Scatter unmarried quorum members and older quorum members throughout all the groups; their observations, either as sons or as experienced fathers, will be valuable. Invite each group to discuss the question, "How can I improve discipline in my home?" The purpose of these small-group discussions is to encourage and train and provide the setting for quorum members to help one another. Care should be taken to preserve home-teaching confidences and to consider only those problems that are volunteered.

▪ Invite a quorum member to read and to lead the quorum in a discussion of Ephesians 6:4. This discussion question may be helpful: Why would it be better for a father to wait until his anger has subsided before he proceeds to discipline the child, even if he still feels that some form of physical discipline is necessary? Compare Proverbs 15:18.

▪ Assign a member of the quorum presidency to lead the quorum in a discussion of timing in discipline. This question may be helpful: How can being sensitive to timing help a father in disciplining his children?

▪ Invite a quorum member to read and lead the quorum in a discussion of these passages: Doctrine and Covenants 84:46; 19:20. Discussion questions may include the following:

Can the light of Christ, or conscience, help in discipline? How?

Occasionally some physical punishment may be necessary to get the attention of the child or to bring about the necessary humility without which the light of conscience can have little effect. Why?

■ Consider the following counsel from Brigham Young for quorum discussion: "How often we see parents demand obedience, good behavior, kind words, pleasant looks, a sweet voice and a bright eye from a child or children when they themselves are full of bitterness and scolding! How inconsistent and unreasonable this is! If we wish our children to look pleasant we should look pleasant at them; and if we wish them to speak kind words to each other, let us speak kind words to them" (R. Clayton Brough, *His Servants Speak*, p. 56).

■ Review "Love Is the Power That Will Cure the Family," *Ensign,* May 1982, pp. 69–70, or Conference Report, Apr. 1982, pp. 96–99, for an example of how Elder F. Enzio Busche disciplined one of his children. Discuss how this approach could be applied in the homes of quorum members.

Be Subject to the Powers That Be

D&C 134

Personal Study

Seek to uphold and sustain the law and the leaders wherever you live.

On 24 August 1977, in Warsaw, Poland, President Spencer W. Kimball dedicated the land of Poland for missionary work. The local members had worked for more than a year with government officials to bring this about. In part of the dedicatory prayer, President Kimball said:

"Our Father, our desire to be associated with this land is to create a love for Thee and to cause the people in this nation to love their fathers and their leaders and love their land and to live honorable, righteous lives. . . .

"Now, Father, we pray that Thou wilt bless these fathers and mothers in this nation, that they may bring up their children that they grow up to be honorable, peaceful, loving parents themselves" (*Deseret News Church Almanac*, 1978, p, 5).

What could the local members of the Church in Poland do to help open their country to the Church? Was it better for them to stay in Poland or move to the headquarters of the Church? Where is Zion? If they stayed there, what was their responsibility toward their government? What is the priesthood bearer's responsibility to his country?

1 Zion Shall Be the Pure in Heart in the Stakes throughout the Earth

■ D&C 97:18–26. What destiny is promised to the latter-day Zion? What are the conditions upon which the establishment of Zion throughout the world shall rest? _____

_____

No matter where Zion is geographically, what must be the predominant characteristic of Zion's people, as described in these passages? _____

_____

■ 1 Nephi 22:3–5, 11–12. Through how much of the world was Israel to be scattered? Was ancient Israel scattered simply to be gathered again, or was there another purpose (see Abraham 2:11)? _____

_____

■ 2 Nephi 9:1–2; see also Jeremiah 23:3–8; 1 Nephi 14:12–14. When the gathering of Israel has been completed, how many lands of promise shall Israel have been gathered to? _____

_____

Among how many peoples and nations shall Zion be established? _____

_____

■ 1 Nephi 14:12–14. In Nephi's great vision of the future, where did he see that congregations of Saints had been established?

_____

Why is it true that members of the Church can "gather out" from the wickedness that may surround them and still remain and live and worship in their own lands? _____

_____

President Harold B. Lee quoted a statement of Elder Bruce R. McConkie:

"The gathering of Israel consists of joining the true church; of coming to a knowledge of the true God and of his saving truths; and of worshiping him in the congregations of the Saints in all nations and among all peoples. . . .

"The place of gathering for the Mexican Saints is in Mexico; the place of gathering for the Guatemalan Saints is in Guatemala; the place of gathering for the Brazilian Saints is in Brazil; and so it goes throughout the length and breadth of the whole earth. Japan is for the Japanese; Korea is for the Koreans; Australia is for the Australians; every nation is the gathering place for its own people" (in Conference Report, Apr. 1973, pp. 6–7; also *Ensign,* July 1973, pp. 4–5).

145

2 Sustain the Laws and Leaders Wherever You Live

■ Twelfth article of faith. As members of the Church gather into the true fold of God and worship God in congregations established in every land, they are still citizens of the country in which they reside. What are their obligations to their country as described in this passage? _____

_____

■ President Marion G. Romney said: "A Latter-day Saint . . . is not a member of the Church only: he is also a subject or citizen of the state in which he lives. As such, his attitude must be in harmony with the twelfth Article of Faith" (*Ensign*, Jan. 1971, p. 16).

■ President David O. McKay declared:

"The three significant words used in the 12th Article of Faith express the proper attitude of the membership of the Church toward law. These words are—obey, honor and sustain.

" . . . Obedience implies a higher attitude than mere submission, for obedience has its root in good intent; submission may spring from selfishness or meanness of spirit. . . .

" . . . In honoring the law, we look upon it as something which is above selfish desires or indulgences.

"To sustain signifies to hold up; to keep from falling. To sustain the law, therefore, is to refrain from saying or doing anything which will weaken it or make it ineffective" (in Conference Report, Apr. 1937, p. 28).

■ Elder Howard W. Hunter said:

"Regardless of whether sovereignty is administered by an individual or by the people, citizens become subject to that supreme power. They have the rights and privileges afforded them under the law, and they have the duty to comply with the provisions of the law. . . .

" . . . Citizens do not have the right to take the law into their own hands or exercise physical force. The sovereign laws of the state must be sustained, and persons living under those laws must obey them for the good of the whole. In this regard The Church of Jesus Christ of Latter-day Saints takes a strong

position" (in Conference Report, Apr. 1968, p. 63; or
Improvement Era, June 1968, p. 79).

■ D&C 134:1, 5–6. Who instituted governments? _____

_____

For what purpose? _____

_____

What responsibility do members of the Church have toward the
government under which they live? _____

_____

What would be the effect in society if there were no
governments, either local or national? _____

_____

■ D&C 134:3–7. Could anyone believe in and worship God
according to the revelations God has given in the last days and
at the same time be guilty of sedition and conspiracy against the
government under which he lives? The message of the Church
has always been to sustain the government in the land of your
residence. President Brigham Young and his counselors in the
First Presidency issued the following statement which is still
applicable today: "Sustain the government of the nation
wherever you are, and speak well of it, for this is right, and the
government has a right to expect it of you" (*Millennial Star*
14:325).

■ Matthew 22:20–21. What is implied in these teachings of the
Master? What would be implied by disobedience to the Savior's
teachings? President Harold B. Lee taught:

"Today we are constantly hearing from the unenlightened and
misguided . . . that they have their agency to do as they please
or to exercise their own self-will to determine what is law and
order, what is right and wrong, or what is honor and virtue.

" . . . When one sets himself up to make his own rules and
presumes to know no law but his own, he is but echoing the
plan of Satan" (Conference Report, Apr. 1972, p. 121: also
Ensign, July 1972, p. 31).

3 Strive to Make Your Country Strong and Worthy of God's Blessings

■ D&C 98:16, 22. In the midst of the early persecutions of the Church, the Saints sought earnestly to know how they were to meet the threats of their enemies. What were they commanded to do? What could turning the hearts of the fathers and children to each other do to make a stronger and more peaceful country?

_____

What promise was made to these early Saints if they obeyed the Lord's counsel? _____

_____

■ Ether 4:11–12. Do the principles of these verses apply to all people anywhere in the world? Why? _____

_____

■ Elder Howard W. Hunter said: "Laws enacted to promote the welfare of the whole and suppress evil doing are to be strictly obeyed. We must pay tribute to sustain the government in the necessary expense incurred in the protection of life, liberty, property, and in promoting the welfare of all persons" (in Conference Report, Apr. 1968, p. 65; or _Improvement Era_, June 1968, p. 80).

■ Elder Ezra Taft Benson said: "We should pray for our civil leaders and encourage them in righteousness" (in Conference Report, Apr. 1972, p. 50; or _Ensign_, July 1972, p. 60).

■ Malachi 3:11–12. Why can the blessings described in this passage apply to all the nations of the earth? _____

_____

Will acceptance and obedience to the gospel bless any man or woman, in any nation or country, who accepts and lives the commandments of God? How can your living the gospel wherever you are bless and help your own homeland? _____

_____

■ D&C 58:21–22. Is there any excuse for disregarding the laws of the land? Why is one not obeying the laws of God if he disregards or willfully violates the laws of the land? _____

_____

It Will
Make a Difference

Whatever nation we live in, it will be made better and stronger if our own home is strong and good. Our good homes will make good citizens, and good citizens will make our nation a better place in which to live. President Joseph F. Smith said, "The home . . . is more than a habitation, it is an institution which stands for stability and love in individuals as well as in nations" (*Gospel Doctrine*, p. 300).

Quorum Training Suggestions

As priesthood leaders you are responsible to teach and train your quorum members to support and sustain the government under which you live. Emphasize the responsibility of members to sustain and honor leaders and rulers and to strive always and in every way to be good citizens. Encourage quorum members to study the self-instructional portion of the lesson beforehand so that they will be prepared to participate in the activities that you plan for the quorum hour.

▪ To encourage individual study, select three or four questions from the self-study materials, and invite the quorum members to share the answers they found to those questions. The review questions might include the following:

What should our attitude be toward governments?

Where is Zion? What is our duty regarding the building of Zion?

What effect can a solid, righteous home and family have on the stability of any nation?

▪ Display the poster "Articles of Faith" (OC014).

▪ Discuss the following statement by a former member of the First Presidency, Stephen L. Richards: "A threat to our unity derives from unseemly personal antagonisms developed in partisan political controversy. The Church, while reserving the right to advocate principles of good government . . . exercises no constraint on the freedom of individuals to make their own choices and affiliations. . . . Any man who makes representation to the contrary does so without authority and justification in fact" (in Conference Report, Oct. 1951, pp. 114–15).

▪ Present and discuss this statement by President David O. McKay:

"Reverence [is akin] to the respect for law and a contributing factor toward it is reverence for sacred things. . . .

"Reverence and obedience to law should begin at home. . . .

"I speak of reverence in connection with obedience to law because a reverent person is law-abiding. . . .

" . . . The time calls for Latter-day Saints everywhere to demonstrate by deeds as well as by words that we love God, revere sacred things and places, and obey, honor and sustain the law" (in Conference Report, Apr. 1937, pp. 30–31).

Where is the best place to teach reverence?

Why does teaching reverence contribute to the stability and order of nations?

What is the best age for beginning to learn reverence?

▪ Encourage a respect for the law and leaders of the country in which you live by activities such as the following:

Invite anyone who may be qualified to come and present to the quorum a discussion on some of the great patriots in the history of your country.

Invite a quorum member who may be qualified to make a presentation in the quorum on a cultural history of your region or nation.

Display and review the history of local, regional, or national flags.

▪ Discuss these questions:

How can a strong home and family contribute to peace and orderliness in the nation?

Why is it true that good members of the Church make good citizens of whatever nation they live in?

"Man May Become like God"

D&C 132:20

Personal Study

Strive to obey the gospel and become like God the Father.

"But what is the purpose of it all?" Frank blurted out to his quorum president as they walked home together after an interview. "Why do we do all the things we are supposed to do? Yes, I know the Church is true and that we will be judged in eternity for how well we do here. But the requirements here are so precise, and the promises about future rewards are so vague. What are we seeking, really?"

Have you ever felt like Frank? Is it easy for us to sometimes forget the actual objectives that we have in the Church? Do we ever get so busy attending meetings, paying tithing, holding home evenings, and trying to do all the rest that God has required that we forget what our ultimate destiny can be if we remain faithful?

President Lorenzo Snow was one who sought earnestly to learn and did come to know the ultimate eternal opportunity which can be ours through our devotion and labor in the gospel plan. Study these passages and statements carefully, and ponder upon the significance of their meaning for you.

1 God Was Once a Man As We Are Now

▪ When he was a young man, Lorenzo Snow was promised by the Lord through the Patriarch to the Church that through obedience to the gospel he could become as great as God, "and you cannot wish to be greater" (Eliza R. Snow Smith, *Biography and Family Record of Lorenzo Snow*, pp. 9–10).

▪ President Lorenzo Snow recorded this experience that occurred when he was still a young elder: "The Spirit of the Lord rested mightily upon me—the eyes of my understanding were opened, and I saw as clear as the sun at noon-day, with wonder and astonishment, the pathway of God and man." Elder Snow expressed this new found understanding in these words: "As man now is, God once was: As God now is, man may be." Later the Prophet Joseph Smith assured him: "Brother Snow, that is true gospel doctrine, and it is a revelation from God to you" (quoted by LeRoi C. Snow, in "Devotion to Divine Inspiration," *Improvement Era*, June 1919, pp. 651–56).

■ The Prophet Joseph Smith said:

"... *It is the first principle of the Gospel to know for a certainty the Character of God, and to know that we may converse with him as one man converses with another, and that he was once a man like us; yea, that God himself, the Father of us all, dwelt on an earth*" (*Teachings*, pp. 345–46; italics in original).

■ President Brigham Young elaborated on this concept: "It must be that God knows something about temporal things, and has had a body and been on an earth; were it not so He would not know how to judge men righteously, according to the temptations and sins they have had to contend with" (as cited by Harold B. Lee, in Conference Report, Apr. 1969, p. 130; or *Improvement Era*, June 1969, p. 104).

■ 3 Nephi 12:48. What are some of the meanings implied in this passage? _____

_____

Could the words "even as" have reference to the way as well as the accomplishment? Does Jesus ask that we do anything that he was not willing to do himself?

2 Our Father Advanced and Progressed Until He Became God

■ President Joseph Fielding Smith said: "*Our Father in heaven, according to the Prophet, had a Father,* and since there has been a condition of this kind through all eternity, each Father had a Father" (*Doctrines of Salvation*, 2:47).

■ President Joseph F. Smith taught: "I know that God is a being with body, parts and passions. . . . Man was born of woman; Christ, the Savior, was born of woman; and God, the Father was born of woman" (*Church News*, 19 Sept. 1936, p. 2).

■ President Wilford Woodruff explained: "[God] has had his endowments a great many years ago. He has ascended to his thrones, principalities and powers in the eternities. We are his children. . . . We are here to fill a probation and receive an education" (*Deseret News Weekly*, 28 Sept. 1881, p. 546).

■ How does it help us to know that the basic elements of God's life in a mortal world were the same as ours? President Brigham Young explained:

"He is our Father—the Father of our spirits—and was once a man in mortal flesh as we are. . . .

" . . . There never was a time when there were not Gods and worlds and when men were not passing through the same ordeals that we are now passing through. . . .

"It appears ridiculous to the world, under their darkened and erroneous traditions, that God has once been a finite being" (*Deseret News*, 16 Nov. 1859, p. 290).

■ Philippians 2:5–12. What does this passage say that Jesus did?

_____

_____

Why did he feel justified in doing it? _____

_____

How does Jesus show us the way and provide us the power, through our obedience, to do just as he has done (compare John 15:1–8)? _____

_____

_____

3 Through Obedience to the Gospel, Man May Become like God

■ Elder S. Dilworth Young attributed in verse the following words to our Father in Heaven as He revealed His plan to us in our premortal home:

"My children all: You see in me
Exalted man, of flesh and bone
And spirit pure. One time, long
Long ago, I was as you, a spirit son
Of an exalted Father. [see HC 6:302–17]
You may become as now I have become
But you must do as I have done."
(In "The Eternal Conflict," *1978 Devotional Speeches of the Year* [Provo, Utah: Brigham Young University Press, 1979], p. 83.)

- What does this mean for you? _____

_____

- John 8:29; 3 Nephi 27:13. What example has Christ given us regarding following the ways of the Father? _____

Why are we not justified in saying that the objectives of the gospel are all right for God and Christ but too high for us? _____

_____

- President Joseph F. Smith said: "We are precisely in the same condition and under the same circumstances that God our heavenly Father was when he was passing through this, or a similar ordeal" (*Gospel Doctrine*, p. 64).
- Psalm 82:6. What does this passage mean for us? _____

Did we receive anything from our Father that could help us become like him? _____

What can a child grow up to be? _____

What can a son of God grow up to be? _____

President Lorenzo Snow said: "We are the offspring of God, begotten by Him in the spirit world, where we partook of His nature as children here partake of the likeness of their parents. Our trials and sufferings give us experience, and establish within us principles of godliness" (*Deseret News*, 17 Feb. 1886, p. 66).
- 3 Nephi 28:10. What is Jesus expressing to these men? _____

What does eternity hold in store for them? _____

Why could Jesus say to anyone what he has said to these men?

_____

■ Revelation 3:21. What does it mean to overcome? _____

What great blessing is promised to those who do? _____

What can be the destiny of a man if he will strive with all his heart to do the best he can? _____

■ What evidence do we have that God does not jealously guard his position and power, but rather seeks to see that his children rise up to the perfection of glory, knowledge, and power that he has obtained (see Moses 1:39)? _____

■ The Prophet Joseph Smith summarized this doctrine by declaring: "Here, then, is eternal life—to know the only wise and true God; and you have got to learn how to be Gods yourselves, and to be kings and priests to God, the same as all Gods have done before you" (*Teachings,* pp. 346–47).

It Can Make a Difference!

It is not sufficient to be born a child of God. One must actively cultivate the characteristics of God in his own life in order to really know him and become like him. Consider this counsel by Elder Gordon B. Hinckley: "That man who knows that he is a child of God, created in the image of a divine Father and gifted with a potential for the exercise of great and god-like virtues, will discipline himself against the sordid, lascivious elements to which all are exposed" (in conference Report, Oct. 1975, p. 57; or *Ensign,* Nov. 1975, p. 39).

Elder Neal A. Maxwell pointed out that "it is much easier to believe in eternal progression than to practice daily improvement" (*All These Things Shall Give Thee Experience,* p. 71). How much easier is it to dream of becoming like God than to do the specific things we need to do today to be better members of the Church, better husbands and fathers, better citizens, and better Christians? What can you do to improve today? Are you striving daily to reach your potential?

Quorum Training Suggestions

As the presiding officers of your quorum or group, you have regular contact with those home teachers who visit the homes of every quorum member. Are any members of your quorum like Frank, busy trying to do what is required, but not always remembering why? Your purpose in this quorum training is to help your quorum members understand and remember the objective for which we are striving. You probably have quorum members who understand that man may become like God, but do you have brethren who do not feel that it is possible for them? Use these other resources to encourage and comfort and reassure your quorum members that they can, if only they will. Encourage quorum members to study the self-study material carefully so that they will be prepared to discuss how this knowledge may help them purify their lives.

▪ To encourage individual study, allow the brethren to share their thoughts from their individual study by asking such questions as:

What are the implications of the statement that God was once as we are now?

Has there ever been a time when men were not passing through what we are now passing through? Why?

▪ Display a picture of Lorenzo Snow (OQ453).

▪ Challenge quorum members to ponder these questions: Why do we so frequently forget the objects that we have in the gospel? What problems could we avoid if we would always remember the ultimate purposes of the gospel? What are some things we could do to keep before us the purpose of the plan of salvation?

▪ Select a member of the quorum presidency to lead the quorum in a discussion of these passages. Analyze each of them and discuss what they contribute to our understanding of the doctrine that man may become like God.

Revelation 3:21

Philippians 2:5–12

D&C 130:18–21

D&C 50:24

D&C 93:11–20, 27–28

■ Discuss the implications of the following statement by President Harold B. Lee: "I . . . charge you to say again and again to yourselves, as the Primary organization has taught the children to sing 'I am a [son or daughter] of God' and by so doing begin today to live closer to those ideals which will make your life happier and more fruitful because of an awakened realization of who you are" (in Conference Report, Oct. 1973, p. 10; or *Ensign*, Nov. 1973, p. 6).

■ Present and analyze this poem written by President Lorenzo Snow.

"Has thou not been unwisely bold,
Man's destiny to thus unfold?
To raise, promote such high desire,
Such vast ambition thus inspire?
"Still, 'tis no phantom that we trace
Man's ultimatum in life's race;
This royal path has long been trod
By righteous men, each now a God:
"As Abra'm, Isaac, Jacob, too,
First babes, then men—to gods they grew.
As man now is, our God once was;
As now God is, so man may be,—
Which doth unfold man's destiny.

. . . .

"The boy, like to his father grown,
Has but attained unto his own;
To grow to sire from state of son,
Is not 'gainst Nature's course to run.
"A son of God, like God to be,
Would not be robbing Deity;
And he who has this hope within,
Will purify himself from sin. . . ."
(*Improvement Era*, June 1919, pp. 660–61.)

■ Present this statement as a summary of President Snow's teaching on the possible destiny of man: "It is our duty to try to be perfect, and it is our duty to improve each day, and look upon our course last week and do things better this week; do things better today than we did them yesterday, and go on and on from one degree of righteousness to another" (in Conference Report, Apr. 1898, p. 13).

■ Be careful in presenting this material that you don't bring God down to man's level. Our objective is to perfect ourselves and *raise* our level to his exalted place.

The Quorum Is a Vehicle for Priesthood Service

D&C 88:80

Personal Study

Counsel and work together as a quorum for the spiritual and temporal welfare of individual members.

Elder Vaughn J. Featherstone related the following account of a brother named George Goates, who was helped by his priesthood quorum when his burdens had become overwhelming. Brother Goates had lost in death four of his family members during the terrible influenza epidemic of 1918, but all of this notwithstanding, the ordinary requirements of life still faced him. Elder Featherstone recounted his story in the words of Les Goates, a son of George Goates:

"After breakfast dad [Bro. George Goates] said to Franz, 'Well, son, we had better get down to the field and see if we can get another load of beets out of the ground before they get frozen in any tighter. Hitch up and let's be on our way.'

"Francis drove the four-horse outfit down the driveway and dad climbed aboard. As they drove along the Saratoga Road, they passed wagon after wagon-load of beets being hauled to the factory and driven by neighborhood farmers. As they passed by, each driver would wave a greeting: 'Hi ya, Uncle George,' 'Sure sorry, George,' 'Tough break, George,' 'You've got a lot of friends, George.'

"On the last wagon was the town comedian, freckled-faced Jasper Rolfe. He waved a cheery greeting and called out: 'That's all of 'em, Uncle George.'

"My dad turned to Francis and said: 'I wish it was all of ours.'

"When they arrived at the farm gate, Francis jumped down off the big red beet wagon and opened the gate as we drove onto the field. He pulled up, stopped the team, and paused a moment and scanned the field, from left to right and back and

159

forth—and lo and behold, there wasn't a sugar beet on the whole field. Then it dawned upon him what Jasper Rolfe meant when he called out: 'That's all of 'em, Uncle George!'

"Then dad got down off the wagon, picked up a handful of the rich, brown soil he loved so much, and then in his thumbless left hand a beet top, and he looked for a moment at these symbols of his labor, as if he couldn't believe his eyes.

"Then father sat down on a pile of beet tops—this man who brought four of his loved ones home for burial in the course of only six days; made caskets, dug graves, and even helped with the burial clothing—this amazing man who never faltered, nor flinched, nor wavered throughout this agonizing ordeal—sat down on a pile of beet tops and sobbed like a little child.

"Then he arose, wiped his eyes with his big, red bandanna handkerchief, looked up at the sky, and said: 'Thanks, Father, for the elders of our ward' " (in Conference Report, Apr. 1973, pp. 46–48; or *Ensign*, July 1973, pp. 35–37).

---

1 The Priesthood Is Organized in Quorums to Serve

God's house is a house of order. Priesthood quorums have been organized to facilitate the work of the kingdom.

■ Elder Boyd K. Packer explained:

"I hope, if I can be blessed, to present something of a primer of ideas on the priesthood quorum . . .

"In ancient days when a man was appointed to a select body, his commission, always written in Latin, outlined the responsibility of the organization, defined who should be members, and then invariably contained the words: *quorum vos unum* meaning, 'of whom we will that you be one.'

"The word *quorum*, which does not appear in either the Old Testament or the New Testament, from that beginning came to mean, that select group without whose consent business could not be transacted, nor work proceed with authority.

"In the dispensation of the fulness of times, the Lord instructed that the priesthood should be organized into quorums; meaning, selected assemblies of brethren given authority that His business might be transacted and His work proceed. . . .

"The quorums are made up of worthy men of whom you are designated to be one" (*A Royal Priesthood*, Melchizedek Priesthood Personal Study Guide, 1975–76, p. 131).

▪ Numbers 1:4, 16. Why must there be heads over the thousands in Israel? Even though the quorum leader has no more priesthood than his fellows why must there be a head, one who presides with directing keys? _____

_____

▪ Deuteronomy 1:13–15. Is the idea of priesthood organization new?

▪ Exodus 24:9–10. Who saw the God of Israel? _____

_____

It is essential to remember that the quorum is an agency for the priesthood bearers who give it being to work in concert. In a sense the quorum is a clearinghouse for priesthood activity.

▪ President Joseph F. Smith said: "There is no office growing out of this Priesthood that is or can be greater than the priesthood itself. It is from the Priesthood that the office derives its authority and power. No office gives authority to the Priesthood. No office adds to the power of the Priesthood. But all offices in the Church derive their power, their virtue, their authority, from the Priesthood" (*Gospel Doctrine*, pp. 148–49). Why was the priesthood restored before the Church was organized? _____

_____

Why is the priesthood more essential than the quorum? _____

_____

2 Priesthood Quorums Promote True Fraternity

▪ President David O. McKay said: "If priesthood meant only personal distinction or individual elevation, there would be no need of groups or quorums. The very existence of such groups, established by divine authorization, proclaims our dependence upon one another, the indispensable need of mutual help and assistance" (in Conference Report, Oct. 1968, p. 84; or *Improvement Era*, Dec. 1968, p. 84).

■ Elder John A. Widtsoe wrote: "The priesthood is a great brotherhood, held together by the eternal immutable laws that constitute the framework of the Gospel. The feeling of brotherhood should permeate the quorum. It should be the first concern of a quorum to help all members who may be in need temporally, mentally, or spiritually. The spirit of brotherhood would be the directing force in all the plans and operations of the quorum. If this spirit be cultivated, wisely, and persistently, no other organization will become more attractive to the man who holds the priesthood" (*Priesthood and Church Government*, p. 135).

■ 1 Samuel 18:1, 3. How strong can true brotherhood be? _____

Thus the quorum has been given to serve the individual priesthood man,—not the other way around—and to strengthen true bonds of brotherhood. Why is it essential to understand these concepts? _____

3 The Quorum as a School of the Prophets

■ Numbers 11:29. How many of the Lord's people should be prophets in their own lives and responsibilities? _____

■ Elder Bruce R. McConkie has said that a priesthood quorum is "an organized body of priesthood brethren who have the same office or calling. It is a church agency that administers salvation to its members and their families. It is a local school of the prophets" (address at Regional Representatives' Seminar, 4 Oct. 1973, p. 3).

■ D&C 107:89. What is the duty of an elders quorum president? Would this apply to leaders of other priesthood quorums? _____

■ D&C 43:8. How can this verse be applied to quorum instruction? _____

▪ D&C 88:77–80 (see also D&C 29:34). How extensively is the priesthood to be instructed, according to these verses? Does it seem that instruction should center only on theory? What things are spiritual unto the Lord? _____

_____

▪ Matthew 18:20. What is the principle here? How could it be applied to a priesthood quorum? The priesthood quorum is meant to be a place where individual members can be more perfectly instructed according to their duties, both temporal and spiritual, under the direction of those who preside over them.

4 Using Quorum Resources to Assist Brethren

Priesthood men working in concert can often more fully focus and concentrate priesthood service. This is a paramount reason for the existence of the quorum. It is essential that a quorum help members who may be in need temporally, mentally, and spiritually.

▪ Elder Boyd K. Packer said, "If his priesthood quorum functions properly, a man sustained by the brethren of his quorum, almost could not fail in any phase of life's responsibility" (address at Regional Representatives' seminar, 4 Oct. 1973, p. 65; see this study guide, appendix 2, pp. 298–305).

▪ Elder Gordon B. Hinckley quoted President J. Reuben Clark in relation to quorum service:

"I am confident that the Lord intended that a priesthood quorum should be far more than a class in theology on Sunday mornings. Of course, the building of spirituality and the strengthening of testimony through effective gospel teaching is an important priesthood responsibility. But this is only a segment of the quorum function. Each quorum must be a working brotherhood for every member if its purpose is to be realized. There must be instruction in principles of personal and family preparedness. If effectively taught, such instruction will become preventative welfare, because the quorum member and his family, equipped with such knowledge, will be better prepared to handle many difficulties that might arise. The teaching of financial and resource management, home production and storage, the fostering of such activities as will promote physical, emotional, and spiritual health might all be the proper and legitimate concerns of the presidency of the quorum in behalf of its members.

"Furthermore, the quorum becomes a resource of organized and disciplined manpower" (*Ensign*, Nov. 1977, p. 86).

■ Exodus 17:8–12. How does this incident from the life of Moses illustrate brotherhood and service? _____

_____

Pure religion includes service. Priesthood is most perfectly expressed in service. Quorums are organized to serve.

Will It Make a Difference?

President Joseph F. Smith said: "We expect to see the day . . . when every council of the Priesthood . . . will understand its duty; will assume its own responsibility, will magnify its calling, and fill its place in the Church, to the uttermost, according to the intelligence and ability possessed by it. When that day will come, there will not be so much necessity for work that is now being done by the auxiliary organizations. . . . The Lord designed and comprehended it from the beginning, and he has made provision in the Church whereby every need may be met and satisified through the regular organizations of the priesthood" (*Gospel Doctrine*, pp. 159–60).

Quorum Training Suggestions

The central idea of this lesson is that the quorum is primarily an agency for priesthood service. Care should be taken to help individual priesthood bearers see the quorum as a means to the end of service and not as an end in itself. The following suggestions could aid in quorum training.

■ To encourage individual study such review questions as the following could be asked: Why is the priesthood organized in quorums? Is there any organization or office more important than the priesthood itself? Why? How could a priesthood quorum be a school of the prophets? What kinds of service can the quorum facilitate for individuals?

▪ Note the basic definition of a priesthood quorum in the *Melchizedek Priesthood Handbook*, 1984 p. 1.

▪ The quorum instructor could elaborate on some of the following purposes of priesthood quorums as given by President Joseph Fielding Smith:

"The quorums of the priesthood are organized for a definite purpose. I've jotted down several of these: first, to keep the members holding the priesthood active and alert in the performance of every duty which the priesthood requires at their hands; second, to teach the members how to assume responsibility and magnify their callings; third, to train them in methods by which they may effectually teach others and officiate in their behalf; fourth, to encourage them in their responsibilities pertaining to the salvation of the dead as well as for the living.

"A quorum, properly anointed, must seek out the needs of every individual member and attempt to supply these needs that may be discovered, both temporally and spiritually. No quorum of the priesthood is assuming the full obligation placed upon it by the Lord which does not sufficently extend temporal need. Each member should dedicate himself and use his talent to advance the cause of Zion. He must be loyal and faithful to the Church, to the quorum, to the priesthood in general, to his family and to every divine principle of eternal truth" (in Conference Report, Oct. 1945, p. 95).

▪ The quorum could be divided into groups. Each group could be given a specific problem and then assigned to design a quorum plan that would solve a problem. Consider such problems as the following: A brother has a runaway son. A widow's house needs painting. A brother has difficulty getting to priesthood meetings because of transportation problems. The wife of a paralyzed brother needs help to care for her husband.

▪ Discuss Romans 15:1–2, relating it to quorum service.

▪ The quorum could sing or at least examine the words of the hymn "Rise Up, O Men of God" (*Hymns*, no. 332).

▪ Discuss the following observations by Elder Stephen L. Richards: Regarding the priesthood quorum, he said, it is "first, a class; second a fraternity; and third, a service unit" (in Conference Report Oct. 1938, p. 118). He also said, "I like to define the Priesthood in terms of service and I frequently call it 'the perfect plan of service' " (in Conference Report, Apr. 1937, pp. 46–45).

■ Review Elder L. Tom Perry's story of how a group of high priests changed the focus of their quorum from passive listening to actively serving ("When Ye Shall Not Fear, *Ensign*, Nov. 1981, p. 37; or Conference Report, Oct. 1981, pp. 53–54).

Unity in Your Family

D&C 93:42–43

Personal Study

Establish goals for increasing family unity.

Lehi "took nothing with him, save it were his family" (1 Nephi 2:4)

How important do you feel Lehi's family was to him? How important is your family to you? What would you be willing to do to unite all the members of your family in love and righteousness?

President David O. McKay said:

"When one puts business or pleasure above his home, he that moment starts on the downgrade to soul-weakness. When the club becomes more attractive to any man than his home, it is time for him to confess in bitter shame that he has failed to measure up to the supreme opportunity of his life and flunked in the final test of true manhood. No other success can compensate for failure in the home. The poorest shack in which love prevails over a united family is of greater value to God and future humanity than any other riches. In such a home God can work miracles and will work miracles" (in Conference Report, Apr. 1964, p. 5; or *Improvement Era,*, July 1964, p. 445).

1 Why Is It Important to Achieve Family Unity

■ Moses 5:12–15. What influences divided members of the first family on earth? _____

_____

What are some influences or conditions that tend to divide families today? _____

_____

▪ D&C 93:41–49. Why did the Lord chastise his servants regarding their families? _____

_____

What are some of the things you can do to preserve order and love in your home? _____

_____

▪ D&C 105:4–5. Since the family is the basic unit of the Church, what is the law of the celestial kingdom with regard to the family? _____

_____

Consider the counsel of President McKay:

"I can imagine few, if any, things more objectionable in the home than the absence of unity and harmony. On the other hand, I know that a home in which unity, mutual helpfulness, and love abide is just a bit of heaven on earth. I surmise that nearly all of you can testify to the sweetness of life in a home in which these virtues predominate. Most gratefully and humbly I cherish the remembrance that never once as a lad in the home of my youth did I ever see one instance of discord between father and mother, and that goodwill and mutual understanding has been the uniting bond that has held together a fortunate group of brothers and sisters. Unity, harmony, goodwill are virtues to be fostered and cherished in every home" (in Conference Report, Oct. 1967, p. 7; or *Improvement Era*, Dec. 1967, p. 34).

What further values of family unity can you suggest? _____

_____

How are the individual members of your family helped when each one feels he is a part of a family group, working together for worthwhile goals? _____

_____

What, in turn, are some consequences of disunity? _____

_____

▪ 2 Nephi 1:14–29. Disunity crept into Lehi's family. Did he "give up" on his family? _____

_____

Why? _____

_____

How long did he try to unite his family in righteousness? _____

_____

Should you ever cease this same effort? _____

_____

■ D&C 6:32. What great blessings does the Lord promise to your family when you are united in efforts toward righteousness?

_____

_____

2 How Can You Promote Family Unity?

■ 1 Nephi 8:10, 12. Why is it significant that Lehi thought first of his family after partaking of the fruit? _____

■ Consider the counsel of Elder A. Theodore Tuttle concerning the priorities of parenthood:

"This decision to be parents means to put *first* the obligation to be baby-sitters, trainers, discipliners, supervisors, teachers, assigners, checker-uppers, planners, story-tellers, exemplars, and, in short, to be common, ordinary, garden variety, old-fashioned, on-the-job, full-time parents. It means that this responsibility as parents comes before social climbing, the newest in gadgets, or conspicuous consumption. It supersedes personal selfishness, propriety, pleasure, even a tidy house. It demands solemn and continual allegiance to a cause greater than self. Fulfillment of this parental duty develops all of the virtues that can be named, and requires the application of all the qualities that make men great. But to participate in the joy of this privilege, as the Lord had intended, requires a *conscious decision* to accept the responsibilities of this sacred obligation—the most sacred and far-reaching obligation assumed by two people" ("And They Shall Also Teach Their Children," *Relief Society Magazine*, July 1963, pp. 484–85.)

- Ephesians 5:23–29 (especially verses 25–28). In what crucial way may a husband promote unity in his family? _____

_____

- Ephesians 6:1–4. How may you as a father further promote love and unity (see verse 4)? _____

_____

How may you as a son encourage unity in your family (see verses 1–2)? _____

_____

- Mosiah 4:13–15. What counsel does King Benjamin give to promote family solidarity? _____

_____

- D&C 121:36–44. What principles are you to follow in exercising the priesthood in your home? _____

_____

How will applying these principles consistently strengthen your family? _____

_____

From the instructions given by the Lord in these verses (D&C 121:36–44), consider what approach you could take to resolve these family situations:

One of your children does not wish to attend Church.

A son or daughter is associating with companions detrimental to his or her spiritual welfare.

A son is not willing to accept a mission call.

A son or daughter is breaking the Word of Wisdom

3 Set Some Goals for Family Unity

It is possible for families to be united in temporal things, such as camping, sports, music, hobbies, or family traditions. These activities are commendable. They are incomplete, however, unless there are spiritual goals as well. Family togetherness alone is not sufficient. Family efforts are to be directed toward both eternal goals and appropriate temporal concerns.

Consider these questions as you think about your family:

How could you improve your regular family prayers in such a way as to increase unity in your family? What goals could you set as a family concerning family prayer?

How could family council meetings help? You might consider making specific assignments in a family council (such as cleaning the house, doing dishes, running errands), and then setting a goal to have all assignments done during the week without having to remind or ask. How might such a program promote your family's unity?

You might set the goal to hold weekly family home evenings. What goals might you set to make your family nights more meaningful to your family?

How may setting aside a time to be alone with one of your children, where you give him your undivided attention, help your family? In what ways might regular individual interviews with family members help? What goals have or can you set along these lines?

**You Can Make
a Difference**

Think carefully about the questions asked in this lesson. Apply them to your own family situation. Jot down some goals or write a brief outline of your plans for increasing and maintaining family unity. Perhaps your family members can help.

Quorum Training Suggestions

Encourage the quorum members to bring their scriptures to quorum meeting. Follow suggestions and directions of your quorum leaders as you prayerfully adapt your teaching of this lesson to the special needs of your quorum members. Avoid discussions of quorum members' personal problems as you relate their needs to the subject.

▪ You might have a quorum member read the statement by President McKay in the introduction, then discuss ways of determining when a person is putting business or pleasure ahead of family responsibilities. Discuss what might be considered success or failure in the home.

▪ Have a quorum member read the statement by Elder Tuttle, and discuss how "fulfillment of this parental duty develops all

171

of the virtues that can be named." List some of these virtues on the chalkboard, and call for illustrations of how family unity helps develop them.

■ Discuss some of the counsel in the scriptures regarding putting your house in order. Then suggest ways, through discussion, in which each priesthood bearer may contribute to family unity as a son, as a brother, as a husband, as a father or grandfather. Each quorum member will find himself in at least one and possibly all five of these roles.

■ Share experiences and ideas about setting goals for strengthening the family. Discuss the types of goals that might be set, how the family might be brought in to share in the planning and setting of goals, and how they might be best carried out. Discuss specific steps.

■ Emphasize the need for each priesthood bearer to commit himself to evaluate his family's unity by identifying areas of weakness and then setting goals that promote and strengthen unity.

■ Show the filmstrip *Father, Consider Your Ways* (OF090).

■ Invite quorum members to look up scriptures in the Topical Guide of the Latter-day Saint Edition of the King James Bible under the heading "Unity" and relate these scriptures to the objective of this lesson.

■ Discuss the following quotation by Elder John H. Groberg: "I know of no single activity that has more potential for unifying our families and bringing more love and divine direction into our homes than consistent, fervent family prayer" (in Conference Report, Apr. 1982, p. 75; or *Ensign*, May 1982, p. 50).

■ Invite quorum members to suggest additional ways in which we can seek unity in the family.

"Go Ye and Do the Works of Abraham"

D&C 132:32

Personal Study

Learn what the Abrahamic covenant is and how you can fulfill the conditions of that same covenant.

In every age of the world the Lord has made covenants with his people. These covenants are contracts, agreements, or mutual promises between God in heaven and men on earth. The Lord, for his part, reveals the terms and conditions of the covenant and then promises to pour out specified blessings upon those who keep it. Man, for his part, agrees to keep the terms and conditions revealed to him in order to obtain the promised blessings.

President Joseph Fielding Smith wrote:

"Each ordinance and requirement given to man for the purpose of bringing to pass his salvation and exaltation is a covenant. Baptism for the remission of sins is a covenant . . .

"Keeping the Sabbath day holy is a covenant . . . All of the Ten Commandments are everlasting covenants. The law of tithing is a form of an everlasting covenant. . . .

"Marriage is an everlasting covenant" (*Doctrines of Salvation,* 1:152–53).

Elder Bruce R. McConkie said: "The new and everlasting covenant is the fulness of the gospel; it is new in every age and to every people to whom it comes; it is everlasting; . . . its laws and conditions never change" (*The Promised Messiah,* p. 438).

What covenants have you entered into? What covenants and promises has the Lord made with those who have gone before you? Have you had planted in your heart "the promises made to the fathers" (D&C 2:2)? What are these promises? Can you obtain similar promises?

1 What Is the Abrahamic Covenant?

■ Genesis 17:1–2. Who were the parties to this covenant? _____

What was the promise made to Abraham at that time? _____

■ Genesis 17:3–6. What was Abraham to become? _____

Did this promise apply only to his mortal existence? _____

Concerning this matter, President Brigham Young said:

"We understand that we are to be made kings and priests unto God; now if I be made the king and lawgiver to my family, and if I have many sons, I shall become the father of many fathers, for they will have sons, and their sons will have sons, and so on, from generation to generation, and, in this way, I may become the father of many fathers, or the king of many kings. . . .

"In this way we can become king of kings, and lord of lords, or father of fathers, or prince of princes" (*Discourses of Brigham Young*, p. 195).

■ Genesis 17:7–8. With whom, besides Abraham, was the covenant to be established? _____

Compare 1 Nephi 22:9–12.

■ Abraham 2:9–11. Who are the seed of Abraham? President Joseph Fielding Smith has answered: *"Every person who embraces the gospel becomes of the house of Israel.* In other words, they become members of the *chosen lineage,* or Abraham's children through Isaac and Jacob unto whom the promises were made. The great *majority* of those who become members of the Church are *literal descendants* of Abraham through Ephraim, son of Joseph. Those who are not literal descendants of Abraham and Israel must *become such,* and *when they are baptized and confirmed they are grafted into the tree and are entitled to all the rights and privileges as heirs."* (*Doctrines of Salvation*, 3:246.) According to verse 11, what are the ultimate blessings associated with the Abrahamic covenant? _____

_____

■ Elder Bruce R. McConkie wrote:

"Abraham first received the gospel by baptism . . . ; then he had conferred upon him the higher priesthood, and he entered into celestial marriage . . . , gaining assurance thereby that he would have eternal increase; finally he received a promise that all of these blessings would be offered to all of his mortal posterity. . . .

"All of these promises lumped together are called the *Abrahamic covenant*. This covenant was renewed with Isaac . . . and again with Jacob. . . . *Those portions of it which pertain to personal exaltation and eternal increase are renewed with each member of the house of Israel who enters the order of celestial marriage."* (*Mormon Doctrine,* "Abrahamic Covenant").

■ D&C 101:4–5. What is another way in which Abraham serves as a pattern for us? _____

_____

What effect can our trials have on us if we submit to them and endure their "chastening" as Abraham did? _____

_____

■ D&C 124:19. Where is Abraham now? What blessings came to Abraham because he fulfilled so honorably the covenant God made with him? What have he and Isaac and Jacob become because they "did none other things than that which they were commanded" (see D&C 132:37)? In the Joseph Smith Translation of the Bible, we read that because Abraham fulfilled all the covenants God had given him, "God blessed Abram [Abraham], and gave unto him riches, and honor, and lands for an everlasting possession; according to the covenant which he had made, and according to the blessing wherewith Melchizedek had blessed him" (JST, Genesis 14:40; compare Alma 7:25). Can we receive the same blessings as Abraham?

2 How Do We Enter into the Same Covenant?

■ Isaiah 51:2. How can we fulfill the Lord's charge in this passage? The Prophet Joseph Smith taught that "the ancients, though persecuted and afflicted by men, obtained from God promises of such weight and glory, that our hearts are often filled with gratitude that we are even permitted to look upon them. . . . If we are the children of the Most High, and are called with the same calling with which they were called, and embrace the same covenant that they embraced, and are faithful to the testimony of our Lord as they were, we can approach the Father in the name of Christ as they approached Him, and for ourselves obtain the same promises" (*Teachings of the Prophet Joseph Smith*, pp. 65–66). Even though we have a right to the blessings of Abraham because we are his heirs (through descent or adoption), what must we do to enter into the same covenant that Abraham did? _____

■ Where can we go to enter into the Abrahamic covenant? Elder Bruce R. McConkie answered:

"We go to the temple and we get married for eternity, and when we do, we are given everything that Abraham received as far as the promises of glory and exaltation are concerned. . . .

"Joseph Smith says that in the temple of God there is an order of priesthood that is patriarchal. 'Go to the temple,' he says, 'and find out about this order.' So I went to the temple, and I took my wife with me, and we kneeled at the altar. There on that occasion we entered, the two of us, into an 'order of the priesthood.' When we did it, we had sealed upon us, on a conditional basis, every blessing that God promised father Abraham—the blessings of exlatation and eternal increase. The name of that order of priesthood, which is patriarchal in nature, because Abraham was a natural patriarch to his posterity, is the New and Everlasting Covenant of Marriage" ("The Eternal Family Concept," *Genealogical Devotional Addresses*, 19–23 June 1967 [Provo, Utah: Brigham Young University Press, 1968], pp. 89–91).

3 How May We Inherit the Blessings of Abraham?

■ The Prophet Joseph Smith said, "Abraham was guided in all his family affairs by the Lord . . . and prospered exceedingly in all that he put his hand unto; it was because he and his family obeyed the counsel of the Lord" (*Teachings*, pp. 251–52). What was the key to Abraham's receiving these blessings? _____

_____

■ Concerning Abraham's obedience, President Spencer W. Kimball has written:

"Abraham recognized the blessings in store for the faithful and sought earnestly to obey the commandments of God. . . .

"There are many examples of Abraham's obedience to the Lord's will. In Genesis we learn that God commanded Abraham to circumcise every male in his household. . . . Instead of . . . procrastinating his obedience, Abraham went out and complied 'in the selfsame day.' (Gen. 17:26.)

"A similar, but even more impressive example is Abraham's obedience to God's command that he sacrifice his only son, Isaac. . . . He arose early the next morning and began the journey to the appointed place.

"How often do Church members arise early in the morning to do the will of the Lord? How often do we say, 'Yes, I will have home evening with my family, but the children are so young now; I will start when they are older'? How often do we say, 'Yes, I will obey the commandment to store food and to help others, but just now I have neither the time nor the money to spare; I will obey later'? Oh, foolish people! While we procrastinate, the harvest will be over and we will not be saved. Now is the time to follow Abraham's example" ("The Example of Abraham," *Ensign*, June 1975, p. 4).

■ Genesis 18:19. What does this passage teach us about Abraham's labor as a father? _____

_____

What is suggested by the words "after him" in this passage? _____

_____

Did Abraham set the example and take the lead in his home? Do you suppose Abraham could ever have received the promised blessings if he had not faithfully discharged his duties as a father? Why?_____

_____

In what way is our obligation today the same as Abraham's anciently? Elder Mark E. Petersen said:

"Obedience is the thing! . . .

"God covenanted with Abraham and Isaac because of their premortal faithfulness. But their children who do not live up to the covenant in this life can lose that advantage, while those not of Abraham may obtain that same advantage for themselves if they will accept and live the gospel" (*Abraham, Friend of God*, p. 110).

**It Will Make
a Difference**

We are, as our father Abraham was before us, husbands, fathers, priesthood bearers, missionaries, and servants of the Lord. To each of us the Lord's invitation is clear and simple: "Go ye, therefore, and do the works of Abraham; enter ye into my law and ye shall be saved" (D&C 132:32).

Quorum Training Suggestions

The doctrines relating to the Abrahamic covenant are important and far-reaching. In this quorum meeting you might emphasize the blessings that are available to the quorum members here and now and emphasize what we all must do to qualify for these blessings. Assign quorum members to study the preceding self-instruction materials carefully as they prepare for the quorum activities suggested below.

▪ Encourage individual study by asking questions such as these: What is the Abrahamic covenant? With whom is it made? What are some of the blessings promised in this covenant? What must we do to obtain these blessings?

▪ Assign a quorum member to review and briefly report on the chapter titled "Everlasting Covenants" in President Joseph Fielding Smith's *Doctrines of Salvation*, 1:152–66. Ask such questions as these: What is a covenant? With whom is a covenant made? What is our obligation when a covenant is revealed to us from the Lord?

▪ Have a quorum member read Abraham 1:2 and describe the blessings that are available to us here in mortality in addition to the marvelous promises reserved for the life hereafter.

▪ Have a quorum member read Doctrine and Covenants 130:20–21 and discuss what we must do to obtain blessings from the Lord. Study carefully and refer to President Spencer W. Kimball's article "The Example of Abraham" (*Ensign,* June 1975, pp. 3–7) to demonstrate Abraham's example of obedience.

▪ Display a picture of Abraham (OQ054, OQ056, OQ057, or OQ058).

▪ Point out that one of the things a man must do to merit the blessings of Abraham is to love his wife with all his heart and to become one with her according to righteous principles.

▪ Show either the film *Strengthening the Home* (MP146) or the filmstrip *Father, Consider Your Ways* (OF090). These messages are also available in brochures (*Strengthening the Home,* PBCT0328; *Father, Consider Your Ways,* PBCT0496) that could be made available to quorum members.

"All Things Shall Be Done by Common Consent"

Lesson 25

D&C 20:65; 26:2

Personal Study

Commit yourself to sustain fully the officers and teachers of the Church at all levels.

"When we sustain officers, we are given the opportunity of sustaining those whom the Lord has already called by revelation. . . .

"The Lord, then, gives us the opportunity to sustain the action of a divine calling and in effect express ourselves if for any reason we may feel otherwise.

"To sustain is to make the action binding on ourselves and to commit ourselves to support those people whom we have sustained. When a person goes through the sacred act of raising his arm to the square, he should remember, with soberness, that which he has done and commence to act in harmony with his sustaining vote both in public and in private" (Loren C. Dunn, in Conference Report, Apr. 1972, p. 19; or *Ensign*, July 1972, p. 43).

How are new Church leaders called? How do we demonstrate our loyalty to the new leaders?

1 Church Officers and Teachers Are Called of God

■ Moses 5:58–59; 6:1–7. How was Adam authorized in the beginning to teach the gospel? _____

The ancient prophets were called and authorized in much the same way (see Isaiah 6:8–9, Jeremiah 1:4–5, and Genesis 12:1–3).

180

▪ Numbers 27:15–23. After Moses led the children of Israel out of Egypt into the wilderness, the Lord informed him that he would not enter the promised land.

How was a successor chosen? _____

_____

How did the people shift their loyalty from Moses to the new leader? _____

_____

How was the new leader given authority? _____

_____

▪ John 15:16. How were Jesus' Apostles chosen and given authority to preach the gospel? ____ _____

_____

Is the procedure for calling and authorizing leaders any different today? _____ _____

_____

Consider this familiar statement in the fifth article of faith: "We believe that a man must be called of God by prophecy, and by the laying on of hands, by those who are in authority, to preach the Gospel and administer in the ordinances thereof."

▪ D&C 84:35–38; 1:38. When a stake, ward, branch, or quorum leader calls us to serve in the kingdom, what may we assume about the Lord's involvement in the call? _____ _____

_____

▪ D&C 36:1–2. Although the Savior is not here personally to call people to serve, according to this example to what extent is he involved in inspired calls? _____

_____

▪ Elder Boyd K. Packer gave this instructive account on the matter of calls to serve:

"Some time ago, late one Sunday night, returning after the reorganization of a stake with Elder Marion G. Romney, we were riding along silently, too weary I suppose to be interested in conversation, when he said, 'Boyd, this gospel is true!' (An interesting statement from a member of the Twelve.) And then

181

he added, 'You couldn't go through what we have been through in the last forty-eight hours without knowing that for sure.'

"I then rehearsed in my mind the events of the previous hours; the interviews we had held, the decisions made. We had interviewed the priesthood leadership of the stake and invited each of them to make suggestions with reference to a new stake president. Virtually all of them mentioned the same man. They indicated him to be an ideal man for a stake president with appropriate experience, a fine family, sensible and sound, worthy in every way. Near the end of our interviewing, with just two or three left, we interviewed this man and we found him equal to all of the estimates that had been made of him during the day. As he left the room at the conclusion of the interview, Brother Romney said, 'Well, what do you think?'

"I answered that it was my feeling that we had not seen the new president yet.

"This confirmed the feelings of Brother Romney who then said, 'Perhaps we should get some more men in here. It may be that the new president is not among the present priesthood leadership of the stake.' Then he said, 'But suppose we interview the remaining few before we take that course.'

"There was another interview held, as ordinary as all of the others had been during the day—the same questions, same answers—but at the conclusion of this interview, Brother Romney said, 'Well, now how do you feel?'

"As far as I am concerned,' I said, 'we can quit interviewing.' Again this confirmed Brother Romney, for the feeling had come that this was the man that the Lord had set His hand upon to preside over that stake.

"Now how did we know? Because we knew, both of us—together, at once, without any doubt. In reality, our assignment was not to *choose* a stake president, but rather to *find* the man that the Lord had chosen. The Lord speaks in an unmistakable way. *Men are called by Prophecy*" (*Follow the Brethren,* Brigham Young University Speeches of the Year, [Provo, 23 March 1965], pp. 6–7).

2 We Sustain Church Officers and Teachers through Common Consent

■ The Prophet Joseph Smith described the kingdom of God as a "theodemocracy." The Lord is the lawgiver and calls those who lead in his kingdom. Those who are properly called and ordained have the rights their office allows and are first responsible to the Lord for how they fulfill their calling. All sustain the leaders that preside over them.

The Lord has given his church the law of common consent, by which those selected by the Lord to govern or teach may be sustained by the membership. Consider the following:

■ D&C 20:65. What procedure did the Lord institute for sustaining new Church officers? _____ _____ _____

_____

What does a person vote to do when he raises his hand in favor of one chosen to serve in the Church? _____

_____

■ D&C 26:2; 28:13. What should accompany our sustaining of these officers? _____ _____

_____

■ President J. Reuben Clark, Jr., said:

"When the presiding authority presents any man to the body of the Church to be sustained, the only power which the assembly has is to vote, by uplifted hand, either to sustain or not to sustain.

"Obviously, neither the body of the Church, nor any of its members, can propose that other men be called to office, for the calling of men is the sole power and function of the presiding authority.

"Therefore all debate, all proposals of other names, all discussions of merit and worthiness, are wholly out of order in such an assemblage" (in Conference Report, Oct. 1940, pp. 28–29).

Regarding when it may be appropriate to cast a negative vote, Elder Joseph Fielding Smith said:

"I take it that no man has the right to raise his hand in opposition, or with contrary vote, unless he has a reason for doing so that would be valid if presented before those who stand at the head. In other words, I have no right to raise my hand in opposition to a man who is appointed to any position in this Church, simply because I may not like him, or because of some personal disagreement or feeling I may have, but only on the grounds that he is guilty of wrong doing, of transgression of the laws of the Church which would disqualify him for the position which he is called to hold" (in Conference Report, June 1919, p. 92).

■ If a person sustains the prophet, he will also sustain those the prophet calls to positions of leadership. Concerning this matter, Elder Boyd K. Packer said: "A man who says he will sustain the President of the Church or the General Authorities, but cannot sustain his own bishop is deceiving himself. The man who will not sustain the bishop of his ward and the president of his stake will not sustain the President of the Church" (*Follow the Brethren*, Brigham Young University Speeches of the Year [Provo, 23 March 1965], pp. 4–5).

■ If we do not sustain a local leader, therefore, we fail to sustain those who called that person to leadership. Elder Delbert L. Stapley commented, "We must remember there is not a single officer in the Church who has selected himself for the position in which he serves; he has been called by a higher authority and often responds at considerable personal sacrifice for a position he did not seek" ("Respect for Authority," *Improvement Era*, Dec. 1957, p. 914).

■ In summary, common consent in the Church is the procedure of accepting new leaders, revelations, and policies by the vote of those affected. The law of common consent accommodates the exercise of free agency within the theodemocratic system of the Church. It is a process by which unity is achieved. The Lord calls his servants, and the people have the opportunity to sustain those called.

3 We Sustain Officers and Teachers through Our Words and Actions

■ 1 Thessalonians 5:12–13. Why should we speak of Church officers only in a spirit of love and esteem? _____

■ Our sustaining vote implies that we will speak and act in support of Church officers. Of this, President Harold B. Lee said, "When you vote affirmatively you make a solemn covenant with the Lord that you will sustain, that is, give your full loyalty and support, without equivocation or reservation, to the officer for whom you vote" (in Conference Report, Apr. 1970, p. 103).

■ Elder Howard W. Hunter admonished, "Our ideas may not always be quite like those who preside in authority over us, but this is the Lord's church and he will bless each of us as we cast off pride, pray for strength, and contribute to the good of the whole" (in Conference Report, Apr. 1976, p. 156; or *Ensign*, May 1976, p. 106).

■ President John Taylor summarized sustaining our leaders by our words and actions as follows:

"What is meant by sustaining a person? . . . It is a very simple thing to me. . . . For instance, if a man be a teacher, and I vote that I sustain him in his position, when he visits me in an official capacity I will welcome him and treat him with consideration, kindness and respect and if I need counsel I will ask it at his hand, and I will do everything I can to sustain him. That would be proper and a principle of righteousness, and I would not say anything derogatory to his character. . . .

"But suppose he should do something wrong, supposing he should be found lying or cheating, or defrauding somebody; or stealing or anything else, or even become impure in his habits, would you still sustain him? It would be my duty then to talk with him as I would with anybody else and tell him that I had understood that things were thus and so and that under these circumstances I could not sustain him; and if I found that I had been misinformed I would withdraw the charge; but if not it would then be my duty to see that justice was administered to him, that he was brought before the proper tribunal to answer for the things he had done; and in the absence of that I would have no business to talk about him" (in Daniel H. Ludlow, *Latter-day Prophets Speak*, pp. 217–18).

It Does Make a Difference

"Who have we for our ruling power? Where and how did he obtain his authority? . . . It is by the voice of God and the voice of the people that our present President obtained his authority. . . . He obtains his authority first from God and secondly from the people. . . . Is there a monarch, potentate, or power under the heavens that undergoes a scrutiny as fine as this? No, there is not; and yet this is done twice a year, before all the Saints in the world. Here are legitimacy and rule. You place the power in their hands to govern, dictate, regulate, and put in order the affairs of the kingdom of God. This is, *Vox Dei, vox populi* [the voice of the people is the voice of God]. God appoints, the people sustain" (John Taylor, in *Journal of Discourses*, 1:229–230).

Quorum Training Suggestions

Discuss briefly the fifth article of faith. Then define the law of common consent, and discuss how it relates to this article of faith.

■ Discuss the difference between voting for someone in a political sense and voting for someone within the Church. In the course of such discussion, you may need to clarify differences between types of political governments and the basic government of the Church.

■ Ask the quorum members to suggest reasons why the Lord would reveal that "all things shall be done by common consent" (D&C 26:2). List them on the chalkboard.

■ Discuss how we express our support of ward and quorum officers by accepting calls and assignments that come from them. Encourage the brethren to offer to the bishop or quorum leader an expression of their support.

■ Assign several quorum members to discuss the scriptures listed under the titles of "Common Consent" and "Sustaining Church Leaders" in the Topical Guide to the Latter-day Saint edition of the King James Bible.

Work for the Dead

D&C 110:12–16; 127:4–8; 128

Personal Study

Begin or continue to engage in activities that redeem the dead.

From the earliest days of the Restoration, members of the Church have been urged to do genealogical research so that they could identify their ancestors and have the necessary temple ordinances performed for them. Elders Howard W. Hunter and Boyd K. Packer reviewed our progress in this important work:

"We have been commanded to perform vicarious ordinances for all who have died. . . .

"Billions have lived and we are to redeem all of them. . . .

"We come now to that time, perhaps for the first time in this dispensation, when we must step back and consider the full proportion of the work.

"If we are staggered by it, we must catch ourselves and straighten ourselves up and face it.

"When we contemplate how big it is, it is astonishing; it is past astonishing, it is overwhelming!

"But it is *not* discouraging. . . .

"To those who sense the size of this challenge to redeem all who have ever lived, and are overwhelmed by it, I say, have faith. We will win the day, and the Lord will provide.

"To those who are hesitant to move, I say, wake up and see the vision of it.

"We can accomplish the things we have been commanded, if we will but get started" ("That They May Be Redeemed," address at Regional Representatives' seminar, 1 Apr. 1977).

Are we fulfilling our individual part of this important priesthood work? Otherwise, as the Prophet Joseph Smith expressed it, "who can abide the day of his coming, and who can stand when he appeareth?" (D&C 128:24). Do we understand what our responsibility is? Are we doing all we can to respond to these important responsibilities?

---

1 The Righteous Dead Will Be Redeemed

■ D&C 110:13–16. Of this appearance, President Joseph Fielding Smith said:

" . . . Elijah came to *restore* to the earth . . . *the fulness of the power of the priesthood. This priesthood holds the keys of binding and sealing on earth and in heaven of all the ordinances and principles pertaining to the salvation of man,* that they may thus become valid in the celestial kingdom of God. . . .

"It is by virtue of this authority that ordinances are performed in the temples for *both* the living and the dead" (*Doctrines of Salvation*, 2:117).

What priesthood keys did Elijah restore? _____

_____

Why are these keys so important? _____

_____

■ President Spencer W. Kimball wrote: "Is it any wonder that the organization and work of the Church and its priesthood in this day are patterned after the keys it possesses? We are a missionary Church, participating to the fullest possible extent in the gathering of Israel. We are a Church founded upon families; . . . And we are a Church that is actively engaged in temple and genealogy work for ourselves and for the infinite numbers of our Father's children who have the promise, but not as yet the opportunity, for the ordinances of salvation" ("The Things of Eternity—Stand We in Jeopardy?" *Ensign*, Jan. 1977, p. 4). Why are genealogy and temple work so important to the members of the Church? _____

_____

■ D&C 128:17–18. What does the Prophet Joseph Smith say will happen to the earth unless the fathers and the children assist each other in the great work of redemption? _____

_____

What other ordinances besides baptism for the dead must be performed to help redeem our ancestors?

2 We Should Diligently Seek to Redeem the Dead

- 1 Corinthians 15:29–30. Referring to the question Paul asks in verse 30, President Kimball observed:

"We as members of the Church also stand in jeopardy if we do not do our temple work. Much of our time is taken up with the mundane details of everyday living, which must be done, of course; but those who are members of His kingdom at this critical time should endeavor to give much time and effort to this important work. . . .

"We wonder about our progenitors. . . . What do they think of you and me? We are their offspring. We have the responsibility to do their temple work, and the beautiful temples of the Lord stand day after day, yet we do not fill them always. We have a grave responsiblity that we cannot avoid, and may stand in jeopardy if we fail to do this important work. . . .

"Some of us have had occasion to wait for someone or something for a minute, an hour, a day, a week, or even a year. Can you imagine how our progenitors must feel, some of whom have perhaps been waiting for decades and even centuries for the temple work to be done for them?" (*Ensign*, Jan. 1977, pp. 5, 7).

Why do we need to give much time and effort to this important work at this time? _____

Regarding the challenge the Church has to redeem the dead through temple and genealogical work, Elder Boyd K. Packer counseled:

"To those who sense the size of this challenge to redeem all who have ever lived, and are overwhelmed by it, I say, have faith. We will win the day, and the Lord will provide.

"To those who are hesitant to move, I say, wake up and see the vision of it.

"We can accomplish the things we have been commanded, if we will but get started" ("That They May Be Redeemed," address at Regional Representatives' seminar, 1 Apr. 1977, p. 10).

189

- D&C 127:4. Does the Lord still expect you to "let your diligence, and your perserverance, and patience, and your works be redoubled"? Is this another way of asking us to lengthen our stride and quicken our pace in this important work? _____

_____

3 What You Can Do to Bless Your Immediate Family and Your Ancestors

Regarding the importance of temple and genealogical work, Elder A. Theodore Tuttle said: "All the righteous men and women who ever lived look to us! We are their only hope for salvation. We hold the key to their prison doors. We must set them free! How can we any longer ignore their right to salvation?" (in Conference Report, Apr. 1980, pp. 59; also in *Ensign*, May 1980, p. 41).

- What specific goals can we personally set to accomplish the following activities? Write goals in the space provided.

Gain the blessings of the temple for ourselves and our immediate families so that *we* may become linked to our ancestors. _____

_____

Complete and verify the correctness of our four-generation sheets as the foundation of our genealogical research. _____

_____

Participate in a family organization to combine resources and avoid duplication in searching out our progenitors. _____

_____

Compile sacred family records and provide other family activities to teach our wives and children to turn their hearts to their fathers. _____

_____

Participate in records extracting and indexing projects whenever we have the opportunity. _____

_____

- President Ezra Taft Benson gave the following counsel regarding family organizations: "Ancestral organizations exist only for the coordination of genealogical activity, which includes family histories" (in Conference Report, Oct. 1978, pp. 42; or *Ensign*, Nov. 1978, p. 31).

President Kimball suggested: "Wouldn't it be wonderful if every Latter-day Saint home had in the bedroom of each boy and each girl, or on the mantle of the living room, a . . . picture of a temple which would help them recall, frequently, the purpose of these beautiful edifices" (*Ensign*, Jan. 1977, p. 7).

■ D&C 128:22. What concluding counsel did the Prophet Joseph Smith have for the Saints as he closed his epistle concerning the work for the dead? _____

_____

What does this imply for us? _____

_____

It Will Make a Difference

"A temple recommend is one of the highest accolades we may receive. To use it regularly permits us to participate in the choicest gifts within the keeping of the Church. Those who attend feel a special spirit there. Peace comes. I know that their service there assists a departed one to gain exaltation. And I know that they in turn qualify for blessings from the other side of the veil. And I know that blessings will follow you home from the temple" (A. Theodore Tuttle, *Ensign*, May 1982, p. 66).

Will we be able to abide the day of the Lord's coming: Will we be able to stand when he appears? The answer can be "yes" if we magnify our priesthood and if we are faithful in keeping the commandments of God, including the commandment to perform genealogical and temple work for our dead.

Quorum Training Suggestions

Encourage quorum members to consider the preceding materials prior to the quorum hour so that the doctrinal foundation will be laid and the quorum hour can deal with specific workshop activities.

The purpose of this lesson is to remind priesthood bearers of their responsibility to search out their ancestors and to suggest some specific activities that can help them carry out this responsibility. As a quorum leader, you should seek for opportunities to promote this vitally important work among your quorum members. Your purpose in the quorum meeeting may be to train quorum members in particular genealogical activities. As you seek to do this, some of the following suggestions may be of help to you:

- To encourage individual study, ask the quorum members to share the answers they found in their study of the self-instructional material. You may wish to ask the following questions:

What must happen in response to Elijah's visit to prevent the earth from being smitten with a curse?

Why should there be a sense of urgency in accomplishing the work for those who have passed on? What reasons were given to indicate that this work should be hastened?

- Distribute blank pedigree charts to the quorum members and allow them a few minutes to record from memory all that they can for four generations (themselves, their parents, their grandparents, and their great grandparents). Whether or not quorum members have been previously involved in genealogical work, this exercise can show each quorum member how much he knows about his family. Do not embarrass quorum members by requiring them to share the information they have written down. After completing the exercise, discuss what sources quorum members can turn to to complete their four-generation sheets, or, if these sheets have already been completed, to verify the accuracy of the information on the sheets.

- Invite a quorum member who is involved in a successful family organization to discuss briefly what his family organization is doing to share resources and avoid duplication in searching out and doing the temple work for their dead. If possible, he might share ideas on how to organize and begin working together as a family.

- Discuss the question, "What can you do as husbands and fathers to involve your wives and children in genealogical and temple work?" You may want to divide the quorum members into smaller discussion groups according to the ages of their children to have them discuss this question. Unmarried quorum members, if there are sufficient numbers, may be assigned to a group to discuss the question, "What are my responsibilities to my parents, brothers, and sisters, and other relatives in genealogical and temple work?"

▪ Challenge the quorum members to set particular, measurable goals to accomplish genealogical and temple activities. Point out that the goals should be challenging, yet realistic. Goals could include such things as—

Attending the temple once a month (where appropriate).

Keeping a journal by writing in it at least weekly.

Updating family group sheets.

▪ Appoint a quorum genealogy committee to coordinate and provide ongoing technical assistance to those quorum members who need it. In this way, those who know how to do genealogical research can help those who do not.

▪ Discuss why we do this work. Your reasons may include these:

When our ancestors are empowered by baptism and the priesthood, they are in a better position to help us.

We have been asked by the Lord through his prophet to do it.

We are drawn closer to our ancestors as we have done this work. Some may wish to share experiences in this regard.

Invite a quorum member who is involved in a records extraction project to discuss briefly his experiences and feelings regarding this program.

"Speak, Lord, For Thy Servant Heareth"

1 Samuel 3:9–10

Personal Study

Help your children to recognize and obey the promptings of the Holy Ghost.

Brother Morris was disturbed about a question presented to him by his nine-year-old daughter, Carol. "Dad," she said, as they concluded their regular personal interview together, "how can you tell when you receive the Holy Ghost? I've been a member of the Church for over a year now, and I don't feel any different. The Holy Ghost doesn't talk to me." As Brother Morris continued to ponder, the words of a Primary song took on added meaning:

Child: "Teach me to walk in the light of his love,
Teach me to pray to my Father above,
Teach me to know of the things that are right,
Teach me, teach me to walk in the light."
Parent: "Come, little child, and together we'll learn
Of his commandments, that we may return
Home to his presence, to live in his sight—
Always, always to walk in the light."
Both: "Father in heaven, we thank thee this day
For loving guidance to show us the way
Grateful, we praise thee with songs of delight!
Gladly, gladly we'll walk in the light"
("Teach Me to Walk in the Light," *Sing with Me*, B–45).

One of a father's great responsibilities is to help his children obtain the gift they were commanded to receive when they were confirmed as members of the Church: "Receive the Holy Ghost."

1 The Holy Ghost Is a Revelator of Truth to the Saints

The mission of the Holy Ghost is to testify of and reveal truth. In scripture this third member of the Godhead is sometimes called the Spirit of Truth. As the Spirit reveals truth to us we are free to walk in the light. Children grow toward perfection when they are filled with truth through the Holy Ghost.

■ Psalm 119:97–105. What can make a man wiser than "the ancients"? How could a young person have more understanding than his teachers? Why is it often easier for the Spirit to reveal truth to young people? _____

_____

■ Luke 2:52. In what four dimensions of life did Jesus mature? In what dimension would the Holy Ghost be helpful to our own children's growth? _____

■ 2 Nephi 28:4, 14. What great danger confronts the Saints, especially in these days? _____

_____

How can this danger be avoided (see 2 Nephi 9:29)? _____

_____

■ Jeremiah 3:4. How does the Father guide young people today or at any time? _____

_____

■ 1 Nephi 10:17–19. How did the youthful Nephi learn the truth of his father's words? _____

_____

Can we prepare our children to do the same? What part does the Holy Ghost play in the "eternal round" of God? _____

_____

2 Learn to Recognize and Receive Promptings of the Holy Ghost

■ Many have never received the Holy Ghost. Receipt of the Holy Ghost depends on obedience to the covenant made at baptism. President Joseph Fielding Smith declared: "We have a great many members of this Church who have never reached a manifestation through the Holy Ghost. Why? Because they have not made their lives conform to the truth" (in *Church News*, 4 Nov. 1961, p. 14).

■ Mosiah 18:8–10. What covenant is made at baptism? _____

_____

What promise is made to those who keep the covenant? _____

_____

■ D&C 20:77. What covenant is renewed when the sacrament is partaken? _____

_____

What promise is renewed? _____

_____

■ D&C 59:14. What principle is described here that leads to greater power in the Holy Ghost? _____

_____

■ Alma 19:6. What does this verse say is one great evidence of the reception of the Holy Ghost? _____

_____

Can we personally experience this same kind of joy?

■ Elder Carlos E. Asay said:

"In the Book of Mormon we read of a people who had an instrument called a ball or director. This compasslike instrument was prepared by the Lord and worked according to the people's faith in God. When they were righteous and exercised faith, the spindles would point the way they should go. When their faith or diligence in keeping the commandments was lacking, the instrument would not work. (See 1 Ne. 16; 18:12.)

"One writer stated that the compass and its operation was 'not without a shadow' or type of things spiritual. . . .

"I fear that many of us rush about from day to day taking for granted the holy scriptures. We scramble to honor appointments with physicians, laywers, and businessmen. Yet we think nothing of postponing interviews with Deity—postponing scripture study. Little wonder we develop anemic souls and lose our direction in living. How much better it would be if we planned and held sacred fifteen or twenty minutes a day for reading the scriptures. Such interviews with Deity would help us recognize his voice and enable us to receive guidance in all of our affairs" (in Conference Report, Oct. 1978, p. 78; or *Ensign*, Nov. 1978, pp. 53–54).

■ Mosiah 4:26. What must be done to retain and maintain the gifts and blessings of God? _____

_____

■ Elder S. Dilworth Young summarized how one receives the Holy Ghost and how the Holy Ghost operates upon the Saints:

"To the member of the Church intent on keeping the commandments, needing personal guidance in his daily affairs . . . the Lord has indicated many times that the answer will come by the 'still small voice.' How may I, then, know how to receive and what to expect?

"First, the Lord will speak by his Spirit, which is the Holy Ghost. . . .

"Secondly, it will come into the mind of the recipient. . . .

"Thirdly. . . . feeling is a big part of the process of revelation.

"Fourthly. . . . the assurance comes through feeling.

"If I am to receive revelation from the Lord, I must be in harmony with him by keeping his commandments. Then as needed, according to his wisdom, his word will come into my mind through my thoughts, accompanied by a feeling in the region of my bosom. It is a feeling which cannot be described, but the nearest word we have is 'burn' or 'burning.' Accompanying this always is a feeling of peace, a further witness that what one heard is right. Once one recognizes this burning, this feeling, this peace, one need never be drawn astray in his daily life or in the guidance he may receive. . . .

"Most of us here have had this experience many times, but there is a great host of our children who have not and who need to be led to understand. . . .

"There are many times as our youth grow when they will need to seek the Spirit to know how to act or what to do. . . . *If [they are] righteous,* the voice of the Lord comes into their minds with a certain feeling in the breast, accompanied by a peace. They are receiving the word of the Lord to them" (in Conference Report, Apr. 1976, pp. 33–35; or *Ensign*, May 1976, pp. 22–23).

3 "Speak, Lord, for Thy Servant Heareth"

It is beautiful to consider that before newly accountable children leave their gardens of innocence and begin to more fully enter into the harsher world of darkness and sin, they can be clothed upon with truth, testimony, and greater purity through the Holy Ghost.

■ 1 Samuel 3:1–10. What evidence is there that Samuel was very young when the Lord first spoke to him. How, apparently, was Samuel prepared? _____

_____

Was it necessary for Eli to be in tune as well as Samuel? _____

_____

Why? _____

_____

What lesson is here for fathers? _____

_____

■ 1 Samuel 16:13; see also Alma 32:23. When the youthful David was anointed, what great blessing came upon him? _____

_____

Can a similar blessing come to our children today?

■ 2 Nephi 2:4. What great blessings came to Jacob in his youth?

_____

_____

What is always the same? _____

_____

■ Enos 1:3–5. What led young Enos to prayer and the reception of the Spirit? _____

_____

■ Mormon 1:15; see also Alma 37:35–37. What did Mormon experience as a teenager? _____

_____

■ Joseph Smith-History 1:49–50. To whom did the young Joseph report? _____

How is this significant for all fathers? _____

■ Shortly after Spencer W. Kimball became a member of the Quorum of the Twelve, a friend, Orville Allen, testified of the influence of Elder Kimball's father on the spiritual development of his son: " 'Spencer, your father was a prophet. He made a prediction that has literally come to pass, and I want to tell you about it.' He continued, 'Your father talked to me at the corral, one evening. I had brought a load of pumpkins for his pigs. You were just a little boy and you were sitting there, milking the cows, and singing to them as you milked. Your father turned to me and said, "Brother, that boy, Spencer, is an exceptional boy. He always tries to mind me, whatever I ask him to do. I have dedicated him to be one of the mouthpieces of the Lord—the Lord willing. You will see him some day as a great leader. I have dedicated him to the service of God, and he will become a mighty man in the Church' " (Spencer W. Kimball, *Faith Precedes the Miracle*, pp. xvi–xvii).

The children of Zion must be born of and taught by goodly parents in the nurture and admonition of the Lord and thus be prepared to receive and recognize the Holy Ghost in their lives.

Will It Make a Difference?

Elder Boyd K. Packer testified to the youth of the Church:

"All of the training and activity in the Church has as its central purpose a desire to see you, our young people, free and independent and secure, both spiritually and temporally.

"If you will listen to the counsel of your parents and your teachers and your leaders when you are young, you can learn how to follow the best guide of all–the whisperings of the Holy Spirit. That is individual revelation. There is a process through which we can be alerted to spiritual dangers. Just as surely as that guide warned you, you can receive signals alerting you. . . .

"If we can train you to listen to these spiritual communications, you will be protected. . . . You can learn what it feels like to be guided from on high. This inspiration can come to you now, in all of your activities, in school, and dating–not just in your Church assignments.

"Learn now to pray and how to receive answers to your prayers. When you pray over some things, you must patiently wait a long, long time before you will receive an answer. Some prayers, for your own safety, must be answered immediately, and some promptings will even come when you haven't prayed at all.

"Once you really determine to follow that guide, your testimony will grow and you will find provisions set out along the way in unexpected places, as evidence that someone knew that you would be traveling that way.

"The basic exercise for you to perform in your youth to become spiritually strong and to become independent lies in obedience to your guides. If you will follow them and do it willingly, you can learn to trust those delicate, sensitive, spiritual promptings. You will learn that they always, invariably, lead you to do that which is righteous" (in Conference Report, Apr. 1976, pp. 46–47; or *Ensign*, May 1976, p. 31).

Quorum Training Suggestions

Fathers must help bring their children to rebirth through the Holy Ghost. It is thus imperative for them to be able to help their children accomplish the goal of this lesson, which is to recognize and obey the promptings of the Holy Spirit. The following material may help the quorum instructor to help fathers and prospective fathers.

▪ Introduce the lesson by quoting D&C 68:25 and discussing the importance of teaching children about the Holy Ghost and how to recognize his promptings.

▪ To aid individual study review the personal study material by asking such questions as these: What is the great purpose of the Holy Ghost? Why is the right to the gift of the Holy Ghost conferred at such a young age? What are some essential steps in receiving the Holy Ghost? What are some ways one can recognize the operation of the Holy Ghost in his life? Must one wait for advanced age to receive the gifts and powers of the Holy Ghost?

■ Discuss practical ways the principles of this lesson could be taught to children in home evening setting (see *Families Are Forever*, Family Home Evening Manual, 1976, pp. 81–85).

■ Quorum members may be invited to share their testimonies.

■ The instructor could familiarize the quorum members with the simple and very straightforward material on the Holy Ghost given in *Gospel Principles*, pp. 131–34.

■ Invite a quorum member's children to sing the children's hymn "The Still Small Voice." Note the words:

"Through a still small voice the Spirit speaks to me
To guide me, to save me from the evil I may see.
If I try to do what's right He will lead me through the night,
Direct me, protect me and give my soul his light.
Listen, listen, the Holy Ghost will whisper.
Listen, listen to the still small voice"
(*Sing with Me*, B–92).

■ Elder Boyd K. Packer's talk on "Spiritual Crocodiles" (*Ensign,* May 1976, pp. 30–32; or Conference Report, Apr. 1976, pp. 44–47) could be discussed in the quorum. It portrays the deadly hazards of the present world and the need for protection, particularly of children.

■ Elder S. Dilworth Young's message to youth, "How the Holy Ghost Can Help You" (*New Era,* Oct. 1971, pp. 4–6), has helpful ideas for teaching young people about the Holy Spirit.

■ The August 1977 *Friend* magazine contains articles for children on the Holy Ghost.

Justification and Sanctification

D&C 20:29–33

Personal Study

Pursue a course of personal righteousness that will enable you to be justified and sanctified.

"A famous sculptor once said that there was nothing to art except just cutting away the marble that he didn't want there. There's nothing to attaining perfection either, except removing all the obstacles and the obstructions which defame or pollute it. We are on the road to perfection.

"In one of the Lord's first sermons was the injunction to become perfect: 'Be ye therefore perfect,' he said, 'even as your Father which is in heaven is perfect' (Matthew 5:48)" (Spencer W. Kimball, "Be Ye Therefore Perfect," in *Speeches of the Year, 1974* [Provo, Utah: Brigham Young University Press, 1975], p. 232).

Does the Lord expect the Saints to be able to live immediately the entire law of the gospel? If not, does he bless or aid us in our struggles along the way toward perfection? How? What do the principles of justification and sanctification mean for us?

1 "Be Ye Therefore Perfect"

The Lord has made it clear that to obtain exaltation in the celestial kingdom, every soul must be in harmony with *every* law, ordinance, and teaching pertaining to that kingdom.

"Any person who is exalted to the highest mansion has to abide a celestial law, and the whole law too. . . .

" . . . To get salvation we must not only do some things, but everything which God has commanded. . . . The object with me is to obey and teach others to obey God in just what He tell us to do" (Joseph Smith, *Teachings of the Prophet Joseph Smith*, pp. 331, 332).

- The Prophet Joseph Smith further declared, *"It is not all* to be comprehended in this world; it will be a great work to learn our salvation *and exaltation even beyond the grave" (Teachings of the Prophet Joseph Smith,* p. 348).

- Of this gradual process toward exaltation, President Joseph Fielding Smith taught:

"I believe the Lord meant just what he said: that we should be perfect, as our Father in heaven is perfect. That will not come all at once, but line upon line, and precept upon precept, example upon example, and even then not as long as we live in this mortal life, for we will have to go even beyond the grave before we reach that perfection and shall be like God.

"But here we lay the foundation. Here is where we are taught these simple truths of the gospel of Jesus Christ, in this probationary state, to prepare us for that perfection. It is our duty to be better today than we were yesterday, and better tomorrow than we are today. Why? Because we are on that road, if we are keeping the commandments of the Lord, we are on that road to perfection, and that can only come through obedience and the desire in our hearts to overcome the world" *(Doctrines of Salvation,* 2:18–19).

Since learning to obey the entire law of the gospel is a process that takes time, what is the status of one who is sincerely striving but still has much to do toward reaching perfection? What provisions has the Lord made in his gospel to assist us in our progress?

---

2 Our Righteous Actions Are Justified As We Strive for Perfection

- The scriptures state that the things a person does can be justified (or accepted) before God (1 Nephi 16:2; D&C 132:1, 62).

- Jacob 2:13–14. What is one thing that people do in which the Lord does not justify them? _____

- "What then is the law of justification? It is simply this: 'All covenants, contracts, bonds, obligations, oaths, vows, performances, connections, associations, or expectations' (D&C 132:7), in which men must abide to be saved and exalted, must be entered into and performed in righteousness so that the Holy

Spirit can justify the candidate for salvation in what has been done. . . . *An act that is justified by the Spirit is one that is sealed by the Holy Spirit of Promise, or in other words, ratified and approved by the Holy Ghost*. This law of justification is the provision the Lord has placed in the gospel to assure that no unrighteous performance will be binding on earth and in heaven, and that no person will add to his position or glory in the hereafter by gaining an unearned blessing.

"As with all other doctrines of salvation, justification is available because of the atoning sacrifice of Christ, but it becomes operative in the life of an individual only on conditions of personal righteousness" (Bruce R. McConkie, *Mormon Doctrine,* "Justification").

■ We know when something is justified because the Spirit will be with us (see Moses 6:60). The companionship of the Spirit, graciously extended by the Lord, is the witness or evidence of justification. If, however, one is not striving to overcome the world, one may "fall from grace" (D&C 20:32). President Joseph Fielding Smith said:

"If a person violates a covenant, whether it be of baptism, ordination, marriage or anything else, the Spirit withdraws the stamp of approval, and the blessings will not be received.

"Every ordinance is sealed with a promise of a reward based upon faithfulness. The Holy Spirit withdraws the stamp of approval where covenants are broken" (*Doctrines of Salvation,* 1:45).

If a person sincerely repents of past mistakes, the Spirit may return and again justify the actions of that man, thus assuring they are acceptable to God.

---

3 The Lord Graciously Sanctifies Us When We Love and Serve Him

■ D&C 20:31; see also 3 Nephi 27:20. What further blessing is extended to those who "love and serve God with all their mights"? _____

■ "To be *sanctified* is to become clean, pure, and spotless; to be free from the blood and sins of the world; to become a new creature of the Holy Ghost, one whose body has been renewed by the rebirth of the Spirit. *Sanctification* is a state of saintliness, a state attained only by conformity to the laws and ordinances of the gospel. The plan of salvation is the system and means provided whereby men may sanctify their souls and thereby become worthy of a celestial inheritance" (Bruce R. McConkie, *Mormon Doctrine*, "Sanctification").

▪ President Brigham Young further described sanctification in this way: "I will put my own definition to the term sanctification, and say it consists in overcoming every sin and bringing all into subjection to the law of Christ. God has placed in us a pure spirit; when this reigns predominant, without let or hindrance, and triumphs over the flesh and rules and governs and controls as the Lord controls the heavens and the earth, this I call the blessing of sanctification" (*Journal of Discourses*, 10:173).

▪ The Prophet Joseph Smith said, "The nearer man approaches perfection, the clearer are his views, and the greater his enjoyment, till he has overcome the evils of his life and lost every desire for sin" (*Teachings of the Prophet Joseph Smith*, p. 51).

Sanctification cannot be achieved by man alone; it requires the power of heaven together with his sincere labors and desires (see Mosiah 3:19; 5:2).

▪ President Young said, "When through the Gospel, the Spirit in man has so subdued the flesh that he can live without wilful transgression, the Spirit of God unites with his spirit, they become congenial companions, and the mind and will of the Creator is thus transmitted to the creature" (*Journal of Discourses*, 9:288).

It Will Make a Difference

Those who sincerely strive to overcome the world, are justified, and continue to grow in obedience are eventually cleansed and sanctified, even until they are finally perfected and able to see God (D&C 88:68). Moroni summarized this salvation process (Moroni 10:32–33). Will you accept Moroni's challenge?

Quorum Training Suggestions

Discuss justification and sanctification as processes and conditions essential to our ultimate perfection, processes that are to be sustained and enlarged through continued spiritual growth. Emphasize that receiving these blessings depends mutually upon (1) the Savior's atonement and grace and (2) our faithfulness.

- On what conditions can the Spirit justify a person's actions and the ordinances performed in his behalf?

- If a person violates a covenant, does the justification he once received for that covenant continue? Is it possible that a sanctified person can falter? Discuss D&C 20:30–34 and 130:23.

- Discuss the fact that both justification and sanctification are manifestations of the grace of Christ (see 2 Nephi 25:23).

- Discuss sanctification as simply a state of grace (consider D&C 93:11–20).

- Review scriptures listed in the Topical Guide of the Latter-day Saint edition of the King James Bible under the headings of "Justification" and "Sanctification."

- Discuss how missionary work or other consecrated service can help sanctify one (see William R. Bradford, "Sanctification through Missionary Service," *Ensign*, Nov. 1981, pp. 49–51; or Conference Report, Oct. 1981, pp. 70–73).

"Through the Channels Which I Have Appointed"

D&C 78:17–18

Personal Study

Seek to develop complete confidence that God is guiding the Church through channels that he has appointed.

In April 1883, President John Taylor received a revelation from which the following is an excerpt: "Thus saith the Lord unto the First Presidency, unto the Twelve, unto the Seventies and unto all ye my holy priesthood, let not your hearts be troubled, neither be ye concerned about the management and organization of my Church and Priesthood and the accomplishment of my work. Fear me and observe my laws and I will reveal unto you from time to time, through the channels which I have appointed, everything that shall be necessary for the future development and perfection of my Church, for the adjustment and rolling forth of my kingdom, and for the building up and the establishment of my Zion" (in *Woman's Exponent*, 15 July 1883, p. 28).

Why is continuous revelation necessary? How should we view changes in the management of the Church? From whom and through whom will such changes come? What can we do to prepare to receive and understand the great and important things that God shall yet reveal concerning the management of his church and kingdom?

1 The Church Is Guided by Continuous Revelation

■ President John Taylor spoke of the need for continuous revelation in the management of the Church: "We require . . . living intelligence, proceeding from the living priesthood in heaven, through the living priesthood on earth. . . . Adam's revelation did not instruct Noah to build his ark; nor did Noah's revelation tell Lot to forsake Sodom; nor did either of these speak of the departure of the children of Israel from Egypt. These all had revelations for themselves, and so had Isaiah, Jeremiah, Ezekiel, Jesus, Peter, Paul, John, and Joseph. And so must we or we shall make a shipwreck" (*The Gospel Kingdom*, p. 34). What are some examples of modern revelation given to help the Church respond to a particular problem or need? _____

- Several years before he became the President of the Church, Elder Harold B. Lee explained how the Church would be guided: "I am sure that by the time we arrive at the place where we need more revelations that the Lord will give that light and knowledge to the prophet whom he has put upon the earth for that purpose" (in Conference Report, Oct. 1962, p. 81; or *Improvement Era*, Jan. 1962, p. 36). Later, as a member of the First Presidency, he added: "Keep in mind that the principles of the gospel of Jesus Christ are divine. Nobody changes the principles and doctrines of the Church except the Lord by revelation. But methods change as the inspired direction comes to those who preside at a given time. If you will analyze all that is being done and the changes that are taking place, you will realize that the fundamental doctrines of the Church are not changing. The only changes are in the methods of teaching that doctrine to meet the circumstances of our time" (*Ensign*, Jan. 1971, p. 10).

- D&C 1:14. What may become of Church members who refuse to "hear" the Brethren? _____

- D&C 78:17–18. Besides the need to respond to changing conditions and circumstances, why is it necessary for the Lord to continually guide his church through revelation? _____

---

2 What Are the Appointed Channels?

- 1 Corinthians 12:14–28; D&C 84:108–10. What do these scriptures teach concerning order in the Church? _____

■ D&C 28:2–8; 43:1–7. Who is appointed to receive revelations and commandents for the Church? _____

_____

How confidently may we follow the instructions of the head of the Church? _____

_____

Elder Marion G. Romney recalled the counsel of President Heber J. Grant: " 'My boy, you always keep your eye on the President of the Church, and if he ever tells you to do anything, and it is wrong, and you do it, the Lord will bless you for it.' Then with a twinkle in his eye, he said, 'But you don't need to worry. The Lord will never let his mouthpiece lead the people astray' " (in Conference Report, Oct. 1960, p. 78).

■ Acts 9:1–6. After Paul's experience on the road to Damascus how did he demonstrate his willingness to submit to the authority of those called by the Lord? _____

_____

Why would this have been especially hard for Paul to do?

_____

■ Why does it sometimes seem easier to sustain and support the General Authorities of the Church than those who are appointed to preside as our quorum leaders, bishops, or stake presidents?

_____

Why is this wrong? _____

_____

■ Luke 10:16. Will a man follow counsel from the leaders of the Church if he refuses or ignores direction from those he lives among and knows so well? Do we reverence the man or the office to which he is called? _____

_____

President John Taylor said: "I acknowledge every man in his place and office, whether president, bishop, priest, teacher or deacon; and then they should acknowledge everybody over them. . . . Do not be too anxious to be too smart, to manage and manipulate, and to put things right; but pray for those that God has placed in the different offices of this church that they may be enabled to perform their several duties. The Lord will sustain his servants and give them his Holy Spirit and the light of revelation" (*The Gospel Kingdom*, p. 167).

■ Consistent with the order of the Church, faithful members of the Church may receive revelation for themselves or their families. President Heber J. Grant said: "The Lord gives to many of us the still, small voice of revelation. . . . It comes to each man, according to his needs and faithfulness, for guidance in matters that pertain to his own life. And for the Church as a whole it comes to those who have been ordained to speak for the Church as a whole. And this certain knowledge which we have that the guiding influence of the Lord may be felt in all the ways of life, according to our needs and faithfulness, is among the greatest blessings God grants unto men. And with this blessing comes the responsibility to render strict obedience to the 'still small voice' " (*Improvement Era*, Dec. 1938, p. 712).

3 Prepare to Receive Revelations through Appointed Channels

■ D&C 21: 4–7. When are we to receive the words of the prophet? _____

_____

Who is to exercise "patience and faith"? _____

_____

Why? _____

_____

What blessings are promised to those who obey? _____

_____

■ At the solemn assembly in which he was sustained as prophet, seer, and revelator, President Spencer W. Kimball said:

"Today you have seen the Church in action. You have seen the mighty works of the Lord, how that everything is done by common consent, and those who are led sustain those who lead them. . . .

" . . . We are grateful, deeply grateful for your sustaining vote. Our only interest now is to advise and counsel the people aright and in total line with the counsels of the Lord as they have come through the generations and dispensations. We love you people and wish for you total progress and joy and happiness, which we know can come only through following the admonitions of God as proclaimed through his prophets and leaders" (in Conference Report, Apr. 1974, p. 65; or *Ensign*, May 1974, p. 46).

How does sustaining the prophets and leaders prepare us to accept new commandments and revelations? _____

_____

■ How does giving heed to that which has been revealed prepare us for additional instruction? _____

_____

President Joseph F. Smith observed: "There are other things . . . yet to be revealed to the people of God. Until we do our duty, however . . . to add commandments, to add light and intelligence to us over that which we have already received, which we have not yet fully obeyed, would be to add condemnation upon our heads. It is enough for us to live in the light of the present inspiration and present revelation" (in Conference Report, Oct. 1917, p. 5).

It Will Make a Difference

President Ezra Taft Benson counseled, "One who rationalizes that he or she has a testimony of Jesus Christ but cannot accept direction and counsel from the leadership of His Church is in a fundamentally unsound position and is in jeopardy of losing exaltation" (in Conference Report, Apr. 1982, p. 90; or *Ensign*, May 1982, p. 64). How well are you following direction received from your Priesthood leaders and how righteously are you seeking and giving proper direction in your responsibilities as father, husband, home teacher, or priesthood leader?

Quorum Training Suggestions

Quorum members may range in their beliefs concerning modern revelation from those who find peace and security in following the prophets to those who view any change from established practice as suspect. The purposes of this lesson are to instill faith that God does now and will in the future reveal his will through appropriate channels and to prepare priesthood holders to receive and intelligently act upon revealed truth.

- To encourage individual study, ask the brethren in the quorum to share insights they received from studying the self-instructional material. You may wish to ask the following questions:

Why, in the management and development of the kingdom today, is it necessary to receive revelation in addition to the commandments and revelations contained in the scriptures?

What are the channels which have been established through which revelation may be received?

How can we prepare to receive personal revelation as well as guidance and instruction from those called to direct the Church?

- Discuss the difference between policies and procedures, which frequently change, and doctrine, which is stable. Discuss some instances where policy has changed. Note that changes always come through proper channels.

- Discuss ways in which we might appropriately resolve doubts and questions concerning counsel and direction from the living prophets. Refer particularly to the instructions given to Oliver Cowdery in the Doctrine and Covenants, sections 8 and 9. In what way should our inquiries to the Lord be limited? What is the importance of study and faith in obtaining a spiritual witness?

- Assign a quorum member to review the deception of Hiram Page, one of the Eight Witnesses to the Book of Mormon, in the early days of the Church (see Joseph Smith, *History of The Church of Jesus Christ of Latter-day Saints*, 1:109–15) and the great principle which was revealed to the Church in connection with this incident (see D&C 28). Why was Oliver Cowdery chastised in connection with these "revelations"? What was the source of revelations which did not come through appointed channels (see D&C 28:11)?

- Discuss this statement by Elder Boyd K. Packer: "The man who will not sustain the bishop of his ward and the president of his stake will not sustain the President of the Church" ("Follow the Brethren," Brigham Young University *Speeches of the Year*, 23 March 1965, p. 5). Why is this so?

- Discuss why fathers should carefully guard against any unkind or improper words being spoken about any of the Lord's anointed servants. Use Doctrine and Covenants 121:16–22 in your discussion.

■ Read and discuss this statement by President Kimball: "It was President Wilford Woodruff, who, in his closing years, made this statement: 'I ask my Heavenly Father to pour out his spirit upon me, as his servant, that in my advanced age, and during the few days I have to spend here in the flesh, I may be led by his inspiration. I say to Israel, the Lord will never permit me or any other man who stands as president of this Church to lead you astray. It is not in the program. It is not in the mind of God. If I were to attempt that the Lord would remove me out of my place, and so he will any other man who attempts to lead the children of men astray from his oracles of God and from their duty. . . . ' (*The Discourses of Wilford Woodruff* [Bookcraft, 1969], pp. 212–13.)" (in Conference Report, Oct. 1972, p. 30; or *Ensign*, Jan. 1973, p. 35).

Why is President Woodruff's statement such a comfort in these last days?

What obligation does this suggest for us?

Love All of God's Children

D&C 112:11

Personal Study

Learn to love and fellowship all people.

In early June of 1978, the First Presidency of the Church announced that a revelation had been received that extended the full blessings of the gospel to all worthy members of the Church. Their statement evidenced the great love the Lord's servants have for all of God's children:

"As we have witnessed the expansion of the work of the Lord over the earth, we have been grateful that people of many nations have responded to the message of the restored gospel, and have joined the Church in ever-increasing numbers. This, in turn, has inspired us with a desire to extend to every worthy member of the Church all of the privileges and blessings which the gospel affords.

"Aware of the promises made by the prophets and presidents of the Church who have preceded us that at some time, in God's eternal plan, all of our brethren who are worthy may receive the priesthood, and witnessing the faithfulness of those from whom the priesthood has been withheld, we have pleaded long and earnestly in behalf of these, our faithful brethren, spending many hours in the Upper Room of the Temple supplicating the Lord for divine guidance.

"He has heard our prayers, and by revelation has confirmed that the long-promised day has come when every faithful, worthy man in the Church may receive the holy priesthood, with power to exercise its divine authority, and enjoy with his loved ones every blessing that flows therefrom, including the blessings of the temple" (in Conference Report, Oct. 1978, p. 22; or *Ensign*, Nov. 1978, p. 16; see also Official Declaration—2).

As a further evidence of the Church's commitment to love all of God's children and to administer the gospel to them, the next general conference of the Church voted unanimously "as a constituent assembly [to] accept this revelation as the word and will of the Lord" (in Conference Report, Oct. 1978, p. 22; or *Ensign*, Nov. 1978, p. 16).

Is there any person anywhere to whom we do not have the fullest obligation to love and serve him and share with him the blessings of the gospel? Are we seeking for the Christlike love that knows no color or nationality or culture? Are we truly becoming "no more strangers and foreigners, but fellowcitizens with the saints, and of the household of God" (Ephesians 2:19)?

1 Go Ye into All the World

▪ Matthew 28:19; Mark 16:15; compare D&C 1:4, 58:64. What was the Lord's command to his disciples anciently? _____

Why does this same command apply to us today? ___ _____

Why does the Lord use such words as "all nations" or "all the world" or "every creature" or "uttermost parts of the earth"?

Will he be pleased with less than total penetration of the whole earth?

▪ President Spencer W. Kimball said:

"Our goal is nothing less than the penetration of the entire world. . . .

"Most of the illustrations of the gospel used by Jesus—salt, light, bread, water, leaven, fire—have one common element—penetration. We are not only to penetrate the world geographically but we are to penetrate the world of government, school, work, and home, the world of entertainment, the intellectual, the laboring man, the ignorant man" (address at Regional Representatives' seminar, 3 Oct. 1974).

What does it mean to *penetrate?*

▪ 4 Nephi 1:2, 15–18. What condition is described in these verses? _____

How wonderful it would be to live in a society where there was no contention or wickedness of any kind. What, according to verse 15, is necessary for such a condition to exist? _____

_____

How can we help bring to pass such a condition in our day?

_____

- Isaiah 2:2–3; compare John 13:35. When will this prophecy come to pass? _____

How may we help it come to pass? _____

_____

What will be one of the distinguishing characteristics of the latter-day Zion that will cause the peoples of the earth to come to us to show them the ways of the Lord? _____

_____

- Elder Rex D. Pinegar told of a friend of his who was traveling home in an airplane:

"His only son would soon be leaving home in just a few days to serve as a missionary. . . . His great love for his son caused him to reflect, 'If my son is going so far away to teach about our Church, this had better be the best church!' Then he took out a note pad and pen and began to list the characteristics or qualities one would look for in the best church. . . .

"His list became long and impressive, and he satisfied himself that his church, The Church of Jesus Christ of Latter-day Saints, offered a program to meet the need of every individual. Truly, he determined, it is the best church his son could represent!

"My friend felt so good about his list of attractive qualities of the best church that he decided to show it to the gentleman seated next to him on the plane. The man . . . responded with interest and respect. Together they reviewed the list, and as they concluded their conversation the businessman asked my friend, 'Would you like to know what I would look for in a church? There is just one criterion: the members of that church would best exemplify the teaching of the Savior—"Love thy neighbor as thyself." ' . . .

"It is that love for the Lord and for our neighbors—all men everywhere—that is the motivating force which prompts my

216

friend's son, and [tens of thousands] like him, to leave home, friends, family, security, and comfort to go among unknown neighbors throughout the world with the message of the gospel of Jesus Christ" (in Conference Report, Oct. 1978, pp. 11–12; or *Ensign*, Nov. 1978, pp. 9–10).

How well do we exemplify that love that will attract the attention of those who are searching for the truth?

2 Learn to Appreciate the Strengths of Other Cultures

■ D&C 88:78–82; compare D&C 90:15, 93:53. What does the Lord expect us to learn? _____

Is there any limit to the things we are to learn? _____

According to verses 80 and 81, why are we to know all these things? _____

How can knowing these things help us in our mission "to testify and warn the people"? _____

■ It is natural for people to study and learn of the history and culture of their own nation and perhaps of the nations of their ancestors. President Kimball suggested, however, that we ought to broaden our awareness now to all the world: "We mention Ghana and Nigeria, but what of Libya, Ethiopia, the Ivory Coast and the Sudan and others? These are names that must become as familiar to us as Japan, Venezuela, New Zealand, and Denmark have become" (address at Regional Representatives' seminar, 29 Sept. 1978).

■ Ezra 1:1–2. Who was Cyrus? _____

What work was the Lord able to perform through him? _____

Do you believe that God raises up men of integrity and virtue among all nations of the earth to help him accomplish his purposes? _____

Must we always assume that we are the only people the Lord can use?

- Alma 29:8. Whom, according to this verse, does the Lord grant to teach his word? _____

Are all such teachers necessarily familiar with or even aware of the gospel of Jesus Christ? _____

Why is it consistent to believe that the great religious leaders of the world, such as Mohammed, Confucius, and the Reformers, as well as philosophers including Socrates, Plato, and others, received a portion of God's light and were thereby able to enlighten whole nations and bring individuals to a higher level of understanding and conduct? _____

- Jacob 3:5–7. What were the Nephites in a position to learn from those whom they considered to be an inferior people?

In our own day, are there qualities of humility, morality, strong family ties, or integrity that we can afford to emulate in cultures other than our own? _____

As a single example from many possible examples, President Kimball spoke of the qualities of the Chinese people:

"The people are intelligent, hopeful, and courteous. They love children, are courteous to parents and women and honor their ancestors. Very like our gospel faithful, they are family-oriented and . . . live in the individual family units. . . .

"The Chinese are a disciplined, industrious, frugal, closely-knit people. Their moral standards are very high by modern western standards. Honesty is assumed as a matter of course. Crime is rare. Drug abuse and prostitution have been virtually climinated. Premarital sex is heavily censured and is rare. Homosexuality and lesbianism are virtually unknown. Family life is strong, with old family members still given great respect and care" (address at Regional Representatives' seminar, 29 Sept. 1978).

Do we need to adopt any of these qualities more fully in our own lives, even in our own Latter-day Saint communities? _____

_____

Wherever we are in the world? _____ _____

_____

Which ones? _____

_____

_____

3 Love and Serve Others Unconditionally

■ Leviticus 19:34. What does the Lord require of us? _____

_____

What is one of the best ways we can do this? _____

_____

President Heber J. Grant said, "The best way in the world to show our love for our neighbor is to go forth and proclaim the gospel of the Lord Jesus Christ" (in Conference Report, Apr. 1927, p. 176). Do you love your neighbors, friends, and others enough to share the gospel with them? Do you love the "stranger that dwelleth with you" enough to share the gospel with him?

■ President George Albert Smith testified: "The gospel of Jesus Christ . . . is a gospel of love and kindness. It will cause us, if we are living as we should, to love our neighbors as ourselves, and go out of our way, if possible, to help them understand better the purpose of life" (in Conference Report, Oct. 1948, pp. 167–68).

■ 1 Timothy 4:12. What is one of the best ways we can share the gospel with all whom we meet? _____

_____

The power of example was stressed by Elder Mark E. Petersen: "I would have you know that your words alone are not enough. I would have you know that it is only your word supported by your righteous lives that can give testimony to the world in such sincere tones that men and women will pay attention to you" (in

Conference Report, Oct. 1963, p. 122; or *Improvement Era*, Dec. 1963, p. 1110).

Will It Make a Difference?

In a revelation given in June 1829, the Lord declared:

"Remember the worth of souls is great in the sight of God; . . . And how great is his joy in the soul that repenteth! . . .

"And if it so be that you should labor all your days in crying repentance unto this people, and bring, save it be one soul unto me, how great shall be your joy with him in the kingdom of my Father!" (D&C 18:10, 13, 15).

"If one labors all his days and brings in save it be one soul!" President Kimball observed, "One soul! How precious! Oh, that God would give us that kind of love for souls!" (address at Regional Representatives' seminar, 3 Oct. 1974, p. 21).

Quorum Training Suggestions

This lesson focuses on the need we have to love and respect and serve all of God's children, all of whom are our brothers and sisters, the children of our Father in heaven. Quorum leaders should encourage the members of the quorum to prayerfully study the personal study material. The following suggestions may be used in the quorum hour to help quorum members to put into practice in their daily lives the principles they have learned.

▪ To encourage individual study, briefly review the personal study material by asking such questions as these: How far-reaching is our assignment to spread the blessings of the gospel? What chief quality or virtue will help us to be successful in this assignment? Why is it so important to understand and appreciate other peoples and their cultures? What is the best way in the world to show our love for our neighbor?

▪ Emphasize that we will be successful in taking the gospel into all the world.

▪ Assign one or more quorum members to study and report on ways we can come to better understand and appreciate those people who are different from us, especially such people who may live in our own neighborhoods or who work with us. If quorum members have had uplifting experiences with befriending other people of other cultures or ethnic groups, perhaps they may be invited to share them with the quorum.

- Discuss this statement from the *General Missionary Handbook* (PBMI4427): "The term *friendshipping* refers to the process of becoming a genuine friend to those who are not members of the Church *regardless of whether they express an immediate interest in the Church*. It involves acts of kindness, service, and love" (p. 15; second italics added.) Why is it important to continue being a genuine friend even to those who are not interested in hearing the gospel? If we genuinely love people, will they be able to resist our efforts to bless their lives?

- Have quorum members pair off in groups of two and discuss with each other how they may learn to love and tolerate others.

- Read the following statement by Joseph Smith and invite quorum suggestions on how its message might be applied to home teaching, fellowshipping, and missionary service: "Nothing is so much calculated to lead people to forsake sin as to take them by the hand, and watch over them with tenderness. When persons manifest the least kindness and love to me, O what power it has over my mind." (*Teachings of the Prophet Joseph Smith*, p. 240).

- Place the following statement on display during the presentation of the lesson and summarize the lesson by discussing its meaning: "Love opens doors" (Marvin J. Ashton, in Conference Report, Apr. 1978, p. 10; or *Ensign*, May 1978, p. 8).

- Read the following statement by President N. Eldon Tanner: "We must do as well enfolding all these new friends in our love and fellowship as we do in enlisting them through our missionary work. We must be as quick to welcome them as we are to witness to them about the Church" (*Church News*, 13 Oct. 1979, p. 5). Discuss ways in which we can make visitors, new members and inactive members feel more welcome in Church activities and meetings.

Priesthood Correlation

D&C 84:108–110

Personal Study

Reach out and strengthen individuals in your family and in other areas of your responsibility.

Satan "maketh war with the saints of God," and his legions are sufficiently numerous to encompass the Saints "round about" (see D&C 76:29). But God will not leave the Saints defenseless against the tidal wave of wickedness and godlessness:

"Today, we are encamped against the greatest array of sin, vice, and evil ever assembled before our eyes. Such formidable enemies may cause lesser hearts to shrink or shun the fight. But the battle plan whereby we fight to save the souls of men is not our own. It was provided . . . by the inspiration and revelation of the Lord. Yes, I speak of that plan which will bring us victory, even the Correlation Program of the Church. And as we do battle against him who would thwart the purposes of God and degrade and destroy mankind, I pray that each of us will *stand in his or her appointed place,* that the battle for the souls of men will indeed be won" (Thomas S. Monson, "Correlation Brings Blessings," *Relief Society Magazine,* Apr. 1967, p. 247; italics added).

Why is it so important that members of the Church be united in righteousness and obedience? Why is it necessary that every member be strengthened and prepared against the wickedness of the times? What has the Lord revealed to help members of the Church and their families remain true and faithful?

---

1 **Correlating Our Effort Will Help Prepare for the Coming of Christ**

■ D&C 84:108–20. Is it possible for each part of the Church to do all the tasks, or is some degree of specialization necessary? Could the President of the Church personally do everything that needs to be done? Could a missionary have time to proselyte if he were expected to perform every other duty at the same time? Why is it appropriate that the work be shared and divided? _____

■ Elder Harold B. Lee described some major parts of the program to unify and coordinate all the strength of the Church:

"We have endeavored to proceed . . . in an orderly and logical manner: first, by placing the priesthood quorums as the Lord has directed us in his revelations; second, by giving strength to the home . . . and third, by a total correlation of the curricula and activities of all the organizations, priesthood, auxiliaries, institutes, and seminaries" (in Conference Report, Oct. 1964, p. 81; or *Improvement Era*, Dec. 1964, p. 1078).

■ 1 Corinthians 12:14–28; compare Ephesians 4:4–16. What great principles about each working for the benefit of the whole does Paul explain in this discourse? _____

■ President Joseph F. Smith said:

"We expect to see the day . . . when every council of the Priesthood in The Church of Jesus Christ of Latter-day Saints will understand its duty; will assume its own responsibility, will magnify its calling, and fill its place in the Church, to the uttermost, according to the intelligence and ability possessed by it. When that day shall come, there will not be so much necessity for the work that is now being done by the auxiliary organizations, because it will be done by the regular quorums of the Priesthood. The Lord designed and comprehended it from the beginning, and he has made provision in the Church whereby every need may be met and satisfied through the regular organizations of the Priesthood" (*Gospel Doctrine*, pp. 159–60).

What must bearers of the priesthood do to faithfully execute the great trust and responsibility that God has given to the priesthood? _____

■ D&C 107:99–100. If we are negligent in discharging our responsibilities in the kingdom, do others suffer? Why? _____

How may the perfect government and system of the Church be affected if someone does not stand in his appointed place and labor in his own calling? _____

_____

2 The Priesthood Is to Watch Over the Church

■ D&C 20:47, 53–55. In the priesthood session of general conference, 30 September 1967, Elder Harold B. Lee prefaced his reading of these verses by stating that the first step in the great correlation work is to put "the priesthood in the place where the Lord had placed it: to watch over the Church" (in Conference Report, 1967, p. 100; or *Improvement Era*, Jan. 1968, p. 27). How do these verses describe the duties of the priesthood of the Church? _____

_____

How would a careful and faithful discharge of those duties help strengthen the membership of the Church throughout the world? _____

_____

■ In the same address explaining some of the fundamental principles of the correlation effort, Elder Lee said:

"Home teaching, in essence, means that we consider separately each individual member of the family. . . . Home teaching . . . is to help the parents with home problems in their efforts to teach their families the fundamentals of parental responsibility. . . .

Quorum leaders were given the responsibility of selecting, training, and supervising quorum members in visiting with and teaching assigned families of their own quorum members" (in Conference Report, Oct. 1967, p. 100; or *Improvement Era*, Jan. 1968, p. 27).

If the priesthood holders were effectively prepared to train fathers in the homes to discharge their responsibilities, how could this strengthen the families of the Church? _____

_____

If the members of the wards and branches understood better that the Church is created to bless and help the family and the individual, rather than the reverse, and all of the programs and resources of a quourum were devoted to strengthening the home and family, how could a father help but want to do better in his assigned responsibilities? _____

■ The responsibility of the Church and priesthood to help the family was emphasized in this statement by Elder Lee:

"Again and again has been repeated the statement that the home is the basis of a righteous life. . . . The priesthood programs operate in support of the home; the auxiliary programs render valuable assistance. . . .

"Much of what we do organizationally, then, is scaffolding, as we seek to build the individual, and we must not mistake the scaffolding for the soul" (in Conference Report, Oct. 1967, p. 107; or *Improvement Era,* Jan. 1968, p. 31).

---

3 Fathers Are to Watch Over and Strengthen Their Family Members

■ Mosiah 4:14–15. What principles are described in these passages? _____

Who is responsible to do the teaching? _____

Who is in the best position to observe and understand the needs of each family member? _____

If a father is having difficulty in meeting his responsibilities to teach and train his family, how could he be helped by a good home teacher with whom he could counsel quietly and privately? _____

■ 1 Nephi 2:16; Enos 1:3. Who taught Nephi the gospel? _____

Who taught Enos the gospel? _____

Who has the responsibility to teach and train family members? _____

- President Spencer W. Kimball said:

"In the divine scheme every soul has been given a father whose responsibility is not only to sire and provide the necessities of life, but also to train for mortality and life eternal.

"Undoubtedly Sariah cooperated with Lehi, but it was the father who called his family together to teach them righteousness" (in Conference Report, Apr. 1965, p. 61; or *Improvement Era*, June 1965, p. 513).

- D&C 93:40, 42. Does it appear to be possible to contribute much strength to the Church if we are not doing everything within our power to teach and train and strengthen our families? Why? _____

President Joseph F. Smith said: "Do not let your children out to specialists in these things, but teach them by your own precept and example, by your own fireside. Be a specialist yourself in the truth. Let our meetings, schools and organizations, instead of being our only or leading teachers, be supplements to our teachings and training in the home" (*Gospel Doctrine*, p. 302).

- In an address to the priesthood, Elder Lee spoke about the blessings of the family home evening program and then restated a promise made by the First Presidency in 1915: "If the Saints obey this counsel, we promise that great blessings will result. Love at home and obedience to parents will increase. Faith will be developed in the hearts of the youth of Israel, and they will gain power to combat the evil influences and temptations which beset them" (in Conference Report, Oct. 1964, pp. 83–84; or *Improvement Era*, Dec. 1964, p. 1079). Although recreation and fun are an important part of family life, can the blessings that God intends for families come to a home where parents do not teach the gospel to their children patiently and regularly?

Will It Make a Difference?

The family is the basic unit of the Church and of society. It is families that may be sealed together for all eternity, not Sunday School classes or Scout troops or choirs or even quorums. All these are aids and helps to assist and strengthen the home. No work is more important than the labor of loving, teaching, guiding, and training that a father has the right and the opportunity to render in his own home and family. Use the programs of the Church to aid you as you seek to teach and strengthen the members of your family.

Quorum Training Suggestions

As our lives become more complex and as the demands upon our time become more consuming, an organized family, an organized quorum, and a correlated Church become more and more imperative. Your responsibility as quorum leaders is to train the members of your quorum to recognize that their responsibility in their home is their greatest responsibility that they shall never be released from, throughout their lives.

Assign quorum members to study the preceding material carefully so that they will be prepared for this very important quorum discussion.

▪ To encourage individual study, invite quorum members to express their insights from reading the personal study guide material. You might also ask:

Why is it necessary that all the programs of the Church be correlated and directed by priesthood authority?

What is the expected result of correlation?

What is the greatest help the Church can give to the family of a man who is inactive and unresponsive to his priesthood duties?

Why is the father the one who bears the foremost responsibility for teaching and training family members?

▪ Present and discuss these questions, which may help to teach the basic principles of correlation to quorum members:

Why must auxiliary workers still work through the home teacher and the father even if they think the father may not be moving as rapidly as they think he should to meet all the needs of the family members?

Why should priesthood and auxiliary officers check with the father before calling or assigning any members of his family to fill any position of repsonsibility? If a family is having problems, what must be strengthened first? How can that be done?

▪ Present and discuss this statement:

"Don't you ever let anyone tell you, the membership of the Church, that the Lord is not today revealing and directing and developing plans which are needed to concentrate the entire forces of this Church to meet the challenge of the insidious forces at work to thwart and to tear down and to undermine the church and kingdom of God.

"I bear you my solemn witness that I know that God is directing this work today and revealing his mind and will. The light is shining through" (Harold B. Lee, in Conference Report, Oct. 1962, p. 83; or *Improvement Era*, Dec. 1962, p. 941).

Why is it so imperative that Church members understand the meaning of the programs being revealed now?

Why can the entire forces of the Church be concentrated only when each member of the Church stands in his appointed place? Refer to Doctrine and Covenants 84:108–10 in your answer.

What are the duties of the auxiliaries? How can they appropriately be involved?

▪ Develop a problem situation for a hypothetical family, the father of which is assumed to be in your quorum. With the quorum members, plan how the quorum might be mobilized to meet that problem.

▪ It may be helpful to refer to some of the basic addresses given by General Authorities and others during the years when the correlation program was first being developed and announced to the Church. Some of these might include:

Conference Report, Oct. 1961, pp. 77–91 (or *Improvement Era*, Jan. 1962, pp. 34–42).

Conference Report, Oct. 1962, pp. 71–83 (or *Improvement Era*, Dec. 1962, pp. 936–41).

Conference Report, Oct. 1964, pp. 80–87 (or *Improvement Era*, Dec. 1964, pp. 1077–81).

▪ Discuss the meaning of correlation to the following statement by Elder Boyd K. Packer:

"If I am failing as a father, help me first, and my children second.

"Do not be too quick to take over from me the job of raising my children. . . .

". . . Get me involved. It is my ministry" (*That All May Be Edified*, p. 94).

▪ Have the quorum leader relate how correlation works in the ward through the ward correlation council.

▪ Invite quorum members to suggest ways in which correlation can work through the family council system. How can this same principle apply to those who are single and share an apartment with others?

Because of the Righteous Few

D&C 103:7–10

Personal Study

Realize that one righteous individual can influence many for good.

Brother Brown sat in stake conference and listened as the stake president announced a realignment of ward boundaries. Many had not expected this. Along with every other member of the stake, Brother Brown raised his hand in support of the change. After the meeting, however, as he was leaving the chapel with his family, some members were criticizing the change and insisting that the action had not been inspired. Brother Brown knew differently. As a member of the high council, he was aware of the long hours of deliberation and prayer that had gone into this decision. He wondered what to do. How would he be received if he spoke out in support of the stake presidency when so many seemed to feel that the change was wrong? Would his conscience be still if he listened to the criticism of the stake presidency and said nothing? Brother Brown knew that he could not keep quiet and still maintain his integrity; so, with a prayer that he would be tactful and not offend, he began to explain to the members that they should support their leaders and that the decision was the Lord's will. He was surprised at how readily they began to understand and to express their appreciation for his explanations. They left the stake conference feeling good about the change and with a renewed determination to refrain from criticizing Church leaders.

What would you have done in a similar situation? Can one voice really make a difference? Can one righteous life make a difference?

1 How Many Is One?

■ Matthew 5:13–16. Can cities or branches or wards or stakes ever respond to this command of the Master if individuals do not respond to it? A candle is a small thing, but if it is lit and held aloft it "giveth light unto all that are in the house." How much influence can one person have? How many, figuratively, can one be if he is determined to honor his covenants and stand for the right? _____

_____

■ Hebrews 11:12. How many did Abraham in effect become, because he believed God, trusted in God's promises, and obeyed God's commandments? How many is one if that one is Jesus Christ? How many lives did he affect when he went into Gethsemane alone and when he hung on the cross alone (see John 12:32)? How many is one if that one is Joseph Smith? How many lives did Joseph affect when he went into the grove alone (see D&C 122:1–2)? _____

■ Isaiah 60:22. What does the Lord say about "one" in this passage? _____

Can one person become as a multitude if he is determined to lengthen his stride and quicken his pace? How many is one if that one is Spencer W. Kimball? How many lives did President Kimball affect because of his strong commitment to taking the gospel to all the earth? How many lives did he affect because of his personal integrity, his love, and his righteousness?

■ An incident that occurred during an East Germany mission conference illustrates how the influence of one inspired man can reach to the ends of the earth:

"Sister Margarete Hellmann had suffered an ailment of the hip since youth. As the years came and went, the affliction brought her an ever-increasing burden of pain. Finally, she could walk only with the aid of a pair of crutches. To facilitate her travel from place to place, and to alleviate the terrible pain she keenly felt with every single step, some of the Saints contributed money and bought her a wheelchair. But this relief was short-lived. Soon, even sitting in her wheelchair was accompanied by almost unbearable pain. Then an inflammation of the nerves of the left side of her face further intensified her suffering. One day she heard the heartening news: the prophet of the Lord was to be in Dresden. She had one all-consuming desire—to attend the conference and touch the prophet. . . .

" . . . 'When our prophet came close to me,' she wrote, 'he warmly shook my hand and looked at me in the spirit of love, as did those who were with him. After that, I did not feel any more pain—not then, nor any to this day. That is the greatest testimony of my life!' " (Joseph B. Wirthlin, in Conference Report, Oct 1978, p. 51; or *Ensign*, Nov. 1978, p. 36).

How many do you suppose may be strengthened by the faith and determination of this good sister? Can each of us, like President Kimball and others of the Lord's servants, stand as symbols of the Savior's love for all men?

---

2 We Should Be a Righteous Influence at Home

■ Joshua 24:15. Who should be first in the family to resolve to worship the Lord? _____

_____

If a father decides that the gospel is unimportant in his life, what effect will this decision have on his children? Why? _____

_____

If a father shows by actions as well as by words that his relationship with his Father in heaven is of great importance to him, what effect will this have on his children? _____

_____

■ A father counseling with his wife sets the standard of worship for the family. President Joseph Fielding Smith counseled: "Bring up your children . . . in light and truth. Teach them by example. Fathers and mothers have to set the example. They cannot say to their children, 'You follow the teachings of the Church, but in our lives we are going to make exceptions.' It cannot be done, not properly. You parents, set the example" (*Take Heed to Yourselves!*, p. 372). How many people can be affected by parents who teach their family properly?

- 3 Nephi 11:29. What does this scripture imply would be the advantage of discussing disagreements calmly? _____

_____

What difference could one man make in the home if he were to always speak calmly and respectfully? _____

_____

- What effect does an orderly, lovely home have on those who live in it or who pass by it daily? Can it be an inspiration to others to improve their surroundings? _____

_____

To what extent can one man make a difference in how an entire neighborhood looks? _____

_____

- Matthew 20:26–28. In what way does this scripture particularly apply to the father as the presiding officer in his home? _____

_____

In what ways should he be a servant to his family? _____

_____

How can his service be a righteous influence in the lives of his family? _____

_____

_____

3 We Should Be a Righteous Influence in Society

- Proverbs 4:18. President Harold B. Lee taught: "Any Latter-day Saint in Church circles, in military service, in social life, or in the business community is looked upon not just as an individual, but as the visible Church today. Someone has said: 'Be careful how you act, because you may be the only Standard Church Works some people may ever read.' . . . The standard . . . in the Church must be visibly higher than the standard . . . in the world" (*Ye Are the Light of the World*, p. 13).

- D&C 101:39–40; compare D&C 103:7–10. How can one be "the salt of the earth"? _____

_____

President Harold B. Lee said: "The Savior's disciples are the salt of society in every dispensation. Salt preserves food from corruption and seasons it, making it wholesome and acceptable; in like manner the Master's disciples are to purify the society in which they move, setting a good example and counteracting every corrupt tendency" (*Ye Are the Light of the World*, p. 11). What are some particular, personal ways in which you can counteract corrupt tendencies in the society in which you live?

- President N. Eldon Tanner taught:

"Now, what must we do? If there is pornography or obscenity in bookstores, on television or radio, or in places of entertainment, if there are those who would make more easily available to the young and inexperienced alcohol and its attendant evils, . . . and if we are threatened with the passage of laws which violate the commandments of God, it is our duty and responsibility as individuals to speak out, to organize, and to protect ourselves and our community against such encroachments. . . . It is . . . important that we react effectively against the immorality and evil in our communities which threaten the morals and the very lives of our children" (in Conference Report, Apr. 1973, p. 59; or *Ensign*, July 1973, p. 10).

- Genesis 18:23–33. What does the Lord promise Abraham, as recorded in this passage? _____

How, as recorded here, can a few righteous people make a difference? _____

Carefully compare Alma 10:22. Does this same principle apply to our day? Is it possible that we are being protected because of the prayers and righteousness of only a few? How important are our individual righteousness and our fervent prayers for the peace, blessing, and salvation of much that we hold dear?

**You Can Make
a Difference**

President David O. McKay taught, "'Man radiates what he is, and that radiation affects to a greater or less degree every person who comes within that radiation" (*Stepping Stones to an Abundant Life*, p. 87). Your life will affect every person with whom you come in contact. Resolve that your influence will be a great and mighty influence for good.

Quorum Training Suggestions

As quorum leaders, you have an opportunity to set an example that will be a factor in the lives of your quorum members. Lead your quorum in a positive and powerful way. Avoid gloom and despair. Each righteous man, no matter where he is or how he serves, can help to bring a glorious day of righteousness.

■ To encourage individual study, have quorum members share insights from their personal study by asking such questions as these: When can one be a multitude? How does a father affect many lives as he teaches and instructs his children? What could be the eternal consequences if he fails to teach effectively? Why is it so sobering to think that our influence will continue throughout eternity? Can one man make a difference in a society? How?

■ Make a list on the chalkboard of the ways in which we can affect the lives of others. Your list might include such things as the following:

Set a good example.

Render service to others.

Radiate Christlike love and concern.

Pray fervently for others, including enemies and persecutors.

Magnify callings as husband and father.

Magnify Church callings.

Speak out when high principles are being attacked.

Be actively involved in politics.

Keep home and yard attractive and clean.

Insist that your community be well-maintained.

■ President Harold B. Lee emphasized the power of one. He said: "There is never a man or a woman of station in this church who falls below the standards he is expected to live without dragging down with him many who have had faith in him. He has wounded their conscience; he has dragged down those of weaker faith, and many count the day of their disaffection in this church when someone in whom they had faith fell below

235

that standard they expected him to maintain" (*Ye Are the Light of the World*, p. 21).

- Present and discuss 2 Kings 6:14–17. When Elisha and his servant faced the horses, chariots, and soldiers of their enemies, were they alone? Who was there to help them? Are you ever really alone? Are you entitled to the same divine help as Elisha if you exercise faith and obey the same standards of worthiness?

- Present this poem by Edward Everett Hale, titled "Patriot's Oath," as cited by President Harold B. Lee:

I am only one—
But I am one;
I cannot do everything
But I can do something.
And what I can do
That I ought to do;
And what I ought to do
By the grace of God,
I will do.
(*Decisions for Successful Living*, p. 205.)

The Fall
of Man

D&C 29:35–43

Personal Study

Understand the blessings of mortality.

In explaining the need for the Fall, President Joseph Fielding Smith said:

"We came here into this mortal world to receive a training in mortality that we could not get anywhere else, or in any other way. We came here into this world to partake of all the vicissitudes, to receive the lessons that we receive in mortality from or in a mortal world. And so we become subject to pain, to sickness. We are blessed for keeping the commandments of the Lord with all that he has given us, which, if we will follow and be true and faithful, will bring us back again into the presence of God our Eternal Father, as sons and daughters of God, entitled to the fulness of celestial glory.

"That great blessing of celestial glory could never have come to us without a period of time in mortality, and so we came here in this mortal world. We are in school, the mortal school, to gain the experiences, the training, the joys, and the sufferings that we partake of, that we might be educated in all these things and be prepared, if we are faithful and true to the commandments of the Lord, to become sons and daughters of God, joint heirs with Jesus Christ; and in his presence to go on to a fulness and a continuation of the seeds forever, and perhaps through our faithfulness to have the opportunity of building worlds and peopling them.

" . . . Let us thank the Lord, when we pray, for Adam. If it had not been for Adam, I would not be here; you would not be here; we would be waiting in the heavens as spirits pleading for somebody . . . to pass through a certain condition that brought upon us mortality.

"We are in the mortal life to get an experience, a training, that we could not get any other way. And in order to become gods, it is necessary for us to know something about pain, about sickness, and about the other things that we partake of in this school of mortality" (*Seek Ye Earnestly*, pp. 4–5).

What was the nature of Adam's transgression? Why was it necessary? How does understanding the doctrine of the Fall help us to endure the difficulties that come to us in mortality?

---

1 The Transgression of Adam

Many Christian sects mistakenly teach that Adam's transgression and fall were contrary to God's plan for his children. They denounce Adam as having introduced evil and sin into the world. Some even suggest that Adam's transgression was a violation of the law of chastity, notwithstanding the fact that Adam and Eve were married by God "while they were yet immortal beings in the Garden of Eden and before death entered the world" (Joseph Fielding Smith, *Doctrines of Salvation*, 1:114–15). As you review the following material, contrast the teachings of the gospel concerning Adam's life and mission with these false teachings and beliefs.

■ 2 Nephi 2:22–23. What was the condition of Adam and Eve in the Garden of Eden? _____

_____

Would Adam and Eve have had children in the Garden? _____

_____

How clearly did they comprehend good, evil, pain, sorrow, or suffering? _____

_____

Why? _____

_____

■ Moses 2:28; 3:16–17. When Adam and Eve were placed in the Garden, they were given commandments that required them to make choices. What was the relationship between these commandments? _____

_____

President Smith explained the nature of the choices: "Just why the Lord would say to Adam that he forbade him to partake of the fruit of that tree is not made clear in the Bible account, but in the original as it comes to us in the Book of Moses it is made definitely clear. It is that the Lord said to Adam that if he wished to remain as he was in the garden, then he was not to eat the fruit, but if he desired to eat it and partake of death he was at liberty to do so. So really it was not in the true sense a transgression of a divine commandment. Adam made the wise decision, in fact the only decision that he could make" (*Answers to Gospel Questions*, 4:81).

■ President Wilford Woodruff said: "Adam and Eve came to this world to perform exactly the part that they acted in the Garden of Eden; and I will say, they were ordained of God to do what they did, and it was therefore expected that they would eat of the forbidden fruit in order that man might know both good and evil by passing through this school of experience which this life affords us" (*Discourses of Wilford Woodruff*, p. 233).

■ President Marion G. Romney dispels any doubt as to Adam's understanding of his action:

"Some men speak of the ancients as being savages, as if they had no intelligence. . . .

"Adam had intelligence, as much as any man that ever lived since or lives now. . . .

"I do not look upon Adam's action as a sin. I think it was a deliberate act of free agency. He chose to do that which had to be done to further the purposes of God" (*Look to God and Live*, p. 251). How did Adam's fall further God's purposes? _____

_____

How do we benefit from it? _____

_____

2 Consequences of the Fall

■ Moses 4:22–31. What conditions of mortal life were placed by the Lord upon Eve? _____

_____

Upon Adam? _____

_____

Upon the earth? _____

_____

Why were Adam and Eve driven from the Garden? _____

_____

- Moses 5:4–5. What did Adam and Eve do, as told in verse 4, before they received commandments? _____

_____

Would the consequence of transgression have been as deeply impressed upon Adam and Eve if they had not been left to labor and plead with the Lord? _____

_____

- Elder Bruce R. McConkie, in explaining some of the important changes in the status of Adam, wrote:

"The first death, in point of time, was spiritual. Spiritual death is to die as pertaining to the things of the Spirit; it is to die as pertaining to the things of righteousness; it is to be cast out of the presence of the Lord, in which presence spirituality and righteousness abound. Adam died this death when he left Eden, and he remained dead until he was born again by the power of the Spirit following his baptism.

"Temporal death is the natural death. It consists of the separation of the body and the spirit, the one going to the grave, the other to a world of waiting spirits to await the day of resurrection. Adam died temporally within a thousand years, which is a day unto the Lord" (*The Promised Messiah*, p. 224).

- Moses 5:13; compare Mosiah 16:3; D&C 20:19–20. What has caused men since the Fall to become carnal, sensual, and devilish? _____

_____

- Moses 5:16. Were our first parents among those who loved Satan more than God? _____

_____

Can we hold our first parents responsible for our sins? _____

_____

Why? _____

_____

■ The mortal state has been variously described by the prophets as wretched and miserable, a place of sickness, sorrow, toil, pain, and death. Why is it necessary for us to experience these things? _____

_____

How does a knowledge of the purpose of trials enable us to have the courage and strength to meet these conditions of mortality? _____

_____

3 Blessings of Mortality

■ 2 Nephi 2:25; Moses 5:10. In what way has being in mortality enabled you to experience some of your greatest joys? _____

Why could Adam and Eve not have experienced these joys in the Garden? _____

Could you describe the sensations of pain or pleasure to someone who has not experienced them? Can there be an intelligent exercise of choice between good and evil without knowledge and experience?

■ The transgression and fall brought about the condition of mortality and brought upon Adam and Eve a multiplicity of sorrow. Eve, like Adam, however, found gladness in their condition: "Were it not for our transgression," she said, 'we never should have had seed, and never should have known good and evil, and the joy of our redemption" (Moses 5:11).

■ Moses 5:9; 14–15. What assurance was Adam given that he and his posterity need not suffer eternally the consequences of his transgression? _____

Would a plan of redemption have been necessary if Adam had not violated the heavenly law? _____

_____

What were the conditions upon which redemption was promised to "even as many as will"? _____

_____

What does this mean to you? _____

_____

Will It Make a Difference?

Understanding the need for the Fall and for its consequences places earthly existence in a glorious perspective. Through earthly trials we gain experience and knowledge essential for eternal progress, just as Adam and Eve did. We may better endure sorrow and pain, rejoice in our children, and appreciate more deeply the love and sacrifice of the Savior.

President Joseph Fielding Smith explained: "Mortality was essential to our eternal exaltation where we would be subject to pain, sorrow, temptation as well as to receive the pleasures and joys of this mortal life. We were to be tried as gold is purified in the crucible. The result of our obedience to the commandments of our Father would be the privilege to return to his presence to become his eternal sons and daughters, clothed with all power and glory, even to the fulness, and be like him" (*Answers to Gospel Questions*, 2:212).

Quorum Training Suggestions

Quorum members may have an incomplete understanding of the fall of Adam. Discussion in the quorum should clarify the doctrine of the Fall and, more importantly, how the lives of quorum members are influenced by it for good.

■ To encourage individual study, briefly review the personal study guide material by asking such questions as these: What was the condition of Adam and Eve in the Garden of Eden? What would have been the consequence had they remained in that condition? Why? What is meant by "original sin" as taught by many Christian religions? Is it a true doctrine? Why? (See James E. Talmage, *Jesus the Christ*, pp. 29–31.) What are the blessings of mortality, agency, experience, and increase? Why does President Joseph Fielding Smith say that we cannot become like God without these blessings?

- Adam's identity as Michael and his role in the creation may be reviewed and discussed to emphasize the greatness of the man chosen by God as our first earthly father (see Joseph Fielding Smith, *Seek Ye Earnestly*, pp. 15–17).

- Prepare and present the following chart or chalkboard diagram:

CONSEQUENCES OF ADAM'S TRANSGRESSION

Adam and Eve before the Fall	Mankind after the Fall (current condition of the world)	Available to mankind through the Atonement
Not mortal	Mortal (subject to physical death)	Immortal through the resurrection
In the presence of God	Cast out of God's presence—spiritual death	May return to the presence of God through faith in Christ, repentance, and obedience
No knowledge of good and evil	Knowledge of good and evil	All knowledge
No posterity	Have children	Eternal increase

- Have a member of the quorum read Doctrine and Covenants 107:53–56. Discuss the doctrine of the Church concerning Adam. Why do we owe him and Eve deep feelings of reverence and gratitude?

- Refer to Elder Mark E. Petersen's excellent discourse, "Adam the Archangel," for insights on the spiritual stature of Adam (in Conference Report, Oct. 1980, pp. 19–23; or *Ensign*, Nov. 1980, pp. 16–18).

- Have members of the quorum share experiences in which they have been blessed through earthly trials. Ask how important health, love, and tranquility have become to those who have endured sickness, rejection, turmoil, and suffering.

- Read the description of Adam under the heading "Adam" in the Bible Dictionary in the Latter-day Saint edition of the King James Bible.

- Invite quorum members to review the scriptures listed under the heading "Fall of Man" in the Topical Guide of the Latter-day Saint edition of the King James Bible.

- Read and discuss Doctrine and Covenants 29:35–43.

- Ask what additional insights about Adam and the Fall we get from the Doctrine and Covenants. Quorum members might be encouraged to look up references to "Adam," the "Fall," and "Michael" in the index of the Triple Combination.

Prepare Your Children for Celestial Marriage

D&C 131, 132

Personal Study

Teach your family of the eternal marriage covenant.

Elder George Q. Morris, referring to the doctrine of eternal marriage, once said:

"Now I believe that . . . our parents . . . must teach these principles. They are as clear as words can make them, as the Lord has explained them. I cannot help feeling that many are . . . not being properly taught. It is not enough to urge temple marriage. They must know what temple marriage means. It is a matter of eternal life and exaltation in the presence of God forever and forever. . . .

"May the Lord help us to awaken our youth and the parents, and all of us, to the need to know what this marriage is, to live worthy of it, to be prepared for it, for our youth to enter into it when they are mature enough, and trained enough, and for all who have been married for time only to prepare themselves for this glorious covenant" (in Conference Report, Oct. 1959, p. 49).

Elder Hugh B. Brown said:

"There should be forthright, frank, and persistent pre-marital instruction by the parents. . . .

"Too many parents avoid this responsibility, some aspects of which are sometimes thought to be too delicate for frank discussion. The fact is, there is no area of human experience, development, and education more necessary, more vital—but more neglected—than is the field of preparation for marriage in all its aspects" (*You and Your Marriage*, pp. 50–51).

1 Entering into Honorable Marriage Is a Commandment of God

Marriage is no mere convenience to be entered into lightly. The gospel teaches that marriage is one of the most important responsibilities of life. Even more than this, it is a commandment of God.

- President Joseph F. Smith said: "God not only commends but he commands marriage. While man was yet immortal, before sin had entered the world, our Heavenly Father himself performed the first marriage. He united our first parents in the bonds of holy matrimony, and commanded them to be fruitful and multiply and replenish the earth. This command he has never changed, abrogated or annulled; but it has continued in force throughout all the generations of mankind" (*Gospel Doctrine*, p. 274).

- Matthew 19:4–6. What did the Savior teach concerning marriage? _____

_____

- President Joseph F. Smith said:

"I want the young men of Zion to realize that this institution of marriage is not a man-made institution. It is of God; it is honorable, and no man who is of marriageable age is living his religion who remains single. . . .

"There are great consequences connected with it, consequences which reach beyond this present time, into all eternity, for thereby souls are begotten into the world, and men and women obtain their being in the world. Marriage is the preserver of the human race. Without it, the purposes of God would be frustrated; virtue would be destroyed to give place to vice and corruption, and the earth would be void and empty" (*Improvement Era*, July 1902, pp. 713–14).

- 1 Timothy 4:1–3. What is one of the signs of the apostasy as given by Paul to Timothy relating to marriage? _____

_____

How is this sign prevalent today? _____

_____

2 Eternal Marriage Is Essential for Exaltation

- D&C 49:15–16. What is the law of God concerning marriage?

- D&C 131:1–4. Who will be exalted to the highest degree in the celestial kingdom? _____

- Speaking of the Lord's law of marriage, President Spencer W. Kimball said: "Brothers and sisters, may I say this is the word of the Lord. It is very, very serious, and there is nobody who should argue with the Lord. He made the earth; He made the people; He knows the conditions; He set the program; and we are not smart enough, any of us, to be able to argue with Him and argue Him out of these important things. He knows what is right and what is true" (" . . . The Matter of Marriage," Salt Lake Institute of Religion devotional address, 22 Oct. 1976, p. 11).

3 Preparing Children to Achieve a Celestial Marriage

- Genesis 18:17–19. Why did the Lord have full confidence in Abraham? _____

What great responsibility rests on priesthood bearers to help their children to prepare for a celestial marriage? _____

- Elder Paul H. Dunn gave the following principles that could be very helpful in effectively teaching children about celestial marriage: "May I testify to all parents in Zion everywhere to the efficacy of these great principles in rearing our children righteously: the power of *precept*, the power of *example*, the power of *love*, and the power of *prayer*" (in Conference Report, Apr. 1974, p. 21; or *Ensign*, May 1974, p. 16; italics added).

- *The Power of Precept in Teaching Children about Celestial Marriage.* D&C 68:28, 31. How, in regard to marriage, can children walk uprightly before the Lord? _____

What are among the greatest "riches of eternity" for a man and wife? _____

_____

Must these things be specifically taught to children? _____

_____

Why? _____

_____

List three or four ways in which parents can teach correct principles about marriage. _____

_____

■ *The Power of Example.* Alma 17:11. Why is example so powerful in teaching? _____

_____

Where will children necessarily look for their example of marriage? _____

_____

■ *The Power of Love.* 1 John 4:19. According to this verse, why do we love God? _____

_____

It has been said that one of the greatest gifts a man can give to his children is to love their mother. Why is this so? _____

_____

Where do children first learn to identify and give love? _____

_____

■ *The Power of Prayer.* James 5:16. Prayer is often described as the "soul's sincere desire." Could there be a better occasion for parents to express their desires concerning the marriages of their children? How, in individual and family prayers, can one help children to achieve a celestial marriage? _____

_____

■ President Ezra Taft Benson noted: "When parents themselves have complied with the ordinances of salvation, when they have set the example of a temple marriage, not only is their own marriage more likely to succeed, but their children are far more likely to follow their example" (in Conference Report, Oct. 1982, pp. 87; or *Ensign*, Nov. 1982, p. 61).

Will It Make a Difference?

Marriage, home, and the family are essential in the quest for perfection. Children need instruction, example, and love to prepare them. Let our children see by our own example that we revere the privilege of proper marriage. Let our children see by the way we treat their mother that we are determined to have a heavenly marriage. Let us teach and train and counsel with our children about the sacred opportunity of marriage.

Quorum Training Suggestions

The purpose of the lesson is to lay down basic principles by which priesthood brethren may effectively teach their children of the eternal marriage covenant. As quorum leaders, illustrate these principles in quorum meeting by relating examples from your own experience and inspiration and by utilizing the experience of exemplary brethren in the quorum. Assign quorum members to study carefully the preceding material so that they will be prepared to discuss how they can help to train their children for proper marriage. Some of the following sugestions for planning the quorum hour might be helpful:

- To encourage individual study, invite the brethren to share what they learned from the personal study guide material. You might ask—

Why is marriage a commandment of God?

What are four important principles that could aid parents in teaching children about eternal marriage?

- Emphasize that although marriage is a commandment of the Lord, none of the Lord's commandments are grievous (see 1 John 5:3). As children are taught, they need to see that marriage is a highway, not an obstacle, to great blessings. Some of the following ideas might be helpful:

Marriage can help a husband or wife overcome selfishness by sharing with spouse and children.

Priesthood is best expressed in service to others. Marriage opens unlimited avenues for service.

When marriage is entered into in the Lord's way, covenants (such as the baptismal covenant and the priesthood covenant) have already been made with the Lord. Keeping these covenants can draw down the powers of heaven to strengthen the marriage bond. The instructor could ask a question such as this: How would a man who keeps his covenants with the Lord be better equipped to be a good husband than one who does not?

▪ There are probably too many in the Church who feel that if they have been married in the temple they have accomplished the will of the Lord. How is this initial step more like a registration for full exaltation than like a graduation? It is written that only those whose marriages are *sealed* by the Holy Spirit of Promise will receive eternal life (see D&C 132:19). On what basis will the Holy Spirit of Promise seal a covenant? (The instructor could discuss this statement by President Joseph Fielding Smith: "Every covenant, contract, bond, obligation, oath, vow, and performance, that man receives through the covenants and blessings of the gospel, is sealed by the Holy Spirit with a promise. The promise is that the blessing will be obtained, if those who seek it are true and faithful to the end. If they are not faithful, then the Holy Spirit will withdraw the blessing, and the promise comes to an end" [*Doctrines of Salvation,* 2:94–95]).

▪ Present these suggestions on how to teach children about the eternal marriage covenant (invite the quorum members to suggest further ideas):

Marry in the temple. (Why is this essential?)

Show love and affection in the home before the children. The working marriage relationship in the home will eloquently teach either negatively or positively.

Have a home evening in which the temple marriage certificate and, perhaps, birth certificates are shown. Explain to the children why the marriage was performed in the temple.

Provide good reading material on marriage, including talks and articles by General Authorities. The conferences issues of the *Ensign* (May and November) are good sources.

Display pictures of temples throughout the home.

Pray that children will be married in the temple, and, in family prayers, thank the Lord in front of children for your own temple marriage.

Teach that eternal marriage and the blessings that go with it are "the very key" to exaltation and that the Lord's way is the only way (see D&C 78:7).

Let children realize the importance of temple ordinances by seeing their parents go frequently to the temple.

▪ The following filmstrips could be obtained from the meetinghouse library and reviewed with the quorum:

The Very Key (OF137, 14 min.)

The House of the Lord (OF098, 12 min.)

▪ Read the words to the song, "The Temple Is a Sacred Place" (*Sing with Me*, B-31). Challenge fathers to see that their children are acquainted with this song.

Spiritual Gifts: Tools of the Priesthood

D&C 46:7–29

Personal Study

Seek to obtain the gifts of the Spirit in your life.

"What man is there of you, whom if his son ask bread, will he give him a stone?

"Or if he ask a fish, will he give him a serpent?

"If ye then, being evil, know how to give good gifts unto your children, how much more shall your Father which is in heaven give good things to them that ask him?" (Matthew 7:9–11).

"God has restored the everlasting Gospel to the earth . . . through this restoration, the gifts, the blessings and the powers that had been bestowed upon believers in ancient days were again enjoyed by the children of men. The burden of the teachings of the Elders of this Church has been to awaken mankind to these solemn and important truths" (George Q. Cannon, *Millennial Star*, 16 Apr. 1894, p. 242).

1 What Are the Spiritual Gifts, and When Are They Bestowed?

A loving Father in Heaven has provided us with spiritual gifts to guide and bless our lives.

■ "The gifts of the Spirit are given by the power of the Holy Ghost. Without the gift of the Holy Ghost, the manifestations of his gifts may not be enjoyed" (Marion G. Romney, in Conference Report, Apr. 1956, p. 72).

■ D&C 46:13–25; Moroni 10:8–16; 1 Corinthians 12:4–10. What are the gifts of the Spirit? _____

_____

- D&C 84:65–72; Mark 16:17–18. What spiritual signs will be evident in the lives of the faithful? _____

_____

- "We are asked if signs follow the believer in our day as in days of old. We answer, they do. The blind see, the lame leap, the deaf hear, the gift of prophecy is manifest, also the gift of healing, the gift of revelation, the gift of tongues and the interpretation of tongues. Jesus said that these signs should follow them that believe. His Church and kingdom always have these signs which follow the believer in all ages when the true Church is in existence" (Brigham Young, in *Latter-day Prophets Speak*, ed. by Daniel H. Ludlow, p. 170).

- Thus, when the Church of Jesus Christ is on the earth, spiritual gifts will be in evidence. When the Church falls into apostasy, these gifts are lost. Note John Wesley's words regarding the apostasy of the early Church:

"It does not appear that these extraordinary gifts of the Holy Ghost were common in the Church for more than two or three centuries. We seldom hear of them after that fatal period when the Emperor Constantine called himself a Christian; . . . From this time they almost totally ceased; . . . The Christians had no more of the Spirit of Christ than the other Heathens. . . . This was the real cause why the extraordinary gifts of the Holy Ghost were no longer to be found in the Christian Church; because the Christians were turned Heathens again, and had only a dead form left" ("The More Excellent Way," Sermon 89, *The Works of John Wesley*, 7:26–27).

- Moroni 10:19. For what reason do these gifts of the Spirit cease to function among men? _____

_____

_____

2 Why Does the Lord Bestow Spiritual Gifts?

- D&C 46:9, 12, 26. What purpose should spiritual gifts serve in our lives? _____

_____

- 1 Corinthians 12:7. Who is benefited by your spiritual gifts besides yourself? _____

_____

- President Brigham Young stated, "Miracles, or these extraordinary manifestations of the power of God, are not for the unbeliever; they are to console the Saints and to strengthen and confirm the faith of those who love, fear, and serve God and not for outsiders" (in Ludlow, p. 172).

- Consider how you might benefit others by appropriately using the following gifts:

1. Faith. In what specific ways might your faith as a priesthood bearer affect for good a wayward Latter-day Saint, members of your ward or branch, or a family member troubled by an undue fear of the evils of today's world?

2. Faith to heal. What positive effects might such a gift have upon a sick person in a family you visit as a home teacher or upon a close relative?

3. Knowledge of the gospel. How might this gift help you help those with serious questions concerning the gospel? How may this gift promote the spiritual welfare of brethren in your quorum?

The exercise of spiritual gifts can bless, edify, and unify us as family members, as priesthood brethren, and as members of the Church.

- D&C 46:7–8. What additional purpose does the Lord give here for bestowing spiritual gifts? _____

_____

- As you receive the gifts listed in Doctrine and Covenants 46:13–25, which ones seem of special value in helping us avoid the false teachings and deceptions of the world? _____

_____

- What gifts could be of special value to a college student as he struggles to discover truth and avoid the false teachings of men?

_____

_____

■ What gifts could be of special importance to a priesthood leader in the selection of quorum members for various assignments or responsibilities or to a bishop in determining the worthiness of members for temple recommends? _____

_____

■ What gifts could be of value in determining the truthfulness of what you are taught? _____

_____

■ What gifts would be of special importance as you seek to give blessings to your wife and children? _____

_____

3 Seek Earnestly the Best Gifts

The Lord has indicated what his greatest gift is and the means whereby we can acquire it.

■ D&C 6:13; 14:7. What is God's greatest gift? _____

_____

How do we obtain this gift? _____

_____

■ 1 Corinthians 12:30–31; D&C 46:8. If you feel that you do not have some spiritual gift, what should your attitude be? _____

_____

■ At the conclusion of Doctrine and Covenants 46, the great revelation on spiritual gifts, the Lord indicates how to acquire the gifts of the Spirit.

D&C 46:28, 30. How do we acquire the gifts of the Spirit? _____

_____

Will It Make a Difference?

President George Q. Cannon stated:

"How many of you, my brethren and sisters, are seeking for these gifts that God has promised to bestow? How many of you, when you bow before your Heavenly Father in your family circle or in your secret places, contend for these gifts to be bestowed upon you? . . .

"There is not that seeking for the gift of healing and for the gift to be healed that there ought to be among the Saints. And so with other gifts and graces that God has placed in His Church for His people. . . .

"Let us seek for these gifts. . . . Let us seek for them with all our might, mind and strength" (*Millennial Star*, 23 Apr. 1894, pp. 260–61).

Quorum Training Suggestions

It would be well to read the counsel given in Doctrine and Covenants 84:73 as you proceed in the quorum discussion on spiritual gifts. Read also verses 65 through 72 of the same section (see also Mark 16:17–18) and discuss the spiritual signs that will be evident in the lives of the faithful.

■ You may wish to summarize the lists of spiritual gifts given in Doctrine and Covenants 46:11–25, 1 Corinthians 12:8–10, and Moroni 10:8–16. List them on the chalkboard.

■ Read President George Q. Cannon's statement found in the section titled "Will It Make a Difference?" and discuss how it relates especially to the lives of priesthood bearers.

■ Review the scriptures in the Topical Guide of the Latter-day Saint edition of the King James Bible under the titles of "God, Gifts of" and "Holy Ghost, Gifts of."

■ Discuss the following statement of Elder Boyd K. Packer as it relates to spiritual gifts: "It isn't seeing is believing; it is believing is seeing" (*That All May Be Edified*, p. 307).)

■ Challenge the quorum to live by the following counsel given by President Marion G. Romney: "Try to live, brethren, so that you can have the Spirit with you in all your activities. Pray for the spirit of discernment that you may hear the promptings of the Spirit and understand them and then pray for courage to do them, to follow the guidance of the Spirit" (in Conference Report, Apr. 1980, p. 71; or *Ensign*, May 1980, p. 50).

Serve God by Serving Your Fellow Beings

D&C 59:5

Personal Study

Perform simple acts of service for your family and those around you.

President Spencer W. Kimball said:

"When I was stake president in Arizona . . . there came to me a never-ending line of people with problems. As I struggled for proper answers to them, I found that by general conference time, I was almost mentally and spiritually exhausted. I felt like a sponge that had been squeezed until it was dry and vacuum-like. Then, we would come to Salt Lake to conference and, after many sessions here, I would return to Arizona still like the sponge, but one that was heavy with wetness and was dripping.

"I have learned that it is by serving that we learn how to serve. When we are engaged in the service of our fellowmen, not only do our deeds assist them, but we put our own problems in a fresher perspective. When we concern ourselves more with others, there is less time to be concerned with ourselves. In the midst of the miracle of serving, there is the promise of Jesus, that by losing ourselves, we find ourselves. (See Matt. 10:39.)" ("Small Acts of Service," *Ensign*, Dec. 1974, p. 2).

1 Why Do You Serve?

Consider first some reasons for service.

- Moses 1:39. In whom does the Lord's "work and glory" center? _____

_____

Whose help does the Lord seek to accomplish his purposes?

_____

- D&C 20:19. Whom are we to love, serve, and worship? _____

_____

In commenting on how to worship properly, Elder Bruce R. McConkie stated: "The Lord is saying to us, 'Here is how you worship. You worship by emulation. You worship by imitation. You worship by patterning your life after mine. You worship by magnifying me and my course, by doing what I have done' " ("How to Worship," *Speeches of the Year*, 20 July 1971 [Provo, Utah: Brigham Young University Press, 1971], p. 6).

- 1 John 4:8. What does John identify as a characteristic attribute of God? _____

_____

What, then, is a most important attribute to emulate as you strive to worship God? _____

_____

Can you truly love, serve, and worship God or become like him without serving his children? _____

_____

- Mark 10:44. Why was the greatest leader of earth also the greatest "servant of all"?

- President David O. McKay spoke of the "noblest calling in life" as follows:

"It is evident that man's noblest work must be impregnated with the greatest of all forces—Love. . . . This power must be directed not for selfish purposes, nor to achieve personal ends. . . .

"The noblest calling in life, then, must be one in which the attribute of love will be manifest, not for self, but for others. . . .

". . . *The most worthy calling in life . . . is that in which man can serve best his fellowman. . . .*

"The noblest aim in life is to strive to make other lives better and happier" ("The Noblest Calling in Life," *Instructor*, March 1961, pp. 73–74).

Why will selfishness or concern only for self ultimately result in unhappiness? _____

• Matthew 10:39. How can we lose our life in service to others?

President Marion G. Romney observed: "We lose our life by serving and lifting others. By so doing we experience the only true and lasting happiness. Service is not something we endure on this earth so we can earn the right to live in the celestial kingdom. Service is the very fiber of which an exalted life in the celestial kingdom is made" (in Conference Report, Oct. 1982, p. 135; or *Ensign,,* Nov. 1982, p. 93).

If serving adds substance to your life, how does this better enable you to bless others? _____

Strive always to sense the importance of learning and loving to serve.

2 Whom Do You Serve?

• President Harold B. Lee recounted the following incident:

"It was just before the dedication of the Los Angeles Temple. We were all preparing for that great occasion. It was something new in my life, when along about three or four o'clock in the morning, I enjoyed an experience that I think was not a dream, but it must have been a vision. It seemed that I was witnessing a great spiritual gathering, where men and women were standing up, two or three at a time, and speaking in tongues. The spirit was so unusual. I seemed to have heard the voice of President David O. McKay say, 'If you want to love God, you have to learn to love and serve the people. That is the way you show your love for God' " (in Conference Report, Apr. 1973, p. 180; or *Ensign,* July 1973, p. 124).

• John 4:11, 20–21. Perhaps one could serve without loving his brother, but can one love and yet not serve? When do we best demonstrate our love for God? _____

- Mosiah 2:17. Whom does King Benjamin say we really serve when we serve our fellow beings? _____

_____

Why is this so? _____

_____

- Ephesians 5:25; 6:4. Whom is it your reponsibility to serve first? _____

_____

- In addition, you are to serve members of the Church. Ponder President Kimball's words:

"God does notice us, and he watches over us. But it is usually through another person that he meets our needs. Therefore, it is vital that we serve each other in the kingdom. The people of the Church need each other's strength, support, and leadership in a community of believers as an enclave of disciples. In the Doctrine and Covenants we read about how important it is to ' . . . succor the weak, lift up the hands which hang down, and strengthen the feeble knees.' (D&C 81:5.) So often, our acts of service consist of simple encouragement or of giving mundane help with mundane tasks, but what glorious consequences can flow from mundane acts and from small but deliberate deeds!" ("Small Acts of Service," *Ensign*, Dec. 1974, p. 5).

- Matthew 25:34–40. Whom else are we to love and serve?

_____

Did the Savior teach us to confine our acts of service only to those of our family, or the Church, or those we like or who like us? _____

_____

- Consider this true personal experience of an early pioneer as an example of whom we should serve:

"Many years ago in a small town in the southern part of the state of Utah, my great grandmother was called to be the president of the Relief Society. During this period of our Church's history there existed a very bitter and antagonistic spirit between the Mormons and the Gentiles.

"In my great grandmother's ward one of the young sisters married a Gentile boy. This of course did not please either the Mormons or the Gentiles very much. In the course of time this young couple gave birth to a child. Unfortunately the mother became so ill in the process of childbirth that she was unable to care for her baby. Upon learning of this woman's condition, great grandmother immediately went to the homes of the sisters in the ward and asked them if they would take a turn going into the home of this young couple to care for the baby. One by one these women refused and so the responsibility fell completely upon her.

"She would arise early in the morning, walk what was a considerable distance to the home of this young couple where she would bathe and feed the baby, gather all that needed to be laundered and take it with her to her home. There she would launder it and then return with it the next day. Great grandmother had been doing this for some time when one morning she felt too weak and sick to go and perform the service that had become her custom. However, as she lay in bed she realized that if she didn't go the child would not be provided for. She mustered all her strength and went. After performing this service she, and I suppose only with the help of the Lord, was able to return to her home and upon entering her living room, collapsed into a large chair and immediately fell into a deep sleep. She said that as she slept she felt as if she were consumed by a fire that would melt the very marrow of her bones. She began to dream and dreamed that she was bathing the Christ child and glorying in what a great privilege it would have been to have bathed the Son of God. Then the voice of the Lord spoke to her saying, 'Inasmuch as ye have done it unto the least of these, ye have done it unto me."

3 How Can You Serve?

As a priesthood bearer, how much of your time is actually spent in performing ordinances, teaching Church classes, or in spectacular service activities? _____

_____

■ As you ponder *how* you can better serve, consider this thought-provoking counsel from President Kimball:

"So often, our acts of service consist of simple encouragement or of giving mundane help with mundane tasks, but what glorious consequences can flow from mundane acts and from small but deliberate deeds! . . .

". . . We should reflect periodically on the qualities of those who have served, led, and taught us. If you were to select just two or three individuals in your life who have been most influential, what specifically did they do that was helpful to you at critical or important times in your life?

"On reflecting for a few moments, you are apt to conclude that such a person really cared for you, that he or she took time for you, or that he or she taught you something you needed to know. Reflect now upon your performance, as I do on my own, as to whether or not we now embody in our own ministry those same basic attributes. It is less likely in stirring through one's memories that someone will be remembered because that individual was particularly influential because of a technique. Most often someone has served and helped us by giving us love and understanding, by taking time to assist us, and by showing us the way through the light of their own example. I cannot stress enough, therefore, the importance of our doing these same things for those who now depend upon us, just as we have depended upon others to serve us in the past by special leadership and special teaching.

"If we focus on simple principles and simple acts of service, we will see that organizational lines soon lose some of their significance" ("Small Acts of Service," *Ensign*, Dec. 1974, pp. 5–7).

You Can Make a Difference

As you evaluate your service in your family, the Church, your quorum, and your neighborhood, how can you better serve? Consider the circumstances and needs of those you might serve. Have you considered helping by a word of encouragement, by helping maneuver a couch through the door, by a warm meal, by a brief visit, by the gift of your attention?

What further ideas can you list for blessing those around you?

Quorum Training Suggestions

Select some scriptures to discuss from the Topical Guide of the Latter-day Saint edition of the King James Bible under the headings "Serve" and "Service."

▪ You may wish to use President Spencer W. Kimball's article entitled "Small Acts of Service" in the *Ensign*, Dec. 1974, pp. 2–7.

▪ Discuss President Kimball's statement from that article: "The more we serve our fellowmen in appropriate ways, the more substance there is to our souls. We become more significant individuals as we serve others. We become more substantive as we serve others—indeed, it is easier to 'find' ourselves because there is so much more of us to find" (p. 2).

▪ Read Matthew 25:31–40, then discuss with quorum members some modern applications of the Savior's instruction.

▪ Invite quorum members to suggest ways in which we can serve others.

▪ Discuss some practical and simple acts of service that quorum members might render in their family, the Church, and their neighborhood, according to the needs of those involved. Challenge the quorum members to be more thoughtful and more aware of others' needs and to perform simple acts of service for those around them.

▪ Discuss the following statement by Elder Loren C. Dunn: " . . . you've got to somehow be involved in helping and strengthening the lives of others. All of the jobs we hold in the Church aim us toward each other so that we can help and strengthen and assist each other. We don't get saved as spectators. We get saved as participants" ("Watch Therefore: For Ye Know Not What Hour," devotional address, Salt Lake Institute of Religion, 10 Nov. 1972, pp. 7–8).

Strengthen the Bonds of Your Family

D&C 75:28

Personal Study

Strengthen family ties.

Concerning the eternal nature of the family, President Joseph F. Smith said: "Our associations (family) are not exclusively intended for this life. . . . We form associations and relations for time and all eternity. Our affections and our desires are found fitted and prepared to endure. . . . Who . . . besides the Latter-day Saints . . . contemplate the thought that beyond the grave we will continue in the family organization? the father, the mother, the children recognizing each other in the relations which they owe to each other and in which they stand to each other? this family organization being a unit in the great and perfect organization of God's work, and all destined to continue throughout time and eternity?" (*Gospel Doctrine*, p. 277).

Do you know the strength you can draw from family members when you keep close to them? Are there brothers or sisters or other family members who could use your help? Why did God organize his mortal children into families?

---

1 We Have an Obligation to Care for Our Parents

■ Exodus 20:12. By the time of the Savior, Israel was no longer keeping this commandment. President J. Reuben Clark, Jr., said:

"Israel had gone so astray that whenever a son or daughter wanted to rid himself or herself of the obligation of caring for father or mother, he proceeded to say to father or mother, 'From this time on,'—this was the effect of it—'I repudiate my obligation, and whatever I give to you is a gift. . . .'

"Now I repeat to you, brethren, that command is without restriction. It runs to Israel, in my view, wherever Israel may be, and its promise as well as its command follows Israel in whatever land they may reside.

" 'Honour thy father and thy mother: that thy days may be long upon the land which the Lord thy god giveth thee' " (pamphlet, "Fundamentals of the Welfare Program"; compare Mark 7:9–13).

■ Regarding modern disobedience to this commandment, President Marion G. Romney stated, "Today the temptation, and all too often the practice, is to turn Father and Mother over to the public welfare and let the state take care of them" (in Conference Report, Oct. 1974, p. 168). What kinds of spiritual and emotional scars may be caused by such a practice? _____

_____

What are the effects on the self-esteem of both children and parents if parents are deliberately abandoned to the state? _____

_____

What would be the effects on family bonds? _____

_____

■ Elder Vaughn J. Featherstone said:

"Some years ago . . . Elder Matthew Cowley said, 'A mother can take care of seven children, but seven children will not later take care of that same mother.' . . .

"Let us review the program, the Lord's program, for the care of our senior Saints. First, the responsibility rests with the individual to do all he or she can to be a contributing member of society and of the Church, and give service to friends and children and loved ones. . . .

"Now, second, the family should do all they can do. Those who have mothers and fathers who are confined should care for them by furnishing those soul needs such as love, care, and tenderness. . . .

"Now, third, after the individual and family have used all their resources, then the Church is called in to assist" (in Conference Report, Oct. 1974, pp. 37–39; or *Ensign,* Nov. 1974, pp. 29–30).

What are some of the excuses children may give to rationalize away their responsibility to care for their parents? _____

_____

Even though families may be forced to turn to outside help after exhausting their own worldly resources, what other kinds of support can they always give? _____

_____

What can be the effects and value of this kind of support? _____

_____

- Mormon 9:31. What implications does this verse have to the family? _____

_____

Is any mortal a completely perfect parent? _____

_____

Does any parent have enough love, or patience, or wisdom, or maturity all of the time? _____

_____

Why is it so important to avoid condemning our parents for their human imperfections? _____

_____

In what ways should we be eternally grateful to our parents?

_____

- This poem by Carol Lynn Pearson perhaps expresses the yearning of every parent:

Look—
Your little fist
Fits mine
Like the pit
In a plum.

I think,
In the time
Before remembering,
These two hands
Clasped companionably,
Then parted.

Help me, child.
Forgive me
When I fail you.
I'm your mother,
True,

But in the end
Merely an older equal
Doing her faltering best
For a dear
Small friend.

("Mother to Child," from *The Search*, by Carol Lynn Pearson. Copyright © 1970 by Carol Lynn Pearson. Reprinted by permission of Doubleday & Company, Inc.)

---

2 We Have an Obligation to Stay Close to Our Brothers and Sisters

■ Elder Marvin J. Ashton stated a goal we should strive for in our family relationships:

"Have family members realize that a brother can be a friend, and that a sister can be a friend, and that a father and a mother can be more than parents, they can be friends. . . .

" . . . Catch the wisdom and the inspiration of building a home so that our members in that sacred unit can look upon a father and say, 'He is my best friend,' or 'My mother is more than a mother, she is my friend.' When we realize that parents and family members can be more than blood relations and are in very deed friends, then we will have a glimpse of how our Heavenly Father wants us to live, not only as brothers and sisters but as very close friends" (in Conference Report, Oct. 1969, pp. 28–29; or *Improvement Era*, Dec. 1969, p. 51). If brothers and sisters are going to be very close friends, how interested must they be in each other's welfare? _____

Why must they get together as often as possible to strengthen their love and family bonds? _____

■ Mosiah 4:14–15. When we permit our children to fight and quarrel with one another, what are we allowing them to do?

Even though disagreements are normal in families because of the many differences in age, wants, and needs, we must not allow such disagreements to degenerate into what? _____

Why, if parents sit by and allow their children to fight and quarrel, are they actually encouraging such behavior? _____

_____

We should teach children positive ways of behaving in order to prevent the quarreling. What kinds of preventive behavior does verse 15 say to teach children? _____

- 1 Nephi 7:19–22. What did Nephi immediately do as his brothers sought reconciliation? _____

What does Nephi's example teach about the way family members should act toward each other? _____

- Genesis 32:1–11. As Jacob sought reconciliation with Esau, what was he willing to sacrifice in order to be one with his brother again? _____

In the eternal perspective, was it worth the price? _____

What was Jacob feeling at this time? _____

Why must we avoid letting such feelings keep us from trying to reconcile differences within our families? _____

- Genesis 33:1–11. How strong were the true, deepest feelings between these two brothers? _____

Does the feeling of being a brother or sister ever leave us? _____

Why was it so important for Esau to accept the gifts of love from his brother? _____

Why is it so vital to be able to receive as well as to give love in a family? _____

■ Genesis 45:1–15. How did Joseph show that he cared for his father and brothers? _____

_____

What principles from Joseph's example could you better apply in your relationship with your family? _____

_____

■ The Prophet Joseph Smith's deep feelings for his brother Hyrum show what kinds of feelings can be developed between brothers and sisters if they are willing to try: "I love him with that love that is stronger than death, for I never had an occasion to rebuke him, nor he me" (*History of The Church of Jesus Christ of Latter-day Saints*, 2:338).

3 Family Organizations Help Strengthen Family Bonds

■ In order to strengthen and achieve our potential as eternal families, we become organized into three distinct family organizations: (1) the immediate family organization; (2) the grandparent family organization; (3) the ancestral family organization. President Ezra Taft Benson described the immediate and grandparent family units and their purposes: "Our responsibility to organize as families at the immediate level begins when a couple is married. The grandparent family organization develops as children from the immediate family marry and have children. Through such family organizations, every family in the Church should become actively involved in missionary work, family preparedness, genealogy and temple work, teaching the gospel, and cultural and social activities" (in Conference Report, Sept.–Oct. 1978, p. 41; or *Ensign*, Nov. 1978, p. 30). These family organizations can exist to meet all of the spiritual and temporal needs of each family member. Each family therefore becomes stronger as family members work together to bring about the individual salvation of each member.

■ President Benson also said:

"Ancestral family organizations are comprised of descendants of a common ancestral couple [and are for coordinating] genealogical activity on common ancestral lines. When ancestral family organizations deviate from this major objective and seek primarily to provide social, cultural or other types of activities, they take over the legitimate domain of the immediate and grandparent organizations. . . .

". . . Ancestral organizations exist only for the coordination of genealogical activity, which includes family histories. Once this function has been accomplished the ancestral family organization might well be dissolved . . . in favor of the immediate and grandparent organizations" (in Conference Report, Sept.–Oct. 1978, p. 42; or *Ensign*, Nov. 1978, p. 31).

What are the advantages of concentrating our efforts within the immediate and grandparent organizations? _____

_____

If we had well organized social, cultural, and spiritual activities within our own families, how would family bonds be affected?

_____

Will It Make a Difference?

The Prophet Joseph Smith wrote of his brother: "There was Brother Hyrum who next took me by the hand—a natural brother. Thought I to myself, Brother Hyrum, what a faithful heart you have got! Oh may the Eternal Jehovah crown eternal blessings upon your head, as a reward for the care you have had for my soul! O how many are the sorrows we have shared together. . . . Hyrum, thy name shall be written in the book of the law of the Lord, for those who come after thee to look upon, that they may pattern after thy works" (*History of The Church*, 5:107–08). Resolve to pattern your ties with all the members of your family after those of Joseph and Hyrum Smith (see D&C 135:3).

Quorum Training Suggestions

This lesson provides an opportunity to emphasize the importance of family ties. Emphasize that we must reach out to family members and that families need to become independent, self-sustaining sources of support and spirituality for each member.

■ Encourage individual study by asking such questions as these: How long are we obligated to care for our parents? What kinds of friendships and loyalties should we develop with our brothers and sisters?

■ Discuss how open, honest, and spiritual family get-togethers can be since we know each other's weaknesses and are therefore able to be more real with each other.

■ Assign a quorum member in advance to present some practical suggestions for strengthening bonds between brothers and sisters. Following his remarks, ask the quorum members for any additional suggestions they might have.

■ There are many articles and statements in the *Ensign,* January 1977, that concern the "why" and the "how" of family organizations, and how such organizations can help strengthen family bonds.

■ Some time in this quorum training session may be devoted to having selected quorum members explain to the quorum particular traditions of their families or ways that they have found to organize themselves to accomplish the family duties for which they are responsible.

■ Discuss ways in which the following counsel by President Spencer W. Kimball could be applied: "It is important for us . . . to cultivate in our own family a sense that we belong together eternally, that whatever changes outside our home, there are fundamental aspects of our relationship which will never change. We ought to encourage our children to know their relatives. We need to talk to them, make an effort to correspond with them, visit them, join family organizations, etc." (in Conference Report, Oct. 1974, p. 161; or in *Ensign,* Nov. 1974, p. 112).

■ To illustrate the importance of strong family ties and their impact on society, show the filmstrip, "The Family and the Home" (OF133).

"It Is the Same"

D&C 1:38

Personal Study

Recognize and accept the voice of the Lord's authorized servants.

(Note to the instructor: Use this lesson to discuss the messages presented by the Brethren in April general conference. Schedule this discussion as close to conference as is convenient.)

- Elder George Albert Smith noted: "When we are instructed by the President of this Church, we believe he tells us what the Lord would have us do. To us it is something more than just the advice of man" (in Conference Report, Oct. 1930, p. 66).

- D&C 1:38. What did the Lord say about the words of his authorized servants? _____

_____

- What are some of the settings in which the Lord's words come to us through his chosen servants? _____

_____

- President Harold B. Lee said: "How in the world is the Lord going to get over to you what He wants you to do if you are not there when He says it, and you do not take the time to read it after it has been said?" (*Stand Ye In Holy Places*, p. 159).

- Many members of the Church do not live close to Church headquarters or to locations where general conference is conveniently broadcast by means of radio or television. All members, however, do have access to the words of the prophets, Apostles, and other leaders through printed materials. Speaking of the importance of reading the written addresses, Elder Spencer W. Kimball admonished: "I hope you will get your copy . . . and underline the pertinent thoughts and keep it with you for continual reference. No text or volume outside the standard works of the Church should have such a prominent place on your personal library shelves" ("In the World But Not Of It," *Brigham Young University Speeches of the Year*, 14 May 1968 [Provo, Utah: Brigham Young University Press, 1968], p. 3).

■ What have you recently read from the writings and speeches of the Lord's authorized servants? _____

_____

What could you do to become more familiar with the *voice* of God's servants? _____

_____

■ President Ezra Taft Benson has said, "Therefore, the most important reading we can do is any of the words of the Prophet contained each week in the Church Section of the *Deseret News* and any words of the Prophet contained each month in our Church magazines. Our marching orders for each six months are found in the general conference addresses which are printed in the *Ensign* magazine" ("Fourteen Fundamentals in Following the Prophets," *1980 Devotional Speeches of the Year*, [Provo, Utah: Brigham Young University Press, 1981], p. 27).

Quorum Training Suggestions

Your purpose as a quorum leader is to encourage the quorum members to study the conference addresses published in the *Ensign* and to incorporate the teachings of the conference in their personal lives. Prayerfully select the topics for quorum discussion that will best meet the needs of your particular quorum or group.

■ Encourage quorum members to bring their copies of the conference edition of the *Ensign* to quorum meeting to use as a resource for discussion.

■ Select several quotations that are of particular value in adding further understanding to the scriptures and share these with quorum members. Invite others to do the same.

■ Cite the following statement by Elder Packer and discuss its relationship to following proper channels of authority in the Church: "Revelation is always vertical. There is no horizontal revelation in the Church. It is all vertical" ("Follow the Rule," *1977 Devotional Speeches of the Year* [Provo, Utah: Brigham Young University Speeches of the Year, 1977), p. 19). (Elder Packer's meaning is that revelation comes *down* appropriate channels, from one higher level to a lower level. No one receives revelation for an area over which he has no authority.)

- Assign several quorum members to make a list of the topics which have been addressed during the conference and the frequency with which they were mentioned. Discuss general themes that may have been evident during this conference. The topical index to the conference talks that appears on the contents page of the *Ensign* conference edition will help with this assignment.

- Invite quorum members to share ideas for personal or family improvement projects which were generated as a result of the counsel given during conference.

- Invite a quartet to sing the hymn, "Come, Listen to a Prophet's Voice" (*Hymns,* no. 46). Discuss the meaning of the words as they relate to D&C 1:38.

- Demonstrate how ideas gleaned from the conference addresses can be filed on cards or in folders for use in future teaching (including home evening) and speaking assignments.

- Point out that one of the three basic purposes of the Church is to "perfect the saints" (the other two being to redeem the dead and to proclaim the gospel). Ask quorum members to point out ways in which following the counsel given at conference can assist us in becoming perfected. Relate this to the following statement by Elder Marion G. Romney: "We have heard enough truth and direction in this conference to bring us into the presence of God if we would follow it" (in Conference Report, April 1954, pp. 132–33).

"Give Heed unto All His Words"

D&C 21:4

Personal Study

Resolve to give heed to all the words of God's servants.

(Note to the instructor: Use this lesson to discuss the messages presented by the Brethren in October general conference. Schedule the discussion as close to conference as is convenient.)

- President Ezra Taft Benson has pointed out that "the most important prophet, so far as you and I are concerned, is the one living in our day and age to whom the Lord is currently revealing His will for us" ("Fourteen Fundamentals in Following the Prophets" *1980 Devotional Speeches of the Year* [Provo, Utah: Brigham Young University Press, 1981], p. 27).

- Why is the living prophet so important? _____

_____

- D&C 21:1–5. What did the Lord command the Church concerning his chief Apostle, the prophet? _____

_____

- Just as many of the Jews rejected Jesus in favor of their dead prophets (see Matthew 3:9; 19:7; John 8:33), in similar fashion many people throughout history have preferred the dead prophets to the living ones. Elder Spencer W. Kimball observed that "even in the Church many are prone to garnish the sepulchres of yesterday's prophets and mentally stone the living ones" (*Instructor*, Aug. 1960, p. 257).

How well do you follow the counsel of the Lord's living prophet? Are you selective in what you give heed to?

- Elder Neal A. Maxwell has said: "Following the living prophets is something that must be done in all seasons and circumstances. We must be like President Marion G. Romney, who humbly said, ' . . . I have never hesitated to follow the counsel of the Authorities of the Church even though it crossed my social, professional, and political life' (*Conference Report*, April

1941, p. 123). There are, or will be, moments when prophetic declarations collide with our pride or our seeming personal interests. . . . Do I believe in the living prophet even when he speaks on matters affecting me and my specialty directly? Or do I stop sustaining the prophet when his words fall in my territory? if the latter, the prophet is without honor in *our* country!" (*Things As They Really Are*, p. 73).

- Luke 16:19–31. What message does this parable give us regarding the importance of following the living prophet? _____

- President Harold B. Lee wisely observed that "the trouble with us today [is that] there are too many of us who put question marks instead of periods after what the Lord says" (in Conference Report, Oct. 1972, p. 130; or *Ensign*, Jan. 1973, p. 108).

- President Wilford Woodruff gave the following assurance, "I say . . . the Lord will never permit me nor any other man who stand as the President of this Church, to lead you astray" (*The Discourses of Wilford Woodruff*, p. 212). Why does such a pronouncement from a prophet of God give us security in giving heed to the words of the living prophets? _____

- At the conclusion of one general conference, President Kimball said: "Now as we conclude this general conference, let us all give heed to what was said to us. Let us assume the counsel given applies to *us*, to me. Let us hearken to those we sustain as prophets and seers, as well as the other brethren, as if our eternal life depended upon it, because it does!" (Spencer W. Kimball, in Conference Report, Apr. 1978, p. 117; or *Ensign*, May 1978, p. 77).

Quorum Training Suggestions

"Your purpose as a quorum leader is to encourage the quorum members to study the conference addresses published in the *Ensign* and to incorporate the teachings of the conference in their personal lives. Prayerfully select those topics for quorum discussion which will best meet the needs of your particular quorum or group.

■ Encourage quorum members to bring their copies of the most recent conference edition of the *Ensign* or the *Church News* to quorum meeting to use as a resource for discussion.

■ Read the words to the hymn "We Thank Thee, O God, for a Prophet," (*Hymns*, no. 196), and emphasize the importance not only of praying for the prophet, but of showing the Lord how grateful we are by following the counsel of His servants.

■ Using President Lee's comment about periods and question marks as a reference point, compile a list of direct admonitions given by the speakers at conference.

■ Emphasize the importance of personal preparation for conference (and other Church meetings) by discussing the following statement from Elder Packer: "In a few days there opens another general conference of the Church. The servants of the Lord will counsel us. You may listen with anxious ears and hearts, or you may turn that counsel aside. . . . What you shall gain will depend not so much upon their preparation *of* the message as upon your preparation *for* them" ("Follow the Brethren," Brigham Young University *Speeches of the Year*, 23 March 1965, p. 10).

■ Read Doctrine and Covenants 68:3–4 along with Doctrine and Covenants 21:1–5, pointing out how the words of the prophets are *scripture* to us. Discuss President J. Reuben Clark, Jr.'s observation that "we can tell when the speakers are 'moved upon by the Holy Ghost' only when we, ourselves, are 'moved upon by the Holy Ghost' " ("When Are Church Leader's Words Entitled to Claim of Scripture?" *Church News*, 31 July 1954, p. 9).

■ Discuss the counsel given in conference in light of the following observation by Elder Boyd K. Packer: "For some reason, we expect to hear, particularly in welfare sessions, some ominous great predictions of calamities to come. Instead, we hear quiet counsel on ordinary things which, if followed, will protect us in times of great calamity" (in Conference Report, Apr. 1982, p. 172; or *Ensign*, May 1982, p. 85).

■ Read the ninth article of faith, and discuss its significance in terms of living prophets and dead prophets.

■ Discuss how general conferences are sources of revelation. Use the following statement by President Joseph Fielding Smith: "It is my humble opinion that we are receiving counsel by inspiration, or revelation, at every general conference of the

Church. Would it not be wise for the members of the Church to pay more heed to these counsels and prepare ourselves for more to come?" (*Answers to Gospel Questions,* 2:205).

■ Invite quorum members to suggest some of the things they learned from conference or identify their favorite addresses and why these were significant to them.

Performing Priesthood Blessings and Ordinances

Appendix 1

The following are guidelines for performing priesthood ordinances.

Publications that give instructions about ordinances and forms of prayer other than those authorized by the First Presidency are not approved.

Baptism and the blessing of the sacrament have a set wording. Other ordinances performed outside the temple do not.

All ordinances have some elements in common. They are performed in the name of Jesus Christ and by the authority of the priesthood. Brethren performing ordinances should live so as to have the guidance of the Holy Ghost. They should seek to use appropriate language to express the thoughts placed in their minds by the Spirit.

When ordinances requiring the Melchizedek Priesthood are performed, only those who hold the Melchizedek Priesthood should stand in the circle. Before ordinances are performed, parents or individuals involved should be counseled in a kindly way so that those who participate are worthy holders of the proper priesthood. The only exception to this policy is that a father, at his request, may hold his child when it is named and blessed. (See *General Handbook of Instructions*, 1983, p. 130.)

---

1 The Naming and Blessing of Children

- Take the child in your arms, or, if it is an older child, place your hands on his head.
- Address our Heavenly Father, as in prayer.
- State the authority (Melchizedek Priesthood) by which the ordinance is performed.
- Give the child a name.
- Add such words of blessing as the Spirit dictates.
- Close in the name of Jesus Christ.

279

2 Baptism

- Stand in the water with the person to be baptized.

- It is suggested that a good way to balance the weight of the one being baptized is to hold the person's right wrist in your left hand, and then have the person hold your left wrist with his left hand.

- Raise your right arm to the square.

- Call the person by his full name, and say the baptismal prayer (see D&C 20:73).

- Place your right hand high on the person's back. Let him hold his nose with his right hand if he wishes. Completely immerse him.

- Help the person come up out of the water.

3 Confirmation and Bestowal of the Holy Ghost

- Lay your hands on the head of the person to be confirmed.

- Call the person by his full name.

- State the authority (Melchizedek Priesthood) by which the ordinance is performed.

- Confirm the person a member of The Church of Jesus Christ of Latter-day Saints.

- Bestow the Holy Ghost by saying to the person being confirmed: "Receive the Holy Ghost."

- Add such words of blessing as the Spirit dictates.

- Close in the name of Jesus Christ.

4 Sacrament

- Blessing on the bread: Kneel and say the prayer in Doctrine and Covenants 20:77.

- Blessing on the water: Kneel and say the prayer in Doctrine and Covenants 20:79, substituting the word *water* for the word *wine*.

5 Conferring the Priesthood and Ordaining to an Office Therein

- Lay your hands on the person's head.

- Call the person by his full name.

- State the authority (Melchizedek Priesthood or Aaronic Priesthood) by which the ordinance is performed.

- Unless it has previously been conferred, confer the Melchizedek or Aaronic Priesthood.

- Ordain to the specific office in the priesthood, and bestow all rights, powers, and authority pertaining to the office.

- Add such words of blessing as the Spirit dictates.

- Close in the name of Jesus Christ.

6 Consecrating Oil

Olive oil should be consecrated before it is used to anoint the sick. A good grade of olive oil should be used. No other kind of oil should be used. Those holding the Melchizedek Priesthood should consecrate it and set it apart for its holy purposes. One man alone can do this.

- Hold the open container of olive oil.

- Address our Heavenly Father as in prayer.

- State the authority (Melchizedek Priesthood) by which the oil is consecrated.

- Consecrate the oil (not the container), and set it apart for the blessing and anointing of the sick and afflicted.

- Close in the name of Jesus Christ.

7 Administering to the Sick

This ordinance is done in two parts.

Anointing

One Melchizedek Priesthood holder anoints with oil as follows:

- Anoint the head of the sick person, using a small amount of oil.

281

- Lay your hands on the person's head.

- Call the person by name.

- State the authority (Melchizedek Priesthood) by which the ordinance is performed.

- State that you are anointing with consecrated oil.

- Close in the name of Jesus Christ.

Sealing the Anointing

Two or more Melchizedek Priesthood holders lay their hands on the head of the sick person. One of them speaks as follows:

- Call the sick person by name.

- State the authority (Melchizedek Priesthood) by which the ordinance is performed.

- Seal the anointing that has already taken place.

- Add such words of blessing as the Spirit dictates.

- Close in the name of Jesus Christ.

---

8 Dedication of Graves

Graves should be dedicated by a Melchizedek Priesthood holder as approved by the bishop after consulting with the family. It is done as follows:

- Address our Heavenly Father as in prayer.

- State the authority (Melchizedek Priesthood) by which the ordinance is performed.

- Dedicate and consecrate the burial plot as the resting place for the body of the person who died (use his full name).

- Pray to the Lord, if the Spirit prompts you to do so, that this spot of earth may be hallowed and protected until the time the body is resurrected and reunited with the spirit.

- Ask the Lord to comfort the family, and add such words of comfort as the Spirit dictates.

- Close in the name of Jesus Christ.

9 Father's Blessings on Children

Fathers should be encouraged to give a father's blessing to their children on such occasions as their going into the military or away from home to school or on missions and on other appropriate occasions.

A father's blessing may be recorded in family records, but it is not to be preserved in the archives of the Church. The procedure for giving a father's blessing is the same as the procedures outlined for blessings of comfort and counsel.

10 Blessings of Comfort and Counsel

On special occasions, Melchizedek Priesthood holders may, on their own initiative or when called upon, give special blessings of comfort and counsel as circumstances suggest. Situations that may call for such blessings include times of stress or trial or times of mental, emotional, or physical difficulty, such as when there has been a death in the family, or when a person is preparing to be hospitalized for an operation. If there is an illness, the blessing may be part of the ordinance of administration to the sick. Otherwise, it may be a blessing of comfort.

There are times when individuals should work out their problems without a special blessing. No clearly defined rule can be made for what to do in every case except to seek inspiration from the Lord.

This is the usual pattern for giving a blessing of this kind:

- Lay your hands on the head of the person to be blessed.

- Call the person by his full name.

- State the authority (Melchizedek Priesthood) by which the blessing is given.

- Give such words of thanks, counsel, exhortation, blessing, and promises as the Spirit dictates.

- Close in the name of Jesus Christ.

Some Counsel
to Consider

"When you receive an ordinance, whether it be baptism, the sacrament, an ordination or setting apart, an endowment or a sealing, you receive an obligation" (Boyd K. Packer,

"Ordinances," *1980 Devotional Speeches of the Year* [Provo, Utah: Brigham Young University Press, 1981], p. 16).

"You priesthood holders . . . should appreciate that you have the great privilege of holding the priesthood, and that as you accepted the priesthood you made a covenant with the Lord that you would honor the priesthood and live worthy of it.

"It is so important that you keep yourselves clean and pure and not participate in any vulgar or unclean or unholy practices. . . . Be sure that you are worthy, that your hands are clean and your hearts are pure, that you have done nothing during the week that would make you unworthy" (N. Eldon Tanner, in Conference Report, Apr. 1975, p. 113; also in *Ensign,* May 1975, p. 76).

Supplemental Readings

Welfare Responsibilities of the Priesthood Quorums

By Elder Gordon B. Hinckley,
in Conference Report, Oct. 1977

I would like to tell you of an experience I had many years ago while serving as a stake president. I received a telephone call from a bishop who reported that a husband and wife in his ward were seeking a divorce. Having gone beyond all limits of prudence in installment buying, they now argued endlessly over money matters.

The husband in his employment faced the constant threat of garnishment of wages, and the wife refused to remain at home because of the harassment of bill collectors. Furthermore, they soon would be without a home because they had received notice of foreclosure. In their mutual frustration, he shouted at her for being a poor manager, and she at him for being a poor provider.

The bishop reported that he had taken care of their emergency needs, and that he had counseled with them at length in an effort to restore the love and respect they once had known. He had reached the point where he felt he had done all he could to help them.

I asked whether the man belonged to a priesthood quorum. The bishop replied that he was an elder. That evening the quorum presidency responded to a call to meet with the bishop. On a confidential basis the problem was outlined. Then the quorum presidency suggested the names of a committee who might work with the family. As I recall, the committee included a lawyer, a credit manager, and an accountant, all members of that quorum.

The couple was then called in and asked whether they would be willing to put their financial affairs in the hands of these brethren. They broke into tears at this sign of help with the burden they had found too heavy to bear themselves.

The men nominated for the committee were then approached and each agreed to serve. What they discovered was a dismal picture indeed. Obligated monthly payments totaled almost twice the monthly income. But these men were accustomed to dealing with problems of this kind. They analyzed the situation thoroughly.

They found, for instance, two cars where one could do at the price of a little inconvenience. There were other things that could be dispensed with.

Then, with the facts before them, they called on the various creditors. They did what the beleaguered husband could not do for himself. They spoke the language of the creditors, and worked out a plan of payment with each. They gave the creditors the assurance that they had control of the assets of the family, and with this assurance and the evident expertise of the committee, the creditors were willing to go along.

While in the process of managing the family's affairs, the committee effectively taught principles of budgeting, financial responsibility, and money management. The problem was not cured in a day. It required many months. But miracles happened. A new and satisfying discipline came into the lives of the husband and wife. The creditors received their just due. The home was saved, and—most important—love and peace returned to that home.

I have recalled this experience to emphasize a principle. That principle was defined by President J. Reuben Clark many years ago:

"The priesthood quorums in their extending of relief have not the obligation prescribed to the bishop. But the relationship of the priesthood, [and] the spirit of lofty unselfish brotherhood which it carries with it, do require that they individually and as quorums exert their utmost means of power to rehabilitate, spiritually and temporally, their erring and unfortunate brethren. In his temporal administrations, the bishop looks at every needy person as a temporary problem, caring for them until they can help themselves: the priesthood must look at their needy brethren as a continuing problem until not only his temporal needs are met, but his spiritual ones also. As a concrete example—a bishop extends help while the artisan or craftsman is out of work and in want; a priesthood quorum sets him up in work and tries to see that he goes along until fully self-supporting and active in his priesthood duties" (J. Reuben Clark, Jr., "Bishops and Relief Society," July 9, 1941, pp. 17–18).

Continuing from President Clark: "[Such] assistance may take the form of helping the needy brother in his actual need and problem, to build a home, or to start in a small business, or, if he be an artisan, to get him a kit of tools, or, if he be a farmer, to get him seeds, or to help him plant or harvest a crop, or to meet some urgent credit need he has, or to supply him with clothing, or shelter, or food, or medical assistance, or schooling for the children, or to give aid in any number of other ways" (Estes Park Address, 20 June 1939, p. 20).

I am satisfied, my brethren, that there is enough of expertise, of knowledge, of strength, of concern in every priesthood quorum to assist the troubled members of that quorum if these resources are properly administered.

It was Kuan Tzu, a Chinese philosopher, who said, "If you give a man a fish, he will have a single meal; if you teach him how to fish, he will eat all his life." This, as I see it, illustrates the principle of Welfare Services. it is the responsibility of the bishop to give emergency help to see that neither the individual nor his family suffers. It is the obligation of the priesthood quorum to set in motion those forces and facilities which will equip the needy member to provide on a continuing basis for himself and his family.

In the words of President Harold B. Lee, spoken many years ago, "All priesthood quorums are 'commanded' [by the Lord] to marshall their forces and, under the spirit and power of the Priesthood, to see to it that every person who is in distress is assisted by his quorum to become self-sustaining" (*Improvement Era*, October 1937, p. 634).

I am confident that the Lord intended that a priesthood quorum should be far more than a class in theology on Sunday mornings. Of course, the building of spirituality and the strengthening of testimony through effective gospel teaching is an important priesthood responsibility. But this is only a segment of the quorum function. Each quorum must be a working brotherhood for every member if its purpose is to be realized. There must be instruction in principles of personal and family preparedness. If effectively taught, such instruction will become preventative welfare, because the quorum member and his family, equipped with such knowledge, will be the better prepared to handle many difficulties that might arise. The teaching of financial and resource management, home production and storage, the fostering of such activities as will promote physical, emotional, and spiritual health might all be the proper and legitimate concerns of the presidency of the quorum in behalf of its members.

Furthermore, the quorum becomes a resource of organized and disciplined manpower available to the bishop and stake president in carrying forward the production and processing of welfare commodities. It is in the quorum that the strong hands of willing men are found to thin the beets, to haul the hay, to build the fences, and to carry forward the myriad requirements of our welfare projects.

I recall a quorum officer in our stake who was an employee of a businessman who was a member of that quorum. The businessman was the quorum president's employer for forty hours a week. It was this same quorum president who called on and assigned the businessman, his boss, to go to the stake farm at five o'clock in the morning to hoe beets. And be it said to the credit of both that each respected the other in his position. They were working brothers in a great fraternity.

I should like to add that this businessman had others of the quorum working for him. The quorum of which they were members operated, as an arm of the Ward Welfare Services Committee, an effective employment program under which job opportunities were found not only for those who were unemployed, but also improvement in the employment of some who in terms of latent ability had been underemployed.

In a revelation given in 1831, the Lord charged the elders to watch over the Church: "And remember in all things the poor and the needy, the sick and the afflicted, for he that doeth not these things, the same is not my disciple" (D&C 52:40).

Each quorum has direct access to the home of every member through assigned home teachers. These brethren of the priesthood have not only the responsibility to teach, but also to inquire, to learn, and even by the power of the Holy Spirit to discern the needs of those for whom they are given responsibility. If there be needs of a temporal nature, the information is brought to the Ward Welfare Services Committee, which is chaired by the bishop, there to receive prayerful consideration and to set in motion those resources which will take care of immediate needs under the direction of the bishop, assisted by the Relief Society president; and long-term remedies under the direction of the quorum president, through the resources available to him.

Brethren, the priesthood quorum is the Lord's organization for men of the Church, just as the Relief Society is the Lord's organization for women of the Church. Each has among its responsibilities, basic to its reason for being, the assisting of those in need.

When the Relief Society was organized the Prophet Joseph said of the women of the Society: "They will fly to the relief of the stranger; they will pour in the wine and oil to the wounded heart of the distressed; they will dry up the tears of the orphan and make the widow's heart to rejoice" (B. H. Roberts, *Comprehensive History of The Church* 4:112). I would hope that the same might be said of the men of the priesthood.

It will be a marvelous day, my brethren—it will be a day of fulfillment of the purposes of the Lord—when our priesthood quorums become an anchor of strength to every man belonging thereto, when each such man may appropriately be able to say, "I am a member of a priesthood quorum of The Church of Jesus Christ of Latter-day Saints. I stand ready to assist my brethren in all of their needs, as I am confident they stand ready to assist me in mine. Working together, we shall grow spiritually as covenant sons of God. Working together, we can stand, without embarrassment and without fear, against every wind of adversity that might blow, be it economic, social, or spiritual."

God help us to increase our efforts toward that day of realization, I humbly pray, as I leave with you my testimony of the divinity of this work in the name of the Lord Jesus Christ, Amen.

Strengthening the Father in the Home

By President Ezra Taft Benson,
in Spencer W. Kimball, et. al., *Priesthood*

In the priesthood, we are engaged in the greatest work in all the world: the building of men of character, men of strength and courage, men of deep spirituality, God-like men.

Each father in the Church is establishing, or should be establishing, his patriarchal order—an order that will extend into the eternities. As priesthood bearers and priesthood leaders, we have an opportunity to draw close to our brethren and help strengthen them in their priesthood duties.

The Lord has given us the broad outline of organization. He has set forth the objectives and purposes, but he leaves to us pretty much the working out of the methods. Here are some basic principles to guide us in this program of strengthening the fathers in their families.

1. *The home and family is the eternal unit and the basis of the righteous life.*

The home is the rock foundation, the cornerstone of civilization. The church, the school, and even the nation stand helpless before a weak and degraded home. No nation will rise above its homes, and no nation will long endure when the family unit is weakened or destroyed.

President David O. McKay wisely said, "No other success in life can compensate for failure in the home." If this nation is to endure, then the home must be safeguarded, strengthened, and restored to its rightful importance.

2. *The father is the presiding authority in the home. He is the patriarch or head of the family.*

President Harold B. Lee gave us the foundation for this principle when he stated: "The most important of the Lord's work that you will ever do will be the work that you do within the walls of your own home."

The worthy priesthood holder who magnifies both his priesthood and his fatherhood, who is a true patriarch in his family, may inherit great blessings, for the Lord has said:

"Ye shall come forth in the first resurrection; and if it be after the first resurrection, in the next resurrection; and shall inherit thrones, kingdoms, principalities, and powers, dominions, all heights and depths . . . and if ye abide in my covenant . . . it shall be done unto them in all things whatsoever my servant hath put upon them, in time, and through all eternity; and shall be of full force when they are out of this world; and they shall pass by the angels, and the gods, which are set there, to their exaltation and glory in all things, as hath been sealed upon their heads, which glory shall be a fulness and a continuation of the seeds forever and ever" (D&C 132:19).

3. *The mother is the helpmate, the counselor.*

Through the Prophet Joseph Smith, the Lord said to Emma Smith, "Thou art an elect lady, whom I have called. . . . And the office of thy calling shall be for a comfort unto my servant, Joseph Smith, Jun., thy husband, in his afflictions, with consoling words, in the spirit of meekness . . . . Wherefore, lift up thy heart and rejoice, and cleave unto the covenants which thou has made. . . . Keep my commandments continually, and a crown of righteousness thou shalt receive" (D&C 25:3, 5, 13, 15).

In establishing this great patriarchal order, the mother must be considered a counselor, a close companion, in planning the execution of the program for the benefit and the blessing of the family.

4. *You cannot talk about father without talking about the role of the mother—they are one, sealed for time and all eternity.*

I make it a practice, whenever I perform a marriage, to suggest to the young couple that they return to the temple as soon as they can and go through the temple again as husband and wife. It isn't possible for them to understand fully the meaning of the holy endowment or the sealings with one trip through the temple, but as they repeat their visits to the temple, the beauty, the significance, and the importance of it all will be emphasized upon them. I have later had letters from some of these young couples expressing appreciation because that item was emphasized particularly. As they repeat their visits to the temple, their love for each other tends to increase and their marriage tends to be strengthened.

5. *The quorum is organized to teach, inspire, and strengthen the father in his responsibility and help him to do his duty.*

This suggests involvement—involving each priesthood holder in the programs of the Church, giving him something to do, assuring him that he is needed and wanted in the Church. Concerning our duty, the Lord has said: "Now let every man learn his duty, and to act in the office in which he is appointed, in all diligence. He that is slothful shall not be counted worthy to stand, and he that learns not his duty and shows himself not approved shall not be counted worthy to stand" (D&C 107:99–100).

6. *If the father fails in his responsibility, the home teacher must work with him to strengthen and help him to do his duty.*

This involves, of course, a lot of person-to-person work and informal contacts. It also involves love for our fellowman and concern for him. "Let every man esteem his brother as himself" (D&C 38:25).

"By this shall all men know that ye are my disciples, if ye have love one to another" (John 13:35).

7. *The father has the responsibility for the physical, mental, social, and spiritual growth and development of himself, his wife, and each of his children.*

A young man once came to my office for a blessing. He had problems—not moral problems, but he was confused; he was concerned and worried. We talked for a few minutes and I said to him, "Have you ever asked your father for a blessing?" "Oh," he said, "I don't know that Dad would do a thing like that. He is not very active." I said, "But he's your father." "Yes." "Does he hold the priesthood?" "Yes, he is an inactive elder." "Do you love him?" And he said, "Yes, I love him. He is a good man, he's good to the family, good to the children." I said, "Do you ever have family prayer?" He said, "It has been a long time since we had family prayer." I said, "All right, would you be willing to go home and watch for an opportunity, and ask your father if he will give you a blessing? And if it doesn't work out, you come back and I will be glad to help you."

So he left, and in about three days he came back. "Brother Benson, this has been the sweetest thing that's happened in our home," he said. "Mother and the children sat there, my younger brother and sisters, with my mother wiping the tears from her eyes. She expressed her gratitude later. Father gave me a lovely blessing." He added, "I could tell it came from his heart."

There are a lot of fathers who would enjoy giving their own children blessings, if they had a little encouragement. As patriarchs of their families, that is one of their obligations and duties, responsibilities, and, of course, opportunities.

8. *A father cannot be released from his responsibility.*

Bishops are called and serve for a while and then are released, but a father is never released. He may release himself through sin, but his is an eternal calling.

"I appeal to you parents, take nothing for granted about your children," said President J. Reuben Clark. "The great bulk of them, of course, are good, but some of us do not know when they begin to go away from the path of truth and righteousness. Be watchful every day and hour. Never relax your care, your solicitude. Rule kindly in the spirit of the priesthood, but rule, if you wish your children to follow the right path."

9. *A father has the responsibility to lead his family by—*

—loving God and looking to him for daily counsel and direction. That means he must have family prayer as well as personal prayer. I often wish there were some way to measure accurately the value of family prayer. What it would mean to little Mary, who is giving her first talk in Sunday School or perhaps her first little talk in Primary, to have the family go onto their knees that morning and make special mention of her that she will do her best and not be too frightened. What it would mean to a special teenage son who is facing a stiff examination in high school, to have him specially mentioned in family prayer. Family prayer can greatly increase the unity and solidarity in the family.

—loving his wife and being one with her. One of the greatest things a man can do for his children is to love his wife and let them know that he loves her.

—desiring to have children and loving them. If he really loves them, he will want the home evening, he will want the family council, he will want them to be exposed to the programs of the Church.

—letting virtue garnish his thoughts unceasingly. This is one of the great needs today particularly. We have so much sin, so many men attracted by a pretty face, and untrue to their companions.

—being an example of all he wants to teach.
—teaching and training his children in the word of the Lord, in light and truth.

—teaching them repentance, faith in Christ, baptism, the gift of the Holy Ghost, enduring to the end, praying vocally and in secret (see D&C 68).

—governing, commanding, correcting, nurturing, and blessing them in meekness, tenderness, and love, and upon the principles of righteousness (see D&C 121).

—not provoking any family members so that they become discouraged.

—creating an environment in the home conducive to order, prayer, worshipping, learning, fasting, growth, happiness, and the Spirit of the Lord. I often like to refer to section 29 of the Doctrine and Covenants, where the Lord gives the assurance that Satan has no power over little children until they reach the age of eight; a father has the opportunity during those eight years, without interference from the adversary, so far as the child is concerned. I am grateful for that. . . .

10. *The father must hunger and thirst and yearn to bless his family, go to the Lord, ponder the words of God, and live by the Spirit to know the mind and will of the Lord and what he must do to lead his family.*

It is soul-satisfying to know that God is mindful of us and ready to respond when we place our trust in him and do that which is right. There is no place for fear among men and women who place their trust in the Almighty, who do not hesitate to humble themselves in seeking divine guidance through prayer. Though persecutions arise, though reverses come, in prayer we can find reassurance, for God will speak peace to the soul. That peace, that spirit of serenity, is a great blessing.

Rearing eleven vigorous children to honorable manhood and womanhood on a small farm is no easy accomplishment. Yet, as my father and mother devoted themselves to this task, they never seemed to have any fear of the future. The reason was their faith—their confidence that they could always go to the Lord and he would see them through.

"Remember that whatever you do, and wherever you are, you are never alone," was my father's familiar counsel. "Our heavenly Father is always near. You can reach out and receive his aid through prayer."

All through my life the counsel to depend on prayer has been prized above any other advice I have ever received. It has become an integral part of me, an anchor, a constant source of strength.

11. *The Church exists to assist the father in getting his family back into the presence of our Father in heaven.*

Long after the Church has performed its mission, the celestial patriarchal order will still be functioning. This is why President Joseph F. Smith said, "To be a successful father or a successful mother is greater than to be a successful general or a successful statesman," and President David O. McKay added, "When one puts business or pleasure above his home, he, that moment, starts on the downgrade to soul weakness." And this is why President Harold B. Lee said, "The Church must do more to help the home carry out its divine mission."

Never has the devil been so well organized, and never in our day has he had so many powerful emissaries working for him. We must do everything in our power to strengthen and safeguard the home and family.

The adversary knows "that the home is the first and most effective place for children to learn the lessons of life: truth, honor, virtue, self-control; the value of education, honest work, and the purpose and privilege of life. Nothing can take the place of home in rearing and teaching children, and no other success can compensate for failure in the home" (President David O. McKay, letter to parents in *Family Home Evening Manual*, 1968–69, p. iii).

12. *Our pattern or model for fatherhood is our Heavenly Father.*

When Saul was on the road to Damascus, he was stopped by a heavenly vision and the voice of the Lord Jesus Christ. Saul responded with these momentous words: "Lord, what wilt thou have me to do?" (Acts 9:6). To this the Lord responded by sending Saul to see one of his authorized servants to receive direction and a blessing.

A man can ask no greater question in his life than that which Paul asked: "Lord, what wilt thou have me to do?" A man can take no greater action than to pursue a course that will bring to him the answer to that question. The Lord has already suggested an answer to each of us when he said, "Be ye therefore perfect, even as your Father which is in heaven is perfect" (Matthew 5:46), and "Therefore, what manner of men ought ye to be? Verily, I say unto you, even as I am" (3 Nephi 27:27).

Christ, then, has set us the example of what we should be like and what we should do. While many men have admirable qualities, there is only one man who ever walked the earth who was without sin, and who had the power to resurrect his own body. This Jesus is our exemplar and has commanded us to follow in his steps. He is the way, the truth, and the light, and no one can come back into the presence of our Father in heaven except through him. That man is greatest who is most like Christ, and those who love him most will be most like him.

How, then, does a man imitate God, follow his steps, and walk as he walked? Through studying the life of Christ, learning his commandments, and doing them. God has promised that to follow this course will lead a man to an abundant life, a fulness of joy, and the peace and rest for which those who are heavy-burdened long. To learn of Christ necessitates the study of the scriptures and the testimonies of those who know him. We come to know him through prayer and the inspiration and revelation that God has promised to those who keep his commandments.

And how do we learn the commandments? Through the words of the Lord in the scriptures, through the revelations received by his authorized servants, through the Light of Christ, that inspiration which comes to every man, and through personal revelation by the Holy Ghost.

The family is under attack today as perhaps never before, and it is very real. Yet the family is the rock foundation, the cornerstone of civilization. The Church will never be stronger than its families. Home teachers, quorum leaders, all of us, need to get the father to recognize his great responsibility to perform his duty as a father and as a patriarch to his own children.

At a stake presidency's meeting in Boise, Idaho, years ago, we were trying to select a president for the weakest and smallest elders quorum in the stake. Our clerk had brought a list of all the elders of that quorum, and on the list was the name of a man whom I had known for some years. He came from a strong Latter-day Saint family, but he wasn't doing much in the Church. If the bishop made a call to do some work on the chapel he'd usually respond, and if the elders wanted to play softball, you would sometimes find him out playing with them. He did have leadership ability; he was president of one of the local service clubs and was doing a fine job.

I said to the stake president, "Would you authorize me to go out and meet this man and challenge him to square his life with the standards of the Church and take the leadership of his quorum? I know there is some hazard in it, but he has the ability."

The stake president said, "You go ahead, and the Lord bless you."

After Sunday School I went to the man's home. I'll never forget the look on his face as he opened the door and saw a member of his stake presidency standing there. He hesitantly invited me in; his wife was preparing dinner, and I could smell the aroma of coffee coming from the kitchen. I asked him to have his wife join us, and when we were seated, I told him why I had come. "I'm not going to ask you for your answer today," I told him. "All I want you to do is to promise me that you will think about it, pray about it, think about it in terms of what it will mean to your family, and then I'll be back to see you next week. If you decide not to accept, we'll go on loving you."

The next Sunday, as soon as he opened the door I saw that there had been a change. He was glad to see me, and he quickly invited me in and called to his wife to join us. He said, "Brother Benson, we have done as you said. We've thought about it and we've decided to accept the call. If you brethren have that much confidence in me, I'm willing to square my life with the standards of the Church, a thing I should have done long ago." He also said, "I haven't had any coffee since you were here last week, and I'm not going to have any more."

He was set apart as elders quorum president, and attendance in his quorum began going up—and it kept going up. He went out, put his arm around the inactive elders, and brought them in. A few months later I moved from the stake.

Years passed, and one day on Temple Square in Salt Lake City, a man came up to me, extended his hand, and said, "Brother Benson, you don't remember me, do you?"

"Yes, I do," I said, "but I don't remember your name."

He said, "Do you remember coming to the house of a delinquent elder in Boise seven years ago?" And then, of course, it all came back to me. He said, "Brother Benson, I'll never live long enough to thank you for coming to my home that Sunday afternoon. I am now a bishop. I used to think I was happy, but I didn't know what real happiness was."

When we bring the fathers back into activity, we bring them happiness in this life, to say nothing about the eternal blessings that are opened up to them. My heart goes out to those men, heads of families, who are inactive, prospective elders. I don't believe we have a greater challenge in the Church today than to activate those men and bring them to the point where they can take their families to the house of the Lord and have opened to them the richest blessings known to men and women in this world, and closely related to the blessings in the world to come.

The Quorum

By Elder Boyd K. Packer,
in Spencer W. Kimball, et. al., *Priesthood*

In ancient days when a man was appointed to a select body, his commission, always written in Latin, outlined the responsibility of the organization, defined who should be members, and then invariably contained the words *"quorum vos unum,"* meaning "of whom we will that you be one."

The word *quorum,* which does not appear in either the Old Testament or the New Testament, from that beginning came to mean that select group without whose consent business could not be transacted, nor work proceed with authority. In the dispensation of the fulness of times, the Lord instructed that the priesthood should be organized into quorums, meaning selected assemblies of brethren given authority that his business might be transacted and his work proceed.

The word *quorum* is so recognized in *Webster's Dictionary* as "a Mormon body comprising those in the same grade of priesthood."

The government of the Lord's affairs in this dispensation rests in The Church of Jesus Christ of Latter-day Saints, which by his own declaration is "the only true and living church upon the face of the whole earth, with which I, the Lord, am well pleased, speaking unto the church collectively and not individually" (D&C 1:30).

The priesthood, which is always associated with God's work, "continueth in the church of God in all generations, and is without beginning of days or end of years" (D&C 84:17).

It continues in our day. Men, young and old, are called out of the world and received into the Church by baptism. With limitations and standards of worthiness established by the Lord, men may qualify by making themselves worthy for ordination into that comparatively small body of men on this earth who are commissioned to hold authority and transact the business of the Lord at this time.

The Melchizedek Priesthood

"There are, in the church, two priesthoods, namely, the Melchizedek and the Aaronic, including the Levitical Priesthood.

"Why the first is called the Melchizedek Priesthood is because Melchizedek was such a great high priest.

"Before his day it was called *the Holy Priesthood, after the order of the Son of God*.

"But out of respect or reverence to the name of the Supreme Being, to avoid the too frequent repetition of his name, they, the church, in ancient days, called that priesthood after Melchizedek, or the Melchizedek Priesthood" (D&C 107:1–4).

"The Melchizedek Priesthood holds the right of presidency, and has power and authority over all the offices in the church in all ages of the world, to administer in spiritual things" (D&C 107:8).

"All other authorities or offices in the church are appendages to this priesthood" (D&C 107:5).

"And this greater priesthood administereth the gospel and holdeth the key of the mysteries of the kingdom, even the key of the knowledge of God.

"Therefore, in the ordinances thereof, the power of godliness is manifest.

"And without the ordinances thereof, and the authority of the priesthood, the power of godliness is not manifest unto men in the flesh" (D&C 84:19–21).

There are in the greater priesthood these offices:

1. The *elder*, who is a standing home minister.

2. The *seventy*, who is a traveling minister.

3. The *high priest*, who is to administer in spiritual things and to preside as his calling in the Church requires.

4. The *patriarch*, who seals blessings upon the members of the Church.

5. The *apostle*, who is a traveling councilor and a special witness of the name of Christ in all the world.

6. The *presidency of the high priesthood*, who have the right to officiate in all the offices of the priesthood (see *A Guide for Quorums of the Melchizedek Priesthood*, Council of the Twelve, 1930, p. 13).

There are five quorums mentioned in the Doctrine and Covenants relating to the greater priesthood. They are:

1. The *quorums of elders*, "which quorum is instituted for standing ministers; nevertheless they may travel, yet they are ordained to be standing ministers" (D&C 124:137). A full quorum consists of ninety-six elders, presided over by a quorum presidency called by the president of the stake. Those brethren now designated as prospective elders affiliate with the quorums of elders.

2. The *quorums of seventy*, "which quorum is instituted for traveling elders to bear record of my name in all the world" (D&C 124:139). This quorum numbers seventy brethren, presided over by seven presidents called by the stake president after conferring with the First Quorum of the Seventy. Their assignment is missionary work, in which they receive some guidance from the First Quorum of the Seventy.

3. The *quorums of high priests*, each with a membership of all high priests residing within the boundaries of a stake, including patriarchs and bishops [see D&C 124:133, 136). The stake president and his counselors form the presidency of this quorum.

4. The *Quorum of the Twelve Apostles*, made up of those men ordained as apostles and sustained as members of that quorum (D&C 107:23–24).

5. The *quorum of the First Presidency* of the Church, consisting of the president and his two counselors (D&C 107:22).

The Aaronic Priesthood

"The second priesthood is called the Priesthood of Aaron, because it was conferred upon Aaron and his seed, throughout all their generations" (D&C 107:13).

This priesthood "holds the keys of the ministering of angels, and of the gospel of repentance, and of baptism by immersion for the remission of sins" (D&C 13:1).

"Why it is called the lesser priesthood is because it is an appendage to the greater, or the Melchizedek Priesthood, and has power in administering outward ordinances" (D&C 107:14).

There are four offices in the Aaronic Priesthood:

1. The *deacon*, who is to "watch over the church," and to be a standing minister to the church. (D&C 84:111. See also D&C 20:57–59.)

2. The *teacher*, who is to "watch over the church always, and be with and strengthen them" (D&C 20:53).

3. The *priest*, who is to "preach, teach, expound, exhort, and baptize, and administer the sacrament, and visit the house of each member" (D&C 20:46–47).

4. The *bishop*, who presides over the Aaronic Priesthood and "administers in all temporal things" (D&C 107:68, 71).

There are three quorums of the Aaronic Priesthood:

1. The *deacons quorum*, to consist of twelve deacons (D&C 107:85), with a presidency called by the bishop from among their members.

2. The *teachers quorum*, to number twenty-four members (D&C 107:86), with a presidency called by the bishop from among their numbers.

3. The *priests quorum*, to number forty-eight priests (D&C 107:87), presided over by the bishop of the ward to which the quorum belongs (D&C 107:88).

The bishop is a high priest and belongs to the high priests quorum.

In both priesthoods, a majority of the required number may constitute a quorum. When the number specified for a quorum is exceeded, the quorum may be—and perhaps generally should be—divided.

It is intended that every holder of the priesthood have membership in a quorum. It is a sacred privilege that comes with the bestowal of the priesthood. Priesthood and quorum membership are virtually synonymous.

In some cases a man may be ordained in an area where there are insufficient brethren to constitute a quorum. He has his priesthood file leader, and his channel of authority leads, as with those who belong to quorums, to the prophet and president of the Church.

When a young man reaches the age of twelve, he has conferred upon him the Aaronic Priesthood and is ordained to the office of deacon. Automatically, immediately, he becomes a member of a deacons quorum. From then on through life, it is contemplated that he will hold membership in a quorum of the priesthood.

Quorum membership is not optional. A man may not present himself to be ordained to an office in the priesthood and yet choose at once not to belong to a quorum, or choose to affiliate with a quorum made up of brethren holding a different office in the priesthood. He is a member of the appropriate quorum, and by his actions he either sustains or degrades it. He maintains his membership in the quorum until he is ordained to another office in the priesthood and automatically becomes a member of another quorum. If he moves from the area of his quorum, he is at once eligible for membership in the appropriate quorum in the area where his church membership is located.

A man who becomes inactive does not lose his membership in the quorum. He may lose interest in the quorum, but the quorum must never lose interest in him. The quorum is responsible always and continually for each of its members. To ignore an inactive member, to wihdraw interest in and contact with him, is an abrogation of his rights as a holder of the priesthood. He cannot be denied membership or participation in a quorum except by proper court action. A man guilty of transgression is subject to disciplinary action. He may be disfellowshipped, in which case sanctions are employed that prevent him from exercising his priesthood until repentance has been completed and those privileges restored. If he is excommunicated from the Church, he no longer holds the priesthood nor membership in a quorum.

If a quorum member is guilty of transgression, to fail to take proper disciplinary action when it is warranted is to offend the privileges of that man. Each of us should have the right to proper discipline. Discipline is an expression of love. In the priesthood, it may become an exalted expression of love, for the word "discipline" comes from the word "disciple."

If his priesthood quorum functions properly, it is almost impossible for a man sustained by the brethren of his quorum to fail in any phase of life's responsibility.

I repeat, all other authorities or offices in the Church are appendages to the higher priesthood.

A worthy priesthood holder may be called as an ecclesiastical officer in the Church, such as stake president, high councilor, or bishop, or be called as an officer, teacher or board member in an appendage organization, without altering his status as a member of the quorum. Such service neither enlarges nor can it diminish his membership in a quorum.

Though he may be called to and released from such assignments, his membership in his quorum is a steady, sustaining citizenship that becomes his right as a holder of the priesthood. And the holding of the priesthood, including the attendant membership in the quorum, ought to be regarded as a sacred privilege.

To be called to preside over a quorum, to be called as the secretary of a quorum, or to be called to any other assignment to sustain the quorum, is in and of itself a signal spiritual honor. It is likewise a monumental responsibility.

Each person who holds the priesthood ought to energetically determine to maintain his standards in order to be worthy of such membership. Priorities in his thinking ought to be so arranged that he regards the priesthood he holds, from which all other offices and authorities must draw their power, as having preference and priority in his feelings and his attentions.

I can easily think of our Sunday School, for instance, as a priesthood Sunday School. It is presided over by a Sunday School president who is a holder of the priesthood and is himself a member of a quorum. His calling, which is relatively temporary, is an honorable service that he renders for a time and a season. He is a credit to his quorum in rendering it. He will, of course, one day be released from it, but it is not contemplated that he will spend a day on this earth without being a member of a quorum.

When a priesthood holder is called to a position in an appendage organization, he is representing his quorum in that sacred reponsibility. He is not taken away from his quorum to fulfill the assignment.

These appendant services round out a fulness of life and provide members of the quorums and their families a fulness of experience, activity, and training. They are, in a very real sense, priesthood functions and activities.

Such callings in the Church are important and ought so to be esteemed. Their relative importance, however, does not and must not give them presumed ascendency over those offices in the priesthood and those callings to govern the quorums of the priesthood. The priesthood is the source of all strength and authority for all organizations and offices in the Church.

One can become careless with his quorum membership. Just as membership in a family or patriotism toward one's country may weaken and fail, so may quorum membership if it is taken for granted. In our day there is an urgent need for every single holder of the priesthood to bolster his spiritual patriotism or allegiance to his quorum.

Stake presidents cannot devote their time and attention to those organizations which are appended to the priesthood to the neglect of the priesthood and the quorums of the priesthood, and succeed in establishing godliness among our people.

They cannot fund those appended organizations with a disproportionate amount of time, or of talent, or of funds, and succeed in bringing godliness to the people.

The strength in the quorum is the key to the strength of the stake. The quorum will be as strong as the individual member. We all have the obligation and responsibility to honor our priesthood, to be worthy citizens of the priesthood quorum.

"For whoso is faithful unto the obtaining these two priesthoods of which I have spoken, and the magnifying their calling, are sanctified by the Spirit unto the renewing of their bodies.

"They become the sons of Moses and of Aaron and the seed of Abraham, and the church and kingdom, and the elect of God.

"And also all they who receive this priesthood receive me, saith the Lord;

"For he that receiveth my servants receiveth me;

"And he that receiveth me receiveth my Father;

"And he that receiveth my Father receiveth my Father's kingdom; therefore all that my Father hath shall be given unto him.

"And this is according to the oath and covenant which belongeth to the priesthood.

"Therefore, all those who receive the priesthood, receive this oath and covenant of my Father, which he cannot break, neither can it be moved" (D&C 84:33–40).

God grant that all of us who hold the priesthood and each of us who is a member of a quorum will honor that priesthood, will sustain that quorum, to the end that godliness may be found in the lives of all Latter-day Saints.

Books Cited

Brown, Hugh B. *You and Your Marriage*. Salt Lake City: Bookcraft, 1960.

Doxey, Roy W. *The Latter-day Prophets and the Doctrine and Covenants*. 4 vols. Salt Lake City: Deseret Book Co., 1963–65.

Green, P. R. *Science and Your Faith in God*. Salt Lake City: Bookcraft, 1958.

Journal of Discourses. 26 vols. London: Latter-day Saints' Book Depot, 1854–86.

Kimball, Spencer W. *Faith Precedes the Miracle*. Salt Lake City: Deseret Book Co., 1972.

————. *The Miracle of Forgiveness*. Salt Lake City: Bookcraft, 1969.

————, et. al. *Priesthood*. Salt Lake City: Deseret Book Co., 1981.

Lee, Harold B. *Decisions for Successful Living*. Salt Lake City: Deseret Book Co., 1973.

————. *Stand Ye in Holy Places*. Salt Lake City: Deseret Book Co., 1974.

————. *Ye Are the Light of the World*. Salt Lake City: Deseret Book Co., 1974.

Ludlow, Daniel H. *Latter-day Prophets Speak*. Salt Lake City: Bookcraft, 1948.

Maxwell, Neal A. *All These Things Shall Give Thee Experience*. Salt Lake City: Deseret Book Co., 1979.

————. *Things As They Really Are*. Salt Lake City: Deseret Book Co., 1978.

McConkie, Bruce R. *Doctrinal New Testament Commentary*. 3 vols. Salt Lake City: Bookcraft, 1965–73.

————. *Mormon Doctrine*. 2d. ed. Salt Lake City: Bookcraft, 1966.

————. *The Promised Messiah*. Salt Lake City: Deseret Book Co., 1978.

McKay, David O. *Gospel Ideals*. 2d printing. Salt Lake City: Improvement Era, 1954.

————. *Man May Know for Himself.* Compiled by Clare Middlemiss. Salt Lake City: Deseret Book Co., 1967.

————. *Stepping Stones to an Abundant Life.* Compiled by Llewelyn R. McKay. Salt Lake City: Deseret Book Co., 1971.

————. *True to the Faith.* Compiled by Llewelyn R. McKay. Salt Lake City: Bookcraft, 1966.

1978 Church Almanac. Salt Lake City: Deseret News, 1978.

Packer, Boyd K. *Teach Ye Diligently.* Salt Lake City: Deseret Book Co., 1975.

————. *That All May Be Edified.* Salt Lake City: Bookcraft, 1982.

Petersen, Mark E. *Abraham, Friend of God.* Salt Lake City: Deseret Book Co., 1979.

Pratt, Parley P. *Key to the Science of Theology.* 10th edition. Salt Lake City: Deseret Book Co., 1966.

Romney, Marion G. *Look to God and Live.* Salt Lake City: Deseret Book Co., 1971.

Roberts, B. H. *A Comprehensive History of The Church of Jesus Christ of Latter-day Saints, Century One.* 6 vols. Salt Lake City: The Church of Jesus Christ of Latter-day Saints, 1930.

Smith, Eliza R. Snow. *Biography and Family Record of Lorenzo Snow.* Salt Lake City: Deseret News Co., 1884.

Smith, George Albert. *Sharing the Gospel with Others.* Salt Lake City: Deseret Book Co., 1948.

Smith, Joseph. *History of The Church of Jesus Christ of Latter-day Saints.* 7 vols. 2d ed. rev. Edited by B. H. Roberts. Salt Lake City: The Church of Jesus Christ of Latter-day Saints, 1932–51.

————. *Teachings of the Prophet Joseph Smith.* Selected by Joseph Fielding Smith. Salt Lake City: Deseret Book Co., 1977.

Smith, Joseph F. *Gospel Doctrine.* 5th ed. Salt Lake City: Deseret Book Co., 1939.

Smith, Joseph Fielding. *Answers to Gospel Questions.* 5 vols. Compiled by Joseph Fielding Smith, Jr. Salt Lake City: Deseret Book Co., 1957–66.

————. *Church History and Modern Revelation.* 2 vols. Salt Lake City: The Council of the Twelve Apostles, 1953.

————. *Doctrines of Salvation.* 3 vols. Compiled by Bruce R. McConkie. Salt Lake City: Bookcraft, 1954–56.

————. *Seek Ye Earnestly.* Salt Lake City: Deseret Book Co., 1970.

————. *Take Heed to Yourselves!* Salt Lake City: Deseret Book Co., 1966.

————. *The Way to Perfection.* 6th ed. Salt Lake City: Genealogical Society of Utah, 1946.

Talmage, James E. *Jesus the Christ.* 3d. ed. Salt Lake City: The Church of Jesus Christ of Latter-day Saints, 1916.

————. *Sunday Night Talks by Radio.* Salt Lake City: The Church of Jesus Christ of Latter-day Saints, 1931.

Taylor, John. *The Gospel Kingdom.* Selected by G. Homer Durham. Salt Lake City: Bookcraft, 1943.

Wesley, John. *The Works of John Wesley.* 14 vols. (1872; reprint ed., Grand Rapids, Michigan: Zondervan Publishing House, n.d., 7:26–27).

Widtsoe, John A., comp. *Priesthood and Church Government.* Salt Lake City: Deseret Book Co., 1965.

Woodruff, Wilford. *Discourses of Wilford Woodruff.* Selected by G. Homer Durham. Salt Lake City: Bookcraft, 1946.

Young, Brigham. *Discourses of Brigham Young.* Selected by John A. Widtsoe. Salt Lake City: Deseret Book Co., 1941.

Index to Melchizedek Priesthood Personal Study Guides, 1982–1985

Entries refer to year and page number. For example, 1982 (85–90) refers to pages 85 through 90 of the 1982 Melchizedek Priesthood Personal Study Guide.

(90–94); doctrine of, 1984 (44); earthly ministry of, 1983 (55–60); faith in, 1984 (104–10); Light of, 1985 (39–43); Messianic prophecies, 1982 (109–14); pure love of, 1984 (168–73); second coming of, 1984 (225–30); suffering of, 1984 (61–63); walking in the light of, 1983 (79–83).

Church: succession in Presidency of, 1984 (133–39).

Church authorities: follow advice of, 1985 (272–78); sustaining of 1985 (180–86).

Church courts: 1982 (155–56); established by the Lord, 1984 (155–56); understanding purpose of, 1985 (154–60).

Civic responsibilities: 1984 (220–24).

Commitment: to the Lord, 1982 (39–44).

Common consent: law of, 1985 (183–84).

Communication, family: 1982 (71–76); in a positive, loving manner, 1983 (209).

Conference: general, 1985 (272–78), 1984 (237–40).

Confession: role of, in repentance, 1985 (91–92); to proper authorities, 1984 (156–59).

Consecration: of oil, 1985 (281).

Correlation: priesthood, 1985 (222–29).

Counseling with your children: 1984 (119–25).

Covenant: Abrahamic, 1985 (173–76); marriage, 1985 (85–88); priesthood oath and, 1984 (27–33); sacramental, 1984 (72–76); to do missionary work, 1984 (186–88).

Cultures: learn to appreciate other, 1985 (214–21).

D

Daniel: interprets dream, 1985 (69–70).

Dead: dedicate grave of 1985 (282); redemption of the, 1985 (187–93), 1984 (20–26).

Deceit: avoiding Satan's, 1984 (97–100).

Deseret Industries: 1985 (20–21).

Discipline: of children, 1985 (136–43).

Doctrine and Covenants: value of, 1985 (1–2).

E

Elijah: mission of, 1984 (8–13).

Employment: to assist members out of work, 1985 (20).

Endowment: purpose of, 1984 (140–44).

Enduring: to the end, 1984 (231–37); trials with patience, 1985 (115–19).

Enoch: characteristics of the people of, 1985 (9–10).

Exaltation: loss of, 1985 (86–87); requirements for, 1985 (247).

Example: Saints should be, 1985 (230–36).

F

Faith: in God, 1984 (109–10); power in, 1984 (104–07); required to heal sick, 1983 (79-83).

Fall of Adam: consequences of, 1985 (239–41).

Family: counseling together brings unity, 1983 (133–38); Elijah's mission concerning, 1984 (8–13); fathers responsible to spiritually nourish, 1985 (225–26), 1982 (162–63); having effective family home evenings, 1983 (139–46); home teaching to bless, 1985 (62–65), 1982 (20–21); husband and wife to counsel together, 1983 (133–38); husband and wife

to preside together, 1985
(46–48), 1984 (113–15);
organizing, 1985 (269–70), 1984
(14–19); records, value of, 1984
(179–84); resources to help, 1985
(62–66), 1982 (22–27);
responsibility to do work for
dead, 1984 (23–24); strengthen
bonds of, 1985 (264–71);
strengthen through
unconditional love, 1983 (198);
suggestions for effective family
councils, 1983 (133–38); teach
and practice obedience in, 1984
(209–13); teach chastity to, 1984
(161–65); teach light and truth
to, 1984 (209–13); teach mission
of Joseph Smith to, 1984
(126–32); teach that sabbath day
is holy, 1984 (55–60); teach that
to partake of sacrament they
must be worthy, 1984 (72–76);
teach Word of Wisdom to, 1984
(214–19); unity, 1985 (167 73).
Fast, law of the: 1982 (115–20).
Fast offerings: 1985 (21–22);
blessing of, 1982 (116–17);
purpopsc to bless others, 1984
(93–94).
Father: Christ as the, 1984 (44);
worship of, 1984 (42–43).
Fathers: blessing of children, 1985
(283); helping to spiritually
nourish families, 1985 (225–26);
home teachers should support,
1984 (177–78); most important
work of, 1984 (111–18);
priesthood responsibility, 1985
(46–52); priesthood
responsibility to wife, 1984
(203–08); presiding with wife,
1985 (46–48), 1984 (113–15).
Fear: righteous need not, 1984
(77–81).
Fellowshipping: in the quorum,
1984 (194–95); others, 1982
(192–94).

Finances: proper use of, 1984
(82–89), 1982 (197–202).
Foreordination: in premortality,
1985 (130–31).
Forgiveness: gift of, 1984 (67–64);
may require a Church court,
1984 (156–59); miracle of, 1984
(63–64, 66–71); of others, 1983
(114–20).
Free agency: 1985 (53–59).
Freedom: in Christ, 1985 (55–58).

G

Gathering of Israel: 1985 (144–45).
Genealogy: family responsibility
for, 1983 (160); individual
responsibility for, 1983 (160–65),
1982 (223–28).
God: man may become like, 1985
(151–52); resist Satan by serving,
1984 (101–02); reverence for,
1984 (147–53); seek to know,
1983 (45); sustaining servants of,
1985 (210–11); will preserve the
righteous by his power, 1984
(77–81); will forgive, 1984
(66–68); worship of, 1984
(42–46).
Godhead: truth of, 1984 (41–42).
Gospel: teaching with power of,
1985 (109–13); sharing with
others, 1985 (95–101), 1984
(188–90); to all the earth, 1985
(71), 1982 (191–96).
Government: support of, 1985
(144–50).
Gratitude: expressing, 1983 (74).
Grave: dedication of, 1985 (282),
1984 (244).
Guidance: of the Holy Spirit, 1984
(197–202); of the Lord in Church
callings, 1984 (49–54).

H

Handicapped, helping: 1985
(26–27).
Holy Ghost: and Light of Christ,
1985 (39–45); bestowal of, 1985
(280), 1984 (242); is revelator

and santifier, 1984 (45); receiving guidance of, 1985 (41–43, 110), 1984 (45, 50–51, 197–202); recognize and obey, 1985 (195–98); seek promptings of, 1985 (195–98); teach children gift of, 1985 (194–201).

Holy Spirit: See Holy Ghost.

Home: creating a wholesome environment in, 1985 (232–33); father presides in, 1985 (46–48), 1984 (111–18); strengthen fathering, 1985 (289–98).

Home teaching: duties of, 1982 (11–27, 163–64); receive the Lord's servants, 1985 (62–66); responsibility to help family members repent, 1984 (174–78); strengthening and nourishing families, 1985 (62–64), 1983 (101); to assist father, 1985 (62–66, 224–25); to support fathers, 1982 (12); .

Honesty: 1984 (34–40).

Hope, doctrine of: 1982 (135–40).

Humility: 1982 (185–90).

Husbands: home teacher to assist, 1985 (62–64); to become one with wife, 1985 (49–50); to love and be faithful to wife, 1984 (203–08).

I

Iniquity: none to be in the Church, 1984 (175–76).

Inspiration: how to recognize, 1984 (199–201).

Integrity: personal, 1984 (34–40).

Interviews: by fathers with children, 1984 (175–76).

J

Journals: keeping of, 1984 (179–84).

Judgments: 1982 (153–58); final 1985 (80–82).

Justification: by faith and good works, 1985 (203–04).

K

Keys: Apostles receive all, 1984 (134).

Kingdom of God: building the, 1985 (69–79).

L

LDS Social Services: 1985 (19–20).

Laws of the land: honor, 1985 (146–47), 1984 (220–24).

Leadership: 1982 (173–78); leading as the Savior led, 1983 (155).

Light of Christ: understanding, 1985 (39–43).

Love: for God and neighbor, 1985 (219–20); quorum provides opportunities to, 1984 (194–95); seek to obtain pure, of God, 1984 (168–72); shown by service, 1985 (257–63); toward wife, 1985 (90–91), 1984 (203–08); use of, in guiding children, 1985 (137–38).

Lucifer: methods of, 1984 (98–100).

Lust: avoid thoughts of, 1985 (88–90).

M

Man: may become like God, 1985 (151–53); role of, 1985 (46–48).

Marriage: blessing of proper, 1984 (205–07); enriching of, 1982 (95–101); teach children of temple, 1985 (245–48); partners to become one, 1985 (49–50).

Melchizedek Priesthood quorum: 1985 (299–300).

Mission: of Elijah, 1984 (8–13); of Joseph Smith, 1984 (128).

Missionary work: befriending nonmembers, 1983 (19); done with love, 1985 (95–101); every member responsible for, 1984 (185–91), 1982 (191–96); preparation for, 1983 (25); responsibility to do, 1985 (72–73), 1983 (13); rewards of, 1985 (97), 1983 (13).

Purity of heart: 1982 (32–37); necessary for pure communication, 1982 (73).

Q

Quorum: brotherhood, 1983 (61); duty of, 1982 (203–08); duty of presidency for instruction of, 1982 (x–xi); lifting spirituality, 1984 (192–96); meaning of, 1985 (298–305); missionary responsibility, 1985 (72–73); opportunities to give service, 1985 (159–61), 1983 (61–66, 95–100); to strengthen priesthood holders 1983 (61–66); welfare responsibilities, 1985 (285–89).

R

Records: keeping, 1984 (179–84).
Redeemer: Christ is, 1984 (44).
Redemption: of dead, 1984 (20–26).
Repentance: and forgiveness, 1984 (63–64, 66–71), 1982 (147–52); home teachers to encourage, 1984 (174–78); may require a Church court, 1984 (157–59); resolving sins through, 1985 (91–92), 1984 (66–71).
Resurrection: Christ made possible, 1983 (173–79); all will rise again, 1983 (173–79).
Restoration: 1982 (167–72); Joseph Smith's part in, 1985 (132–33), 1984 (126–32).
Revelation: Church guided by, 1985 (207–10); receiving personal, 1985 (195–98), 1984 (197–202).
Reverence: 1984 (147–53).
Righteous: need not fear, 1984 (77–81).
Righteousness: faith gives men power to work, 1984 (105–07).

S

Sabbath day: guidelines for proper observance, 1984 (56–57), 1982 (121–27); teach family to keep holy the, 1984 (55–60).
Sacrament: blessing of, 1985 (280), 1984 (245); renewing covenants in, 1984 (73–74); worthiness to partake of, 1984 (72–76).
Salvation: for the dead, 1984 (20–26).
Sanctification: doctrine of, 1985 (204–05).
Satan: father of lies, 1984 (97–103); methods of, include Ouija board, astrology, spiritualism, 1984 (98–100); resisting temptations of, 1984 (101–02).
Savior: will come again, 1984 (226–27).
Scriptures: live the teachings of, 1983 (1–6); search the, 1985 (v), 1984 (1-7), 1983 (1), 1982 (1–9); study of, 1985 (2–4), 1984 (1–7), 1982 (1–7); teaching from, 1982 (4–5); value of, 1985 (1–2), 1984 (1-2).
Second coming of Christ: preparing for, 1985 (222–24), 1984 (225–30); signs of, 1982 (209–15).
Service: giving self-initiated as well as assigned, 1983 (95–100); Savior's perfect example of, 1983 (95–100); serve God by serving, 1985 (257–62); to quorum members 1985 (160–61); to those with special needs, 1985 (18–24); welfare, 1985 (9–31).
Sick: administering to, 1985, (281–82).
Sin: repent of, 1982 (147–52).
Smith, Joseph: prophets testified of his mission, 1985 (130–35), 1984, (126–32).
Social Services: See LDS.
Spirit: receiving the, 1985, (41–43),

1984 (198–99); teaching with the, 1985 (109–13).

Spiritual gifts: 1985 (225–53); obtaining, 1985 (253–55).

Spirituality: in priesthood quorum, 1984 (192–96).

Succession: in Church presidency, 1984 (133–39).

Sustaining: Church officers, 1985 (183–86, 210–11); leaders of the land, 1985 (146–47).

T

Teach: as Jesus taught, 1983 (203); improve ability at, 1982 (179–84); methods of the Savior, 1983 (203–08); with power and authority, 1985 (109–14); with the Spirit, 1985 (109–10).

Teaching children: how to honor parents, 1982 (65–67); how to recognize promptings of Holy Ghost, 1985 (184–201); obedience, 1984 (209–13).

Teaching family members: of the blessings of the Word of Wisdom, 1984 (214–19); to care for the poor, 1984 (90–96); to keep the Sabbath holy, 1984 (55–60).

Temples: blessings and knowledge received in, 1982 (51–56); ordinances for the dead, 1985 (187–93), 1984 (20–26); reverence for, 1984 (151–52); teach children of marriage in, 1985 (245–48); why we build, 1984 (140–46); worship in, 1984 (140–46).

Testimony: 1982 (129–34); testify of Joseph Smith in your, 1984 (129).

Thoughts: avoid immoral, 1985 (88–90); purify our, 1982 (32–37).

Time: wise use of, 1982 (93).

Tithing: 1982 (217–22).

Transgression of Adam: 1985 (238–39).

Trials: enduring, 1985 (118–19).

U

Unity: in the family, 1985 (167–72).

V

Virtue: protect, 1985 (86–88); taught in the home, 1984 (161–67).

W

Wealth: to bless others, 1984 (83–88); use of material, 1984 (85–88).

Welfare program: and family preparedness, 1985 (10–13), 1982 (59–60); basic principles of, 1984 (90–96); principles of, 1985 (10–17); to care for poor and needy, 1985 (18–24), 1983 (101); to help those with special needs, 1985 (25–31).

Welfare services, quorum's role in: 1985 (285–89), 1982 (206–07).

Witness: bearing of false, 1984 (35–36).

Wives: husband to become one with, 1985 (49–50); husbands to love and be faithful to, 1985 (46–48), 1984 (203–08); presiding with, 1985 (46–48), 1984 (13–14); to become one with husband, 1985 (49–51).

Womanhood: role of as wife and mother, 1985 (48–49); supporting women in divine roles, 1985 (46–48), 1983 (147).

Word of wisdom: living the, 1984 (214–19).

Words: sustain leaders with our, 1985 (185–86).

Work: principles of, 1984 (91–92); teaching children value of, 1982 (77–82); for the dead, 1985 (187–93).

Worship: in the temple, 1984 (140–46); through the Son, 1984 (44); what and how to, 1984 (41–48).

Z